Praise for Alex Kotlowitz's

An American Summer

"Alex Kotlowitz doesn't provide solutions to the violence that plagues Chicago. Instead, he eloquently bears witness to a single summer on its streets, chronicling a community's ongoing struggle with murder, misery, and rage. This deeply empathetic and perceptive book isn't easy to read. But we can only see into the neglected corners of America when someone shines a light."
                              —*The Christian Science Monitor*

"Kotlowitz has a ruminative, almost poetic sensibility. . . . The violence is made palpable but never romanticized. Kotlowitz's approach is empathetic in this bold, unflinching depiction of an ever-lengthening crisis."   —*Publishers Weekly* (starred review)

"*An American Summer* is an archive of the war—like finding a shocking but beautiful bundle of letters and photographs in the attic. Except that these dispatches reflect the daily violence that many Americans are experiencing, right now, in too many of our cities. Alex Kotlowitz dispenses with wooden categories of *criminal* and *victim*. With his uncommon warmth and sensitivity, he makes us understand that violence doesn't happen in a moment; it's a state of affairs."   —Sarah Koenig, host of *Serial*

"This is shoe leather reporting at its finest. The author does not appeal to sentiment. Rather than offering opinion or conjecture, he writes matter-of-factly about the people who live and die on the periphery of American society."   —*Pittsburgh Post-Gazette*

"This book is revelatory and brilliant. *There Are No Children Here* changed me when I read it years ago. *An American Summer* has done it again."   —Wes Moore, bestselling author of *The Other Wes Moore* and CEO of the Robin Hood foundation

"In his latest powerful sociological exploration, [Kotlowitz] masterfully captures the summer of 2013 in neglected Chicago neighborhoods, rendering intimate profiles of residents and the 'very public' violence they face every day. . . . A fiercely uncompromising—and unforgettable—portrait."

—*Kirkus Reviews* (starred review)

"Alex Kotlowitz, America's preeminent narrative journalist, has written a searing, profound, and profoundly human book about the gun violence that plagues American cities. Everyone who cares about the future of our cities and of our country will come away deeply moved, and with a deepened understanding of the long shadow cast by substandard schools, housing, and job opportunities. It's not a call to action, but the stories Kotlowitz tells cry out to all readers to start acting."

—Sara Paretsky, *New York Times* bestselling author of *Shell Game*

"A heartfelt and, at times, surprisingly hopeful portrait of a city battling intractable ills. By giving each and every person he talks to the time and respect to tell his or her story, Kotlowitz evokes fully dimensional human beings rather than the statistics or caricatures most of us are used to in reports on 'bad' neighborhoods."

—*Chicago Reader*

"What remains after the deaths, the funerals, the court hearings, the jail sentences, the mourning? This is the question at the heart of Alex Kotlowitz's compassionate and unflinching new book, and what emerges speaks to a stubborn, immovable, singular drive toward hope and forgiveness. Kotlowitz reminds us again and again that what happens in Chicago reflects the best and worst of our nation. This spectacular book is an urgent call to bear witness, not to the dying that violence breeds, but to the love that stands tall amidst the debris."

—Maaza Mengiste, author of *Beneath the Lion's Gaze*

"*An American Summer* is at turns shocking, heartrending, and deeply moving. But it is always important. This is about the soul of our country."   —Luis Alberto Urrea,
author of *The House of Broken Angels*

"It's a testament to Kotlowitz's skill that many of the stories he tells are surprising. All of them are gripping. There are no easy answers here, just people you can't forget, living in a world many Americans can't even imagine."   —The Marshall Project

Alex Kotlowitz

An American Summer

Alex Kotlowitz is the author of three previous books, including the national bestseller *There Are No Children Here*, selected by the New York Public Library as one of the 150 most important books of the twentieth century. *The Other Side of the River* was awarded the *Chicago Tribune*'s Heartland Prize for nonfiction. His work has appeared in *The New Yorker*, *The New York Times Magazine*, and on *This American Life*. His documentary work includes *The Interrupters*, for which he received a Film Independent Spirit Award and an Emmy. His other honors include a George Polk Award, two Peabodys, the Helen Bernstein Book Award for Excellence in Journalism, the Robert F. Kennedy Journalism Award, and the Harold Washington Literary Award. He teaches at Northwestern University.

www.alexkotlowitz.com

An American Summer

An American Summer

LOVE AND DEATH IN CHICAGO

Alex Kotlowitz

ANCHOR BOOKS
A DIVISION OF PENGUIN RANDOM HOUSE LLC
NEW YORK

FIRST ANCHOR BOOKS EDITION, MARCH 2020

The Library of Congress has cataloged the Nan A. Talese/
    Doubleday edition as follows:
Name: Kotlowitz, Alex, author.
Title: An American summer : love and death in Chicago /
    Alex Kotlowitz.
Description: First edition. | New York : Nan A. Talese/
    Doubleday, 2019.
Identifiers: LCCN: 2018014026
Subjects: LCSH: Youth and violence—Illinois—Chicago. | Violent
    crimes—Illinois—Chicago. | Victims of violent crime—Illinois—
    Chicago. | African American youth—Illinois—Chicago—Social
    conditions—21st century. | African Americans—Illinois—
    Chicago—Social conditions—21st century. | Chicago (Ill.)—
    Social conditions—21st century.
Classification: LCC HQ799.2.V56 K68 2019 |
    DDC 364.150835/0977311—dc23
LC record available at https://lccn.loc.gov/2018014026

Anchor Books Trade Paperback ISBN: 978-0-8041-7091-8
eBook ISBN: 978-0-385-53881-7

Author photograph © Kathy Richland

www.anchorbooks.com

Printed in the United States of America
10   9   8   7   6   5   4   3   2   1

Contents

An American Summer

Prelude to a Summer

Near midnight on August 19, 1998, the phone rang, an unusual occurrence at my parents' home in upstate New York, where I was visiting with my wife and infant daughter. I got out of bed and scrambled to the hallway to grab the phone. The voice on the other end sounded familiar, but I couldn't quite place it. "It's Anne Chambers," she said. Anne was a Chicago violent crimes detective whom I knew. She told me she was calling from the kitchen in our home in Oak Park, a suburb bordering Chicago. She told me that Pharoah was there with her, and that he may have been involved in a murder. My legs buckled. I sat down to catch my breath.

This was the Pharoah from my book *There Are No Children Here*, a boy who stepped cautiously, who loved school, and who was so charming and vulnerable that adults went out of their way to protect him. Shortly after the book came out, Pharoah, who had grown up in one of the city's housing projects, had moved in with me—for what I thought would be a short period. I'd helped get him into Providence St. Mel, a college prep school on the city's West Side, and he was struggling, understandably. He couldn't find quiet in his first-floor public housing apartment, as rivers of people flowed in and out daily, mostly family and family friends. He called and told me he just wanted to catch up with his schoolwork. *Could I stay with you, just for a while?* he asked. *Maybe a week or two?* I was single at the time, unencumbered and with a spare bedroom, so I invited him to stay. Though only twelve, he knew what he needed. He brought with him a garbage bag filled with clothes—and his school backpack. Those two weeks turned into six years.

When I got married, Pharoah walked my wife, Maria, down the aisle, along with her dad. We moved to Oak Park as we wanted to be near his school, and we figured it was a community that wouldn't look askance at this unusual arrangement. His adolescent years were rocky. I didn't anticipate how this living situation would pull at his sense of identity. While his mother, LaJoe, supported his decision to live with Maria and me, others in his family didn't. One time his mother called and after leaving a message forgot to hang up, and so on my answering machine I listened to a five-minute rant by a friend of their family berating LaJoe for letting Pharoah live with a white couple. *He don't belong there,* the woman told LaJoe. *He ain't white.*

I knew it had to be hard for Pharoah. He undoubtedly heard these harangues as well. It's tough enough to be a teen in the best of circumstances, grappling with who you are and who you want to be, and here Pharoah had to figure out who he was while living with two white adults who were not related to him by blood, who were not his parents, who were not even his legal guardians. In particular, he had an older brother—I gave him the pseudonym Terence in the book—who clearly resented Pharoah's decision to live with us, and so he would try to pull Pharoah into his activities in the street. There was also a measure of opportunism here, as he knew that Pharoah, who had never been in trouble with the law, would not likely draw the attention of the police. It felt like a tug of war, and

I often felt on the losing end. At one point Pharoah knew he had to get away, to find some reprieve from these forces pulling at him, and so at his request we sent him to a boarding school in Indiana, a military academy where he had attended summer camp.

A week after he left, I was tidying up his bedroom, picking clothes off the floor, making his bed, and finally cleaning his closet, where on the top shelf I noticed a worn black leather bag the size of a medicine ball. I reached to pull it down. It was bloated with cash. I mean lots of cash. Tens. Twenties. Hundreds. All of it stuffed into the bag without much concern for appearance or organization. I knew right away that it belonged to Terence, that he had probably asked Pharoah to hold it for him. I called a friend, an attorney, for advice. His words were simple: "Get rid of it." He called me back a few minutes later and clarified: "I don't mean throw it away." So I called Terence and told him I had something of his which he needed to retrieve. He refused to come to Oak Park, worried that I'd set him up with the local police, so I agreed to meet him on the city's West Side, and there in the middle of a one-way residential street in the early afternoon, in the open so that we both felt protected, I handed over to him what turned out to be somewhere in the neighborhood of $18,000. (Terence later accused me of taking $300 from the bag, but that's another story.)

This is what Pharoah was up against—and what we were up against as well. Pharoah got kicked out of the boarding school for selling marijuana and eventually graduated from our local public school. He was accepted at Southern Illinois University and had decided not to visit New York with us during this summer trip because he wanted to get ready for school. Classes began the following week. And then I got this call.

I knew the detective, Anne Chambers, from my time reporting *There Are No Children Here*. Anne, whom everyone in the neighborhood called Mary (for reasons I never could discern), had been a member of the plainclothes tactical unit in the neighborhood and had a reputation as a fair-minded officer. She was tough, but cared deeply about the kids. She was a single mother, and we used to talk about her son, who at the time was headed off to Harvard with ambitions to be a police officer. She pleaded with him to do something different.

Here's what she told me in that short midnight phone call: Pharoah had taken a taxi from our house to his mother's home on the West Side, and when the cab pulled up, two young men pulled Pharoah out of the backseat and then jumped in. One of them held a pistol to the cabbie's head, demanding his money. The cabbie must have panicked, and when he pressed down on the accelerator, one of the assailants shot him in the back. Anne told me that some detectives suspected Pharoah might have set up the driver. Fortunately, Anne knew Pharoah from her time in the projects and knew that he wasn't that type of kid. I told her that I, too, couldn't fathom Pharoah pulling such a stunt—though privately I worried that maybe his brother had put him up to it.

By the next morning, Anne and her colleagues had determined that in fact Pharoah knew nothing of the robbery. Pharoah's sister had seen much of what transpired and could identify the assailants. For my part, I tried to reach Pharoah. This was before cell phones. His mother said he was out, but she wasn't sure where. I tried calling regularly throughout the day. Both Maria and I were concerned. He'd just seen someone murdered. It wasn't the first time, I knew, but I also imagined how disorienting it must be. Morning came and went. As did the afternoon. Finally that evening I reached him at our house.

Where have you been? I asked.

Shopping.

Shopping?

At Marshall Field's. For school.

Shopping? I was incredulous.

Yeah.

Pharoah, how are you doing?

Okay. Why?

Why? You just saw someone murdered.

I'm okay. I got to go. I need to get packed for school.

I hung up, shaking my head. I was dumbfounded—and angry. How could he not be grieving? How could he not be upset? Shopping? I told my wife that if it was me, I'd be curled up on our couch in a fetal position. I thought to myself, something must be terribly wrong with Pharoah. How can you not feel? How can you not cry? How can you not express gratitude for not getting killed yourself? Pharoah gets yanked out of the backseat of a taxi by two men with a pistol and then watches as they shoot and kill someone he's just shared time with. Something, I thought, was off. Out of kilter. And for the longest time I thought Pharoah was without heart, that he'd become hardened, if not numb, to the violence around him. This of course is the mistake we all make, thinking that somehow one can get accustomed to it.

I feel like I've been working my way to this book for a long while. In reporting *There Are No Children Here,* it was the violence that most unmoored me. Since the publication of the book in 1991, four of the kids I befriended have been murdered, including Pharoah's nephew, whom even at the age of twenty-one everyone called Snugs, short for Snuggles. He was killed in retaliation for someone else getting shot; he was the last person murdered before the Henry Horner Homes, a public housing complex, was razed. Another young man, Jojo Meeks, had joined me, along with Pharoah and his brother Lafeyette, on a fishing trip one summer. He had a smile so wide you felt like you could just walk right in. Jojo became a stick-up artist, of drug dealers mostly, and was killed when he tried to rob some drug dealers with a BB gun. They were better armed.

The numbers are staggering. In Chicago, in the twenty years between 1990 and 2010, 14,033 people were killed, another roughly 60,000 wounded by gunfire. And the vast majority of these shootings took place in a very concentrated part of the city. Let me put this in some perspective, if perspective is possible; it's considerably more than the number of American soldiers killed in combat in Afghanistan and Iraq. Combined. And here's the thing: Chicago is by no means the most dangerous city, not even close. Its homicide rate doesn't even put it in the top ten. But the city has become a symbol for the personal and collective wreckage—a kind of protracted cry of distress—in the streets of the nation's most impoverished and segregated neighborhoods. Citizens killing citizens, children killing children, police killing young black men. A carnage so long-lasting, so stubborn, so persistent, that it's made it virtually impossible to have a reasonable conversation about poverty in the country and has certainly clouded any conversation about race. One friend who worked for a local antiviolence organization—the fact that such groups even exist speaks volumes to the profound depth of the problem—calls it "a madness." What's going on?

Let me tell you what this book isn't. It's not a policy map or a critique. It's not about what works and doesn't work. Anyone who tells you they know is lying. Consider that in Chicago the police have tried community policing, SWAT teams, data to predict shooters, full saturation of troubled neighborhoods, efforts to win over gang members. And the shootings continue. Antiviolence gurus insist they have the answers. I've seen one—the founder of a local program—take credit for the reduction of shootings in the years before his organization even existed. What works? After twenty years of funerals and hospital visits, I don't feel like I'm much closer to knowing.

And so what you have here, in these pages, is a set of dispatches, sketches of those left standing, of those emerging from the rubble, of those trying to make sense of what they've left behind. A summer in the city: 2013. There's nothing special about this particular summer other than it's the one I chose to immerse myself in. Over the course of three months, 172 people were killed, another 793 wounded by gunfire. By Chicago standards it was a tamer season than most.

I need to be upfront with you, the reader. When I told friends about this book, they'd roll their eyes. Such grimness. Such despair. Such darkness. I know what they were thinking: Why would I want to go there? Why would you want to go there? Indeed, this is a book about death—but you can't talk about death without celebrating life. How amid the devastation, many still manage to stay erect in a world that's slumping around them. How despite the bloodshed, some manage, heroically, not only to push on but also to push back. How in death there is love. It's also about who we are as a nation. After the massacre at Newtown and then at Parkland we asked all the right questions. How could this happen? What would bring a young man to commit such an atrocity? How can we limit access to guns? How do the families and the community continue on while carrying the full weight of this tragedy? But in Chicago neighborhoods like Englewood or North Lawndale, where in one year they lose twice the number of people killed in Newtown, no one's asking those questions. I don't mean to suggest that one is more tragic than the other, but rather to point out that the national grieving and questioning don't extend to corners of this country where such carnage has become almost routine. It's in these, the most ravaged of our communities, among the most desperate and forlorn, that we can come to understand the makings of who we are as a nation, a country marked by the paradox of holding such generosity beside such neglect.

Look at a map of the murders and shootings in Chicago and it creates a swath through the city's South and West Sides, like a thunderstorm barreling through the city. How can there not be a link between a loss of hope and the ease with which spats explode into something more? There was a moment when we were filming the documentary *The Interrupters* when Ameena Matthews, one of the three violence interrupters whose work we chronicled, reflected on what she called "the thirty seconds of rage." She described it like this: "I didn't eat this morning. I'm wearing my niece's clothes. I just was violated by my mom's boyfriend. I go to school, and here comes someone that bumps into me and don't say excuse me. You hit zero to rage within thirty seconds, and you act out." In other words, these are young men and women who are burdened by fractured families, by lack of money, by a closing window of opportunity, by a sense that they don't belong, by a feeling of low self-worth. And so when they feel disrespected or violated, they explode, often out of proportion to the moment, because so much other hurt has built up and then the dam bursts. They become flooded with anger.

Then there's the rest of us, who, reading the morning newspaper or watching the evening news, hear of youngsters gunned down while riding their bike or walking down an alley or coming from a party, and think to ourselves, *They must have done something to deserve it, they must have been up to no good.* Virtually every teen and young man shot, the police tell us, belonged to a gang, as if that somehow suggests that what goes around comes around. But life in these communities is more tangled than that. It's knottier and more lasting than readings of a daily newspaper or viewings of the evening news would suggest.

The numbers don't begin to capture the havoc wreaked on the soul of individuals and on neighborhoods, nor do they grapple with the discomforting fact that the vast majority of the shootings are of African-Americans and Hispanics by African-Americans and Hispanics. What to make of all this? I don't know that I fully know myself, but what I've come to realize is that if you're black or Hispanic in our cities, it's virtually impossible not to have been touched by the smell and sight of sudden, violent death. And again—and this seems rather obvious—the violence occurs in communities for which a sense of future feels as distant and arbitrary as a meteor shower, communities that in fact have been shunted aside precisely because they are black and Hispanic.

It's my hope that these stories will help upend what we think we know. Trauma splinters memory. Soldiers who have fought in war speak of holding on to fragments of remembrance, like a disjointed slide show which periodically gets stuck on a single image, on a single moment. This collection of stories, I realize now, mirrors that. It's how I remember the summer, in slivers which I keep coming back to, trying to make sense of the moments I've witnessed and the stories I've heard, trying to sort out what is true and what I and others have misremembered. The novelist and Vietnam veteran Tim O'Brien has talked about how the atrocities and nastiness of battle get in your bones. The same can be said for young and old living in certain neighborhoods in our cities. You have to fight—and fight hard—not to let the ugliness and inexplicability of the violence come to define you. With just one act of violence the ground shifts beneath you, your knees buckle, and sometimes all you can do is try as best you can to maintain your balance. There are those who right themselves and move on, but for most, their very essence has been rattled.

Not long ago, over lunch at a restaurant, I asked Pharoah how much he remembered of that evening from nearly twenty years ago. "I can't get it out of my mind," he told me. He said the cabdriver, a middle-aged white man whose name I later learned was Michael Flosi, engaged him in conversation, that he wanted to know all about Pharoah. When Pharoah told Flosi he was headed to Southern Illinois University, Flosi told him, "God must have really blessed you." Flosi shared with Pharoah that he'd been saving for years to move his family to Texas and that the move was imminent. "He seemed so happy," Pharoah told me. When they pulled up to Pharoah's mom's house, the young men leaped into the cab as Pharoah was getting out.

It's here at this restaurant that I come to realize how much this incident is a part of him. In recounting that afternoon, Pharoah seems in a different place. One minute he is sitting across from me in the booth, and then he scoots out as if he's getting out of a cab. He recoils as if someone's just jumped in front of him. He's not present. Instead he's there, in that moment. Pharoah tells me he ran to the porch, and then after he heard the gunshot he returned to the cab, which had rammed a parked car. Flosi, he says, was slumped over the steering wheel, and the windshield was splattered with blood. (What Pharoah doesn't remember is that according to court records he later called the cab company to find out whether Flosi had lived.) Pharoah at this point looks around. His eyes are wide with fright. He's hyperventilating. In the middle of the restaurant he's crouching, as if trying to disappear. I tell him to sit down. I have to tell him again. "It's like I'm there," he says. "I'm out of breath." The violence is in his bones.

There are so many like Pharoah who carry the violence, who keep moving forward enshrouded in its aftermath. Yet there doesn't seem to be a sense of urgency, especially among the rest of us. "We're in the midst of an epidemic," Don Sharp, a Baptist pastor and longtime friend, told me. "If people were dying of some kind of disease, there'd be all kinds of alerts, but it's become a way of life for us, and that's dangerous." I often think of a *Chicago Sun-Times* front page from a number of years ago. The banner headline read "Murder at a Good Address." The story reported on a dermatologist who was discovered bound and brutally stabbed at his office on luxurious Michigan Avenue. I admired the headline for its brazenness and honesty. Its subject was one of 467 murders that year in the city, though the others didn't warrant such attention, mostly because who would want to read a feature with the headline "Murder at a Bad Address"? In Chicago, the wealthy and the well-heeled die headline deaths and the poor and the rambling die in silence. This is a book, I suppose, about that silence—and the screams and howling and prayers and longing that it hides. Over lunch that day, Pharoah told me, "There's a lot of stuff I want to forget." This book is written with the hope that we won't.

Chapter 1

The Tightrope, a story in four parts

MAY 4 . . . MAY 5 . . . MAY 6 . . .

Marcelo Sanchez's memory of the next twenty-four hours is hazy, mostly because he'd been drinking. First Hennessy Cognac mixed with the energy drink Monster. Then, later, Heineken. Five days earlier Marcelo had turned seventeen, and I suppose if this night was the first time you'd met him, the events that followed wouldn't seem out of character. Marcelo had recently purchased from Men's Wearhouse a slim-fitting, shimmery blue suit, a black tie, and glistening black dress shoes which he had intended to wear to the junior prom the next night at De La Salle Institute, a prestigious Catholic school on the city's South Side. He'd asked his new girlfriend, Tania, to be his date. He planned to take her to Rosebud, an Italian restaurant downtown, and with a friend had scanned the menu online to figure out in advance what he would order. But because of an incident at school—where he held on to a cell phone stolen by another student before turning it in the next day—the school had barred him from the dance. Nonetheless, he planned to wear the suit to take Tania out to dinner tomorrow night, and was trying it on when a neighborhood friend, Daniel, stopped by to ask if Marcelo wanted to join him at a nearby party.

Marcelo is a handsome teen, his sleepy eyes and dark, full eyebrows lending him an air of thoughtfulness. But his hesitant smile—a small uptick of his full lips—contains a glimmer of mischief, a look as if to say, "Who, me?" He's a bit of a wise guy, someone who teases and jokes, so deadpan sometimes it's not clear where the teasing ends and the jabbing begins. He lacks physical grace. He moves like a marionette, his movements stiff-limbed. He's short—five foot three—and sinewy, his features angular. He has an overbite, which he's self-conscious about—along with his height—but what's most noticeable about Marcelo is his skittishness. He's easily distracted. He often laughs nervously. He bites his fingernails. More often than not, when he's seated, one of his legs—usually his right—drives like a jackhammer, sometimes so exhausting him that he plants a hand on his knee in an effort to halt the pumping, or at least to slow it down. He takes medication—Wellbutrin—for his anxiety. Much of this can be directly attributed to the fact that within the past two years he's been stabbed, coming out of a barbershop, and then shot, just outside his house. But more on that later.

What you need to know here is this: at De La Salle, Marcelo had for the past year gotten all A's, except for a B in math this past semester. He was a remarkably hardworking student. It was, to be sure, a delicate balancing act. During the week he studied two to three hours a night. Come the weekend, he'd hang out with his friends from the neighborhood, and though he'd left his gang, the Latin Kings, he danced along the periphery, still cavorting with his old running mates. He knew that he couldn't keep up this double life for long. Some of his friends referred to him as "the stupid smart kid."

Marcelo can be shy, and so at the party he drank quite a bit. He can't remember how much, but it emboldened him enough to approach a cute girl wrapped in a tight dress and tell her that she looked familiar and that he was eighteen, neither of which was true. Around midnight Marcelo wandered outside and in the gangway alongside the house smoked a Newport with his best friend, Javier. At that point four squad cars pulled up. Marcelo thinks it was because someone had reported a gun there, but he isn't sure. He didn't wait around to find out. He and Javier hopped into the car of Daniel, his friend who had driven them there, and took off. Daniel had a friend with him who was so drunk he was falling in and out of sleep, and Javier, whose cell phone had been stolen a week earlier, swiped the sleeping friend's phone from his pants pocket. Marcelo didn't learn this until they got dropped off at his house for the night, and Javier, who was staying over, proudly displayed his new acquisition. Together they laughed at Javier's slyness. Fully clothed, Marcelo fell asleep in his bed while Javier crashed on the sofa in the living room.

Early the next morning Marcelo awoke to the persistent ringing of his cell phone. It was Daniel, who demanded his friend's phone back, and soon Daniel and his friend showed up at Marcelo's house. Javier returned the phone. Daniel suggested to Marcelo and Javier, *Let's go hit stains.* Let's go rob someone, let's leave our mark, let's leave our stain.

I ain't even trying to go, Marcelo said, reluctant to rob strangers.

Come on, man, what the fuck, I got the whip, Daniel replied, a reference to the fact that he had a car.

Javier, who needed a phone and needed money to help pay his family's rent, seemed excited by the prospect. He nudged Marcelo, who, tired and hungover, relented. The four of them piled into Daniel's SUV, which belonged to his mother, and they drove around the neighborhood looking for a mark.

To be fair, Daniel's memory of the events of this morning differs from Marcelo's. He says that when he came by Marcelo's house, they all jumped in his car to get breakfast at a local taqueria, and that the robberies were in fact Marcelo's idea. Marcelo denies that and told me, "I'm just there, like an idiot."

As they drove by Curie High School, on the city's southwest side, they spotted a teenager wearing headphones, lost to the beat of his music. A half-block ahead they pulled into an alley, and all but Daniel, who was driving, jumped out of the car and rushed the young man, who took off running. Javier hurled an empty beer bottle, hitting him in the back. The victim tripped and fell, and within seconds the three were on him. All Marcelo remembers of the assault is that he kicked the young man while he was on the ground. Javier snatched his iPhone and his wallet. Marcelo felt empowered, in control. It was, he said later, "like a high."

Back in the car, they soon pulled up alongside a teen in a black hoodie, and Marcelo noticed a slash through the teen's right eyebrow, an indication that he belonged to a rival gang. Marcelo leaned out of the passenger-side window and false-flagged, pretending to be a member of the same faction. *What up, Folks,* Marcelo hollered. (For a few decades now, the city's gangs have been divided into two sides, Folks and Peoples, a linguistic distinction which to outsiders seems like splitting hairs. Folks. Peoples. It is almost as if they are declaring that we're one and the same rather than they're on opposite sides.) The young man replied, *That's right. Fifty-nine*—a reference to his street. This was the gang that had shot Marcelo a year earlier, and so at that point nothing else seemed to matter. "This was more personal-type shit," Marcelo recalls. He jumped out of the car and punched the boy hard enough that his nose bled. During the scuffle, Marcelo began to have a flashback, reliving the moment he had gotten shot. This happened periodically and it scared him, an almost out-of-body experience which felt too real. His anger turned to rage, and he kicked the teen while he lay on the ground. "It was instinct," Marcelo told me. "I saw him and lost my mind." They left the teen bloodied, lying on the sidewalk. Marcelo jumped back in the car and they continued trolling.

The next boy they came upon carried a bookbag and wore skinny jeans. "He looked like a lame," Marcelo told me. He handed over his phone, a Cricket, with no resistance. *Here you go,* he said, *I don't want no problems.*

Then at a bus stop they came upon a boy on his phone. He looked to be roughly their age. They piled out of the car, and before the boy could flee, Javier hit him in the face. *Let me see your phone,* Marcelo demanded. The boy handed it to him, and Marcelo threw it back. *What'd you do that for?* Javier asked. *Look at that shit, nigga,* Marcelo replied. *It's that Cricket shit again, worth thirty bucks.* They hit the boy with empty beer bottles, so hard he later needed stitches in his scalp.

Marcelo wanted to go home. He was drained, both physically and emotionally. He didn't so much have regrets as he did a sense that this was no longer him. And yet, if he was being honest, he got a rush from the morning's events, almost a high. What was it about hurting someone that gave him satisfaction? he wondered. He insisted they drop him off at his house, and as they cruised back to their neighborhood, they stopped at a traffic light. An unmarked police car cut them off, and two plainclothes officers ordered them out of the car. They were quickly surrounded by half a dozen squad cars. Marcelo, who had removed his shirt because of the heat, sagged into the car seat, one hand tightly clutching his T-shirt. The police arrested the four friends and charged them each with two counts of robbery, one count of attempted robbery, and one count of aggravated battery.

The next day in bond court, in a hearing that took no more than a few minutes, a judge set Marcelo's bond at $300,000, which meant that his family needed to come up with $30,000 to get him released. That was an impossible amount for his mother, who worked at a Styrofoam cup factory, and so it appeared that Marcelo had hit a dead end, that he would sit in jail until his case came to trial, which, given the way things moved in the county courts, could be anywhere from a year to two in the future. Marcelo thought to himself, *I've been leading a double life. It's over. I fucked up.*

Chapter 2

Mother's Day

On July 24 of last year, the *Southtown Star,* a suburban newspaper, ran a short seventeen-sentence story with the headline: "Man Shot to Death in Park Forest Had Drug, Weapons Convictions." The article went on to rattle off the background of the murder victim, Darren Easterling. It read, in part:

A man who was shot to death Sunday on the street in Park Forest was a felon who in the past two years had multiple convictions on drug and weapons charges, according to officials and court records. . . .

As of late Monday afternoon, Park Forest police had no suspects in custody in connection with the shooting, in which at least one other man was injured. . . .

According to court records, Easterling pleaded guilty to felony possession of a controlled substance and possession of marijuana in January 2010. He also pleaded guilty to unlawful use of a weapon in April 2011 and was sentenced to three years in prison. Easterling was released on parole in November 2011, according to Illinois Department of Corrections records. . . .

Darren Easterling, who was 25 and shot multiple times, died at the scene.

L isa Daniels is long-bodied, willowy, and tall, with a handsome, stoic face atop a long, slender neck. She wears hoop earrings, which sway as she walks, her strides purposeful and quick. She works as an administrative assistant to a vice president at the Museum of Science and Industry. She's thoughtful and preternaturally poised, but on this Sunday morning, this Mother's Day, she lay in bed wracked with self-doubt. Her bedroom sat in the rear of her newly renovated second-floor apartment in Englewood, on the city's South Side. She had closed the blinds to block the sunlight and pulled the covers over her, creating a protective cocoon, all in an effort to keep everything and everyone at bay. A few months earlier she and her husband, to whom she'd been married for fourteen months, had finalized their divorce, and just two days ago a friend had called to tell Lisa that her ex now had a girlfriend. Lisa already knew about the girlfriend, since that was in part the reason for their split, but she was distressed that it was now public knowledge. It stung. She wanted to disappear. She couldn't bear explaining herself to friends or family. She felt like a failure. She had failed her marriage. And she had failed her son.

This was the first Mother's Day since she'd lost her son, Darren Easterling (he had his father's name), ten months earlier, and she thought she had been managing reasonably well. But in the wake of her broken marriage, she felt deep shame. Her husband had left her. So had her son, which is at least how it felt. She had raised him with love and a strong moral compass, but he had wandered. "I just didn't want to get up," she told me. "I didn't want to face anything. That's always been my coping mechanism. When I'm feeling really bad, I close myself off." It was, she said, the darkest she'd felt since the funeral. But it was also a moment when her life began to take another turn.

I met Lisa Daniels through a friend, Kathryn Bocanegra, who's a social worker and who's married to someone you'll meet later. Kathryn, who runs two support groups for mothers of children lost to the city's violence, talks about "complex loss," a term used informally among social workers and therapists working in our cities. They came up with the designation because they didn't believe "post-traumatic stress" captured what people grappled with, since there's nothing "post" about their experience. Grief in places where the conflict is ongoing, Kathryn believes, is messy, without a straight line forward, without a map. "The way that people deal with that loss can vary dramatically," Kathryn told me. "Some want vengeance, some want accountability. Others feel like even with that that won't accomplish anything, so they become activists. And some want to pretend it never happened."

Elisabeth Kübler-Ross wrote that grief takes place in five stages: denial, anger, bargaining, depression, and acceptance. Come to Chicago. I dare you to find those stages. I dare you to chart grief. Someone dies a sudden, violent death and the natural order of things breaks apart. You see it in the streets of the city. When someone's murdered, street shrines arise, in summer with the ubiquity of perennials. They decorate the spots where blood has been shed. On street corners. In an alley. By a porch. In a park. At a gas station. Outside a convenience store. At these locations, on sheets of posterboard taped to buildings or lampposts or fences or trees, friends and family leave notes of love and regret and anger.

We lost one. Heaven gain one. RIP. J-Rae

Dear Brandon, I'm so fucked up right now. I can't start
2 explain. I will always love you. You were my all back in
the day. You didn't deserve this. I love you. Yo Pumpkin

R.I.P. Daddy, love Miracle

The only Angel in our family. Ama miss you Angel Love
Nelly R.

They leave candles and empty liquor bottles, usually the deceased's beverage of choice, often Hennessy Cognac and Moët &
Chandon Champagne and grapefruit juice (which is mixed with
the Moët). To fenceposts and streetlamps they tie balloons,
which soon deflate and droop, making them appear less a celebration of the dead than a statement of fact. People leave objects,
like basketballs or flowers or photographs, or stuffed animals or
toys if the victim is unusually young. I've seen dolls and battery-
powered cars, anything that might comfort the dead—and the
living. It's a kind of community catharsis. The acronym RIP—
rest in peace—is everywhere. It's penned on the sheets of posterboard hanging by these makeshift memorials. It's tattooed on
people's bodies. Painted on the walls of apartments. Scrawled on
the side of buildings. Embossed on T-shirts and jackets. It's as if
these communities are piecing together the equivalent of a war
memorial.

But then there's the personal grief, the turbulence of guilt and
loss and anger, gnawing away at individuals, especially mothers,
exposing the rawest and most unpredictable of emotions and
behavior. One mother I knew, a tall, stately woman, had fled war-
torn Sudan for Chicago with her husband and her son. As the son
grew into adolescence, he made connections in their mostly Hispanic neighborhood. At one point he witnessed a murder committed by an older friend and was so distressed that he couldn't stop
talking, couldn't stop hinting to neighbors what he'd seen. One day

the friend, concerned that all the chatter would get him in trouble, beckoned the teen to meet him behind a garage, in an alley, and there shot him six times. As he lay dying, the friend allegedly whispered, *I love you, but I had to do it.*

His mother was at first invigorated by her own amateur detective work, trying to find evidence to arrest her son's murderer, but the case stalled, and in the weeks and months to follow she pulled into herself, her face tightening like a fist. There would be afternoons I'd stop by and she'd still be in her nightgown, curled up on the couch in her small living room, smoking, her hair uncombed. She looked as if she was wilting. Unwashed dishes lay cluttered around the kitchen sink. In need of money, she sold various items from the house, including her television and some furniture. The house got emptier and emptier. At one point she told me, "If I can't protect my son, I'm worth nothing." She became so depressed, so inward, so sour, that—I'm not proud to admit this—I began to go around less often. "Nobody wants to be with me," she told me, apologizing for not being better company. "It's like lenses. I see everything through this tragedy."

She complained about a bitter, almost metallic taste in her mouth. She couldn't rid herself of it, and she told me that it only intensified when she ate. So she stopped eating. The only thing that helped was candy she could suck on, but even that only diminished the bitterness. It didn't erase it. One day, when she had taken her younger son to Lake Michigan, she reached into her pockets and realized she'd forgotten to bring any candy. The metallic taste was unusually strong, and so she reached down, scooped up a small handful of sand, and slowly sucked on it. It took away the bitterness. The sand gave her taste. It is, I suppose, the equivalent of finding solace in an empty room. It was the only joy—albeit a muted one—she could find. She purchased bags of play sand from Home Depot and told her husband it was for their son to play in, but when he figured it out, he began cooking elaborate Sudanese meals, mostly lamb, which she ordinarily savored; but nothing kept that bitterness away like the sand. She had to stop when, months later, her doctor informed her of an alarming iron deficiency. "This tragedy is like my shadow," she told me. "I'm trying to save what is left of me."

I could tell story after story like this, of mothers who drift on a sea of heartache, without oars and without destination. One young mother I met told me she cuts herself. On a warm summer day she had been sitting on her front stoop, braiding her six-year-old daughter's hair, when her daughter doubled over, caught in crossfire. "The moment I cut myself, it burns," the mother told me. "I'm in so much pain I stop thinking of my daughter—and I have some peace." Many hold on to what anchor they can, a piece of their child no one can take away. One mother I know held her seven-year-old daughter as she died in her arms, and in her closet she keeps her daughter's bloodied clothes in a plastic bag, a kind of talisman. Another had her son's EKG record, his last heartbeats, tattooed on her forearm. Still another propped against her fireplace a life-sized cardboard likeness of her son. A few have convinced the city to name a street or a park after their child: Ryan Harris Memorial Park, Hadiya Pendleton Park, Derrion J. Albert Way, Dantrell Davis Way, Blair Delane Holt Way.

One mother told me, "I didn't know there were so many different ways to grieve." Some try to give purpose to their child's death. They find oars; they imagine a destination. Some, like Afaf, turn into amateur sleuths, searching for the killer. One mother I know took in a troubled girl who she thought could help lead her to her son's killer. They become activists, lobbying for gun control or a greater police presence or longer sentences. They comfort other moms in the immediate turbulence of having their child torn from them. In Chicago there are roughly half a dozen groups of mothers who have lost children to the violence: Parents for Peace and Justice, Sisterhood, Chicago Survivors, Purpose Over Pain, Mothers of Murdered Sons. They hold vigils. They attend each other's court cases. They celebrate their children on the anniversary of their deaths or on their birthdays. They march, hold prayer circles, host barbecues, and release balloons to the heavens. Sometimes they arrange block parties, replete with inflatable bounce houses. One group of mothers held a party where they all received tattoos on their pinkies which read *Promise*—as if to remind themselves and others of all the things they'd promised to do in the wake of losing a child. Because these mothers have each other, they live richly in mourning.

I've asked moms about getting closure, and they shake their heads, as if there were any way to put the death of a child behind you, as if there were any way to heal a wound that opens and reopens at the slightest bump. A mention of your child's name. Hearing of someone else's loss. A dream. (Or not a dream. One mother told me she was troubled because she could never conjure up her son in her sleep.) A memory. A keepsake. There's a lot to keep that wound from closing. But here's the thing, most go on. They continue. They have to. Some have other children and so need to be in the present, to nurture, to comfort, to make others laugh. Some have husbands. Or jobs. Or friends. One mother I know, Myrna Roman, has an uncanny ability to lift everyone around her. Her twenty-three-year-old son, Manny, was killed randomly, stopped at a streetlight by a young man who was angry at things having nothing to do with Manny and who Manny didn't even know. Myrna told me that she used to be all "heels and skirts" and now she was just "gym shoes and sweatpants." She said, "The minute it happens [that you lose a child], you're a different person. We're built different. We see life different."

Years ago I read Rian Malan's *My Traitor's Heart*, a searing account of post-apartheid South Africa. Malan told the story of his country by telling the story of several murders. In death, he was suggesting, you can understand life. At the book's end he tells the story of Creina Hancock. She and her husband, Neil, lived in KwaZulu among the Zulus, tirelessly working toward creating sustainable agriculture, trying to undo some of the harm done by apartheid. Neil was murdered by Zulus in a tribal dispute. Creina, though, stayed on, continuing her and her husband's work. What she told Malan has stayed with me: "The only thing you can do is love, because it is the only thing that leaves light inside you, instead of the total, obliterating darkness." That, I think, is at the heart of Lisa's story—and, honestly, the default setting of most mothers who have lost a child to the violence.

At the age of seventeen, Lisa had her first child, Kevin; then, at the age of twenty-four, she had Darren. The two boys had different fathers and because of the age difference were never particularly close. Lisa raised them herself, first in Bronzeville, a neighborhood on the South Side, and then in the southern suburbs, some of which are more distressed than the most hardscrabble parts of Chicago. Her older son, Kevin, was focused on what lay ahead. He knew what he wanted. He was keyed into school and would go on to the University of Illinois to study electrical engineering. Darren was more unpredictable. Hardheaded. Restless. Impatient. Lisa has tried to figure out where it started, why Darren seemed so agitated all the time. Maybe, she thought, it was because his dad, who had remarried and had three more children, wasn't a part of his life. Maybe that was too pat an explanation. Darren played football in high school, first as quarterback. But he didn't like the pressure, so he switched positions, to running back. He liked to hang out at home and watch documentaries, especially on the Discovery Channel. He had a lot going for him: he was athletic, good-looking, and personable. And he and his mother were close. (So were Lisa and Kevin, though Lisa says her relationship with Kevin, because she was so young when she had him, felt more like that of siblings than that of mother and son.) Darren loved his mother's peach cobbler, and so she'd make it especially for him. He always remembered her birthday and Mother's Day, once giving her a card filled with recipes, which she still has. But he started straying. She can't pinpoint when it started. It began as a trickle and then before long turned into a roaring river.

In high school he got suspended for possession of marijuana. After a football game he and friends got arrested after stealing candy from a corner store. Two days later he got caught in a K-mart slipping a pack of condoms into his jacket pocket. Darren would apologize, assure his mother it wouldn't happen again, tell her *I'm going to get it together.* One birthday he wrote her a card which read:

> Thank you for still loving me after 18 long years even though I was bad for 17. Love you with all my heart. And mom don't forget that I'm still going to make it. And you will see a change. Just watch. You don't have to say nothing. Happy Birthday. Love your baby boy Darren.

He got expelled from three different high schools and never graduated. "It seemed he was always looking for something," Lisa told me. "He couldn't seem to grab hold of what he was looking for, and honestly, I'm not sure what that was." Lisa kicked him out of her house after she found a small bag of crack cocaine in a shoebox which he clearly intended to sell. He spent eighteen months in prison for carrying a gun. And then he continued dealing drugs. He had two children with his girlfriend and was an attentive dad, but his relationship with their mother was on-again, off-again. "We never stopped being close," Lisa recalled. "He was respectful. He said he needed to take care of his kids [as a way to justify selling drugs]. I always told him that was BS. You could do something different. This is not what you need to do. Nobody you know in your family lives like this, so stop it." Lisa was too ashamed to share any of this with those around her, until one day, on the phone with her mother, who had worked as a nurse, she broke down and spilled everything—the expulsions, the drugs, the arrests. She sobbed, barely able to get the words through gasps for air. "My mom said the best thing I probably ever heard my mother say," Lisa told me. "She listened while I cried. When I stopped to take a breath, she said, *Stop. Stop blaming yourself. This is not your journey. Darren has to take his own journey.* It was freeing for me. She also assured me he was going to be okay."

On Sunday evening, July 22 of last year, 2012, Lisa received a phone call from a friend of her son's. The friend said he couldn't reach Darren and that he had heard someone had been shot in the Park Forest suburb where he thought Darren had been heading. Lisa called the Park Forest police, but they had no record of an encounter with a Darren Easterling. Nor did St. James Hospital. Then her husband suggested she call the county morgue. She remembers speaking to a man there who asked Lisa for her son's name and his birthdate. He put her on hold, and when he returned he told Lisa, *Yes, he's here.* His tone was so matter-of-fact that Lisa was about to ask, *Can I talk to him?* When she got off the phone, her husband tried to embrace her, but she told him, *I'm fine. I'm okay.* And when she called Darren's friend back and he burst into tears, wailing, Lisa, uncharacteristically, told him to shut up. *It doesn't make sense to cry,* she thought to herself. *You all chose to live this lifestyle.*

I know this sounds odd, but on some level Lisa felt a sense of relief. Kathryn, the social worker, who has seen this in other mothers, calls it "compassionate relief." Lisa knew where her son was headed. She knew it wasn't good. She worried about him. All the time. Her friend Ernest Johnson remembers that when he called Lisa, "I was expecting her to be really shook up, but she seemed peaceful and calm." In fact, she gave the eulogy at Darren's funeral, chastising his friends for their upside-down priorities. She thanked them for purchasing Darren's outfit—$270 for designer jeans and a plaid button-down shirt—but she said that if they had that money, why didn't they lend it to Darren so he didn't feel he needed to rob someone?

Lisa had learned the circumstances of Darren's death from his friends and then from the police. Early in the afternoon of that Sunday, Darren and a friend had driven to the Park Forest suburb to meet a small-time drug dealer, Michael Reed, to buy two ounces of marijuana. Reed lived in Park Forest, a postwar community of compact, mostly single-story ranch homes, and had agreed to meet Darren and his friend on his way to his job at Burger King. When Darren and his friend pulled up in a car driven by a woman friend of theirs, Reed got into the backseat alongside Darren's friend. Darren sat in the front passenger seat. Here's where the story diverges, depending on whom you talk to.

The prosecution theorized that Reed intended to rob Darren and his friend. Because of what she's heard on the street, Lisa is convinced that Darren and his friend intended to rob Reed. It may well be that they were there to rob each other. Regardless, here's what the police believe happened. When Reed got into the backseat, he saw Darren's friend tap his .380 pistol, tucked under his thigh. The friend might have been reaching for it or simply making sure it was still there. Reed pulled out a 9mm pistol and opened fire. He shot twice through the passenger car seat, hitting Darren in the back and the buttocks. He shot Darren's friend twice, in the thigh. And then, as Reed backed out of the car, his gun extended, Darren's friend shot Reed in the hip and the chest. Darren, with two bullet wounds in his back, pulled himself out of the car and leaned over the roof, shooting a .22-caliber pistol with an extended clip. His gun jammed. This is a lot of shooting in a pretty confined area— sixteen shots total. It would be almost cartoonish in its everyone-shooting-everyone-else way if it weren't so damn real, if it weren't so damn fatal. And as it turned out, Michael Reed did not have the promised two ounces of marijuana on him. Nor did Darren or his friend have the $800 for the purchase. No one, it seemed, had come with good intentions.

Reed, injured, ran to a car driven by friends, who drove him to a nearby hospital. Darren's friend was driven to the same hospital by his woman friend. They left behind Darren, who stumbled to the curb in front of a one-story brick home, where he collapsed on top of his gun, gasping for breath. He died on the patchy grass of the parkway, his hand held by a young woman who happened to be passing by. Reed and Darren's friend were both arrested at the hospital.

Lisa initially felt shame. It could just as easily have been Reed who was killed and her son who faced prison. They had pulled guns on each other. Victim. Perpetrator. The lines blurred. There was no nobility in her son's death, no heroism. He had brought it upon himself. Lisa knew that. She didn't take issue with that. What did bother her, though, was that people, total strangers, thought they knew her son. *What do you know?* she'd ask. When the *Southtown Star* had run its story, readers responded with online comments calling Darren "an out of town thug" and "a clown." One asked, "Where are his parents?" (This is not an uncommon refrain. After a seven-year-old was fatally shot in the chest with a bullet intended for someone else, Chicago's mayor, Rahm Emanuel, publicly asked of the shooter, "Where were you raised and who raised you?") Lisa didn't dispute the facts of the article, but it vexed her that the newspaper and its readers saw her son through the lens of this one incident, that they thought they knew the shape of Darren's narrative, that they thought they knew him, and by inference her. And so she wrote a letter to the paper, which read, in part:

> The beautiful thing I have come to recognize about the
> experience of being Darren's mother, is that his love for me

made me just a little bit happier about being me. I could feel his love and the warmth of his embrace (he never forsook an opportunity to hug his mother).

She wrote about his two children, about his love for football, about how she believed he was more than people imagined:

His legacy will not fall to the ground and wither after a blaze of gunfire. I am positive, however, that even after reading my words many will stand firm on their position as to who Darren B. Easterling was based on what the court records show, and will insist on believing that he was a trash laden thug from another town (we are former residents of Park Forest and he had many associations in the city). However, the truth is that my son, just like many before him, has a mother who loved him (and misses him) dearly, he was a brother, a father, a nephew, a friend to many . . . You all have the right to own your perspective, but I have spoken my son's truth.

The newspaper never published the letter, but Lisa would eventually get a license plate holder that reads: *He was my son. His name was Darren.*

Here's the other thing you need to know: from the day police arrested Michael Reed, her son's killer, Lisa refused to hold a grudge against him. She didn't know Reed, knew nothing about him. What she did know is this: "He was in a messed-up place, like Darren." One week after the murder, she posted on Facebook:

Another mother has lost her son, only this loss is different. Today the man who shot Darren has been charged with first degree murder. There is no victory here and I can only imagine the weight his mother carries. I will fervently pray for her and her son. His name is Michael Reed and he too is someone's son and maybe even someone's father, like Darren was. He too was lost in a dark place just like my son was before he made the decision to receive eternal life. I ask you all to pray for him and his mother, as she grieves the life of her son, just as you have prayed for me.

Moreover, she figured that things would run their course, that "what was going to happen was going to happen." She assumed that "he was going to jail for first-degree murder and that that wasn't going to have any effect on my life." She was wrong. On both counts.

Mother's Day descended. It was as if death knelt down—again—and swept everything aside. Her apartment had recently been renovated, and her kitchen, where she spent most of her time and which overlooked a vacant corner lot, was bathed in sunlight. There were few memories of her son. She displayed only one photo of him, from junior high school, kneeling in his football uniform, long-necked like his mom, thin as a pencil. She also kept on her desk in the living room an ashtray-sized ceramic bowl that Darren had made in middle school. (Lisa is not given to sentimentality; she keeps paper clips in the ceramic bowl.) Her bedroom was in the rear of her apartment, and unlike her kitchen received little light. She lay there in her queen-sized bed, alone, sheltered from the inquiries of friends and from the gusty summer wind which rattled her windows. At one point, in gray sweats and a T-shirt, she shuffled into the kitchen, made herself some coffee, poured in creamer and a touch of sweetener, and went back to bed, propping the pillows against her headboard. She sat there thinking about the late nights when she'd leave the kitchen light on so she would know when Darren arrived home. She remembered Mother's Day from two years ago. Darren was locked up without phone privileges, so he had another inmate call his mom, who in turn called Lisa to wish her a happy Mother's Day from Darren. He never forgot.

Lisa is deeply religious. She attends a nondenominational church and leans on her faith. In bed, she recited aloud one of her favorite proverbs: "Trust in the Lord with all your heart and lean not on your own understanding; in all your ways submit to him, and he will make your paths straight." She found comfort in this passage, and thought the only way she would get through the hurt was to focus on God's love for her and not on her own feelings.

She would've called her mother, but she had developed Alzheimer's, which had so progressed that she often didn't remember Lisa. Lisa had steered away from the mothers' groups, because she worried that they'd say, "Get out of here. Your son could have killed my child. Get out of here with that." She navigated grief by herself, occasionally reaching out. That morning she called a friend who had lost a son to illness, wanting to know how she responded when asked how many children she had. *Two,* Lisa decided she'd answer. Some friends had been warning her that come July 22, the anniversary of Darren's death, she would struggle, that it would bring her back to the day he was killed. It irritated her that people told her how she should feel. *It's just another day,* she thought to herself. *I refuse to give it power over me.*

On this day she knew she couldn't fall any further. She came to realize, "I'm more than a grieving mother. We're all more than the sum total of our worst experience. I won't allow myself to be reduced to that single day. There's so much more to me. There's so much more to my life. So I need to pick up the pieces and keep moving."

It was a rough year that followed. The assistant state's attorney, Cheryl Galvin, who was prosecuting Michael Reed for first-degree murder, told me that Lisa was angry. *No matter how much time he serves, I'll never have my son back,* Lisa told Cheryl. *You know, I want him to raise my son's kids. They don't have a father now.* (Lisa remembers it differently. She says she wasn't agitated, just that she was being direct about her situation.) Lisa didn't show up for the court dates and rarely returned Cheryl's calls. It was complicated. She was irked at her son. "I spent some time being angry with him," she told me. "I could not imagine what he was thinking. The place I got to is, if he hadn't been killed then, he still wouldn't be alive today. You don't rob drug dealers and survive." On the anniversary of Darren's death, two of his friends came by, both to comfort Lisa and to receive comfort from her. But she had little patience for their sorrow. *I'm good,* she told them. *Don't come up here with all that sadness.* By that, she meant that they were all out there taking risks, and they knew the stakes. *Stop feeling sorry for yourselves,* she thought.

Through Facebook she tracked down the young woman whom she'd heard had been with Darren as he lay on the parkway. Lisa wanted to know about those last moments. She wanted to know that her son didn't die alone. The young woman told Lisa that she and her sister were on the way home, just around the corner, when they noticed this young man bleeding on the ground. In a phone call, she told Lisa that while her sister called for an ambulance, she knelt on the ground beside him. *Was he still alive?* Lisa asked. The young woman told her that he was. *Did you tell him it was going to be okay?*

Yes, m'am, she assured Lisa.

She said that Darren was choking on his blood, and that she took his hand. Darren's whole body shook, as if he was seizing, she told Lisa, and then his eyes rolled to the back of his head. Lisa was weeping at this point, but mostly out of relief, knowing that her son didn't die by himself. The young woman said that Darren kept trying to say something but couldn't get any sounds out. Lisa wonders what it was, but "I know it begins with 'Tell my momma . . .'" That's what she keeps telling herself—that he always knew he could count on her.

She finally got the strength to attend a court date. Reed had been charged with first-degree murder, and she thought it a straight-forward case. But it was problematic. The key witness, Darren's friend, had pled guilty to unlawful use of a weapon and so didn't make for the best witness. And Darren himself had three felonies. Cheryl, the prosecutor, had no doubt that the defense attorney would revisit Darren's past and paint him as a thug. Cheryl also told Lisa that Michael Reed argued he had shot Darren in self-defense. *What do you mean, self-defense?* Lisa countered. *He killed my son. They came to rob each other.*

"That was a gut check for me," Lisa told me. "They didn't care about my forgiveness. He was fighting for his life. And their belief was that if my son had not been there, Michael wouldn't be having the issues he's having. 'So, get out of here with your forgiveness. Kick rocks with your forgiveness.' That was a real moment for me. If he was found not guilty—the way I was thinking about it is, he got away with murder."

Cheryl tried to break it gently, but given the problems in the case, she was inclined to let Reed plead guilty to a lesser charge, to second-degree murder. Lisa took her time. "I had to decide whether I believed what I said about forgiveness, whether I believed all the things I'd been preaching," she told me. She prayed, and then told Cheryl she would agree to a plea deal *if* she got to read a victim impact statement at his sentencing. Reed and his attorney agreed to that. Twice the sentencing was postponed because Lisa wasn't prepared, and then the third time Lisa arrived at court, Cheryl asked her for the statement, which she needed to submit to the judge. Lisa told her it was in her head. Cheryl put her in an office so that Lisa could write it out. Cheryl assumed that Lisa, like most family members of victims, would address the suffering of herself and her family. Lisa took the stand and in an unwavering voice read her statement.

"My name is Lisa Daniels and I want to thank you for this opportunity to share my heart today by allowing me to give this victim impact statement. I understand this to be a statement in my own words that informs the offender of how the crime committed has affected me and my family. That crime, being the murder of my son Darren Easterling, has affected us all differently because Darren was more than just my son. He was a father, a brother, a nephew, and a friend to many, and his death has left a void in us all but most importantly is the loss for his son and his daughter who are ages nine and seven right now and as they grow will continue to be affected by no longer having their father.

"My son wasn't perfect. He made bad decisions and lifestyle choices that cost him his life. But at the end of the day none of his choices mattered because he was my son and I loved him and miss him terribly. The morning after he was killed the Southtown newspaper headline read: 'Man shot to death in Park Forest had drug and weapon felony convictions' and from that day to this I awake every day with the mission and purpose that his legacy will not be defined by his worst mistake. No one's should. Not even the defendant.

"Bishop Desmond Tutu is quoted as saying, 'My humanity is bound up in yours, for we can only be human together.' I believe that statement to be true. I believe that we are all connected by our humanity and I cannot speak for my son's humanity without speaking for the same humanity of the man who, by one really bad decision, took his life. I have and will always continue to speak on Darren's behalf but today I speak for you Michael Reed. Because the truth is that things could have gone differently that day and this young man could have just as easily lost his life and Darren would be sitting in this seat needing someone to speak on his behalf. I am a mother and I know the heart of a mother. So I will speak from a mother's heart for a child who made a horrible, horrible choice.

"I don't know all of the details of the encounter between Darren and Michael on July 22, 2012, but there are two things I know for sure. The first is that no matter what he did or the choices he made he didn't deserve to die that day as a result of those choices;

and the second thing I know for sure is that this young man does not deserve to spend another year, day or minute behind bars as a result of a poor choice he made. Darren is not coming back, and fifteen years of his life is not going to change that. And so I ask Your Honor to be lenient to this young man."

The judge sentenced Michael Reed to fifteen years, which, given the time he had served, meant he'd be out in three and a half years. As Reed was led out of the courtroom, his hands cuffed to a shackle around his waist, he turned toward Lisa, put his hands together as if in prayer, and mouthed, *Thank you.*

I want to be careful here. There's a lot to admire in what Lisa did. As Kathryn told me, when you lose a child to the violence, "it pulls out of you who you really are. In Lisa's case, she had to dig deep into herself, figure out what she really believes in. That's the real struggle following a loss: Who am I as a person? The deep drilling into yourself—that's where the forgiveness comes from." But Kathryn also talks about how forgiveness is easier when the line between victim and killer is blurred, where the victim is someone who just as easily could've been on the other side of the equation.

I've sat in on trials where, honestly, there wasn't room for forgiveness. At one trial the accused, Andrew Ruiz, glared at Myrna Roman, whose son he had killed. Ruiz had randomly shot Myrna's son, Manny, as he sat in a car waiting for the traffic light to change. Ruiz didn't know him. He was just angry after a dispute with his girlfriend, and as he got in his car that night, he announced, "It's Halloween, and someone's going to die." In court, Ruiz smirked and sneered, one time throwing a gang sign out of sight of the judge. At the sentencing, Ruiz's father seated himself behind the lead detective in the case and muttered, "Fuck the police." Myrna is generous of spirit. She once took another grieving mother under her wings. She has helped other moms post flyers, helped them find information that might lead to their son's murderer. She has spoken to ex-offenders, offering her support. I asked her whether she could ever forgive Ruiz, who was convicted. "If I felt in my heart that he actually felt remorse or regret for what he did, but I don't think there's any way with this person," she told me. "There's no soft spot in my heart for him." I understood. I felt the same way.

Lisa doesn't want to hold herself up as somehow more open-hearted. She's not. It's just that she knew. Her son and Michael Reed tried to kill each other. One came out alive. Lisa knows how easily it could've come out the other way. In the end, it had more to do with justice than it did with forgiveness. What felt right. What felt just. She has since set up an organization, the Darren B. Easterling Center for Restorative Practices, to work with troubled children and grieving mothers.

"Forgiving Michael wasn't something that I intended to do," she told me. "There was just no other consideration. Michael could've died that day. And Darren could've been facing a long prison sentence. Other people's notion of justice is that a wrong needs to be righted. I wasn't looking for that. I was just looking for the right thing to be done. And for me that was someone speaking up on Michael's behalf. If that had been Darren, I would've wanted someone to speak for him and for others to see my son for more than just the mistakes he made. That same thing I would've wanted for Darren, I had to be able to give to Michael."

Lisa wrote to Reed in prison, telling him that she wanted to help him find a job when he's released, help get his feet back on the ground. Reed wrote her back.

To Ms. Daniels,

You continue to amaze me. I really appreciate everything that you have done for me as far as court. I can't say thank you enough because being a mother and having to go thru what your going thru can really be tough and to have enough strength to forgive says a lot. Then say what you said at the sentencing really shocked me. I never had a chance to tell you how sorry I was. I never meant for any of this to happen. Ms. Daniels I didn't know your son. I had nothing against your son. I only came in contact with your son because of Jameal. I say this to say I did not try to rob your son or his friend. Since I been fighting this case I always wanted to let you know this there is so much stuff I would like to tell you but everything has a time and hopefully when the time is right I could share those things with you face to face. I would love the help that you are offering. That means a lot to me. I would be looking forward to that opportunity if there is any way I could repay I would try my best to do honestly. Once again thank you for your forgiveness and giving me a second chance. I truly am sorry! For all this thank and God Bless. Have a Blessed holiday.

Sincerely, Mike

On her way to work one morning, Lisa pulled Reed's letter out of the mailbox, took it to her car in the driveway, where she sat to read it. She knew then that she didn't need to find out what had happened that afternoon. Nothing was going to change the outcome. She needed to focus on what she could control. And so, a few days later, she wrote him back.

Hi Mike,

Thank you for your letter and please know that your sincere apology means more to me than you can ever possibly imagine. Please forgive my delay in responding but I've been really busy working, and building the organization. I know that there are probably bundles of things that took place the day you met

Darren that I know nothing about and I really appreciate you wanting to share some of that with me moving forward. Darren's death has changed my life (and your life) forever and from that day to this my focus has been on moving forward, helping others do the same and building an organization enabling the light of Darren's life to overshadow the experience of his death. And my prayer for you is that the rest of your life will overshadow the few minutes of that one day. And I am here to help you accomplish that any way I possibly can. That being said, always feel free to reach out to me and share your hopes, dreams and plans for the future but don't feel the need to share anything that happened that day. Let's continue to move forward. Sound like a plan? ☺
I look forward to hearing from you again.

Ms. Daniels

From prison, Reed told me, "I just want her to know I'm not a cold-blooded killer." When I mentioned this to Lisa, she told me she already knew that. "It makes me sad that he got the impression that that's what people thought of him. I never thought anything close to that. I would stand toe-to-toe with anybody who thinks that that's who he is."

Chapter 3

A Conversation: The OGs

It was tough to locate. I was given the intersection, but all I could find was an aged two-story building, its blue paint peeling like a snake shedding its skin. A sheet of plywood covered the first-floor window. The structure looked abandoned. As I stood outside, an older gentleman pedaled by on a three-speed bike. "Methadone?" he asked. "Methadone?" Another man on the corner offered loose cigarettes at fifty cents a smoke. Then I noticed the two cameras above a white door which had a CeaseFire bumper sticker plastered on it. I knocked. I could hear someone remove a security bar, and the door opened a few inches. Through the crack I heard an unwelcoming voice. "What you want?" I told him I was there to see Jimmie Lee. There were muffled sounds, and all I could make out was the word "police." I corrected him. "A friend," I said. "Alex." The door shut. A half-minute later Jimmie Lee opened the door, apologized, and beckoned me in.

The room once held a biker's club called the Western Warriors, but that was before Jimmie began renting the place in 1997, two years after he got out of prison. He rechristened it the Night Prowler, and it became a social club, mostly for old-timers, or OGs as they're known on the street: Original Gangsters. It's not a particularly large space. There's a faux-marble bar to the left lined with red stools, their plastic cushions cracked and ripped. To the right sits a big-screen TV fronted by a worn couch so low to the ground that it takes some work to rise from it. In the middle of the rectangular room, Jimmie has placed a round table for card playing, mostly poker and spades. And in the back he's positioned a homemade green, felt-lined craps table atop a pool table, which Jimmie says has seen better days. Along one wall is an electric stove, which Jimmie uses to cook for parties and repasts, of which there have been many in recent years. Attached to the same wall is a karaoke machine which a friend gave to Jimmie and which as far as I can discern is rarely used.

Jimmie comes here every day, to relax, to get away from what he calls the "craziness" of the streets. The neighborhood around the Night Prowler is rough, and so Jimmie has installed a kind of security system; in exchange for watching over the place, a friend who's homeless sleeps in the club, in a loft, a cavelike room over the bathroom which you wouldn't notice except that Bobby, who has trouble sitting still, is often crawling either in or out of it, contorting his body to avoid the strip of flypaper hanging from the ceiling.

Jimmie has a healthy anxiety about the neighborhood. Every Halloween he holds a party for children of friends and neighbors, as he worries about them trick-or-treating, especially at dusk. It began as just a gathering for children who were kin to him, but these gatherings have expanded, bringing in children of friends, so that some Halloweens over a hundred costumed boys and girls come by. Jimmie says he spends well over $700 at Sam's Club for candy. Twenty years, and Jimmie's had only one fight in the club, years ago, fisticuffs over a woman. Otherwise he's had no trouble, mostly because the clientele is older men who have tired of the streets and who are just looking, like Jimmie, for a place they can retire to, a place which feels unbothered by the goings-on outside.

Jimmie and I sat at the bar, both of us sipping bottled water. Jimmie doesn't drink. He's dressed casually in T-shirt and jeans, along with white socks and a pair of black Crocs. He has a black knit skullcap atop his head, a nod to his conversion to Islam.

I first heard of Jimmie Lee nearly thirty years ago, when I began work on my book *There Are No Children Here*. Jimmie headed a faction of the Conservative Vice Lords, the street gang that controlled the half of the Henry Horner Homes where Lafeyette and Pharoah lived. He was, to the say the least, a complicated man. He ran a robust drug business—heroin and cocaine—and so his members were heavily armed, with pistols, Uzis, and even grenades. Jimmie often could be seen in a bulletproof vest. But he also provided for elderly residents too poor to afford groceries and insisted on a sense of decency on his turf. He once punched a drunken father who had publicly berated his daughter outside a project building, calling her "a bitch."

I never met Jimmie while I was working on the book, since in the midst of my reporting he was arrested and convicted of possession of a controlled substance and intent to deliver. I wrote to him in prison requesting an interview, but he, understandably, declined. My portrait was based on interviews with gang members, with residents, and with the police. (In all the police stations on the West Side, pictures of Jimmie—along with four other high-ranking Vice Lords—hung on the walls with the warning "They are known to be involved in drug traffic, home invasions of dope flats, extortion and other crimes. They have been known to employ fully automatic weapons, travel in car caravans, usually with tail cars for protection.") Jimmie also had an enforcer, Napoleon English, whom everyone called Nap Dog and who was known to carry a .38 revolver in his waistband and a small derringer in his back pocket. He was so feared that I was warned not to engage with him during my time at Horner. So I didn't.

In 2010, while I was visiting an antiviolence organization housed at the University of Illinois at Chicago, a gray-haired gentleman approached me. He was smiling as if he knew something I didn't. "Alex," he said. I apologized and told him I couldn't place where I knew him from. He laughed, so restrained that I thought maybe he was mocking me. He extended his hand. "Jimmie Lee." All I could think to say was, "At least you're willing to shake my hand." Jimmie was wearing his usual inscrutable expression, one that never seems to waver, somewhere between stern and more stern. "I have one request," he said. I thought to myself, *Whatever you want, it's yours,* but I just nodded. "Can I get a copy of *There Are No Children Here*? Signed?"

Jimmie and I became friends after that. We'd periodically get together and talk about his time at Henry Horner, when he pretty much ran his end of the projects, holding more authority than either the police or the Chicago Housing Authority. When I first arrived at Horner, I spent my afternoons at the Boys Club as a way of getting to know the kids in the community, and Jimmie told me that Major Adams, the club's head, had asked him to keep an eye out for me, to ensure my safety, which he had, though I had had no idea at the time.

Jimmie was in prison when the book was published, and he told me that when word got out that he was a major character in a book, he got placed in segregation. He said it was clear the prison authorities were trying to make a point: *You may be a big shot in the outside world, but not in here. Don't let it go to your head.* I apologized, and Jimmie shrugged. "It's the system," he said. Once we were having lunch at a small spot, Ruby's, on the West Side, and an older man sauntered up to Jimmie and introduced himself. It happens a lot, that people who know Jimmie, sometimes just by reputation, approach him like he's a local celebrity, not because of the book but because of who he was on the street. Sometimes they buy him a meal. On this occasion Jimmie made small talk and then introduced me, telling the man that I'd authored this book that Jimmie's in. The man was vaguely familiar with the book and asked Jimmie, "You were one of those boys?" Jimmie shook his head. "No, I was the villain." He looked my way, as if to say, *Hey, that's the truth*. He invited me then to visit him at the Night Prowler.

As we sat on the cracked red stools, a group of four men played hearts at the round table. Jimmie wouldn't tell me much about them except that he said they, too, had all been players at one point. One of them, I noticed, had lost a leg. "Shot," Jimmie explained. "They trailed him. Knew he carried money. They tried to rob him."

Jimmie is now sixty-four, and as for many involved in the street, it got old, it got too dangerous, it got too foolish. When Jimmie got out of prison in 1996, he chose to settle down. He had a bevy of grandkids, and he wanted to be there for them. One of them, Deshon McKnight, gained some fame in Chicago for his poetry. Another became a highly recruited high school football player, a defensive end. Jimmie settled into a routine. In the mornings he goes to the gym to work out, mostly with the stationary bike and light weights. Into his seventh decade, he's still barrel-chested (his grandson, Deshon, boasted that when his grandfather was younger he had such a full chest he could balance a can of pop on it), but his shoulders are hunched, and when he walks he lists to one side, like a ship caught in the crosscurrents. In the afternoons he'll often take a long stroll, walking his daughter's shih tzu, Cotton. And in the evenings, well, he ends up here at his club, and if he's lucky a few old friends might wander in to play cards or shoot dice. But often he's by himself, holed up, away from the unpredictability of the outside.

"That killing stuff, there ain't no sense to it," he told me. "Forty years ago I wasn't in my right mind." I asked what changed for him, and before he could answer, the one-legged gentleman at the card table piped up, "He wanted to live longer. A lot longer." Jimmie smiled, though even when he smiles it feels like there's a lot going on in there.

In one corner a jovial-looking bear of a man played dominoes with Bobby, and he soon joined us. He is one of Jimmie's closest friends, Napoleon English, his former enforcer, who unlike Jimmie is always laughing and who has the ebullience of a little kid, seeming to bounce instead of walk. In the summer of 1986, Napoleon was ambushed by a rival gang and in the ensuing skirmish was shot twice, in the right shoulder and in the left wrist. Recovering in the hospital, he heard that a rival gang, the Gangster Disciples, thought they had killed him and had celebrated outside one of the buildings, chanting *We killed Nap. We killed Nap.* That didn't sit well with Napoleon, and when he got healthy he sought revenge. He walked into a high-rise at Horner and saw someone standing in the corner. *Gangster Stone,* Nap declared, falsely representing his affiliation. *Gangster Stone to the world,* the young man replied. Nap shot Wild Child, who was thirty-one, and as he lay there dying, his voice fading, he asked Nap, *Why you doing this? I ain't never done anything to you.* Nap didn't really have an answer for Wild Child, or for himself. And during his twenty-two years in prison he had trouble sleeping, reliving that moment again and again and again. He also had a recurring dream where he'd find himself shooting at people, but no matter how carefully he aimed, he couldn't hit anyone. He'd wake up in a panic, sweating. "When you start changing for the better and your perspective changes," he told me, "you start wrestling with good and evil. Ain't no murder got no credibility to it. Any murder is madness."

Napoleon joined us. Neither apologizes for his activities when he was younger. They felt they had no choice, though of course that was due in large part to the fact that they were making money in the drug trade, and protecting their enterprise sometimes required the use of force. Both have trouble, though, explaining these present times. "You can't make no sense of it," Napoleon said. "It's like trying to understand God. When we're dead and gone there's gonna be violence. It is what it is. It's the order of the day." What's particularly frustrating to them is that now no one seems in charge.

In the late 1990s and the early 2000s, law enforcement went after the gang chiefs, locking up one after another after another. Cut the snake off at the head. And it worked, for a while. It disrupted the street-corner drug trade and seemed to reduce the violence. But it had unintended consequences, as public policy so often does. In the vacuum, the gangs—at least the African-American gangs—fractured, shattered really, into scores of cliques or crews, organized from block to block. It became virtually impossible not to be associated with one group or another, simply because of where you lived. The police estimate there are 625 different cliques in the city. The names seem pulled out of a comic book: Killer Ward, Bang Bang, Smashville, Suwus, Lamron ("normal" spelled backwards), Hit Squad, Winchester Boys. A former big-time drug dealer, James Highsmith, once shook his head in wonderment at one clique's name. "What the hell you gonna call yourself Brain Dead for?" he asked.

"Now they don't have any kind of structure," Napoleon told me. "Nobody listens to nobody." He and Jimmie seemed perplexed by what's going on. The disputes, they say, are over petty things. "People get into it over nothing," Jimmie says. Someone's stepped on someone's new shoes. An argument over a girlfriend. Someone butting in line at a club. Someone asked to leave a party. Or one clique wars against another clique for reasons no one can explain. *Just because,* is what so many will say. Jimmie Lee and Napoleon English, once feared and revered in their neighborhood, no longer carry the weight they once did, at least among the younger generation. Jimmie tells me the teens in the area call him "old man" or "granddad." Not long ago Jimmie's grandson got into it with others on a nearby block, and despite Jimmie's efforts to intervene, they came around one day looking for his grandson, shooting up Jimmie's front porch. Jimmie's daughter was shot in the hand. "They do their own thing," he explained. "They don't listen to the old-timers." Napoleon gently punched Jimmie in the shoulder, telling him to speak for himself. Napoleon is eighteen years younger.

There's some romanticizing of the past. When Jimmie, Napoleon, and their gang were active in the streets, in the late 1980s and 1990s, the violence was considerably worse. In 1991 the city recorded 927 homicides, more than double what it is some twenty-two years later. I mentioned this to them, and Jimmie shook his head, not in disagreement but in puzzlement. "You say there were more killings back then?" he asked. "But it feels like it's worse now." It does. It may be because then much of the violence occurred in the city's vast acreage of public housing complexes, which were completely out of sight, out of mind. And since those high-rises have been razed, the shootings take place in the neighborhoods and so get more attention. Or it may be because then most of the shootings were over drug turf, clearly directed at opposing gangs, and now it feels more arbitrary, more random. Also, when the organized gangs fought over terrain, they often gave warning to residents, and now the shootings just happen, like a summer rain shower, and so more victims are unintended targets.

I ask them what they think can be done. "That I wish I knew," Jimmie said. "Only thing I can do is, a lot of it start at home. You got to get into the families. If people at home aren't trying to change them, nothing will change them." Both he and Napoleon believe it's considerably easier to get guns these days. In fact, every year for the past ten years the police have taken somewhere in the neighborhood of 7,000 illegal guns off the street, or a gun every seventy-five minutes. "They want that respect," Napoleon explained. I hear this a lot, and while it may seem like an oversimplification, it makes sense. You grow up in a community with abandoned homes, a job-less rate of over 25 percent, underfunded schools, and you stand outside your home, look at the city's gleaming downtown skyline, at its prosperity, and you know your place in the world. And so you look for ways to feel like you're someone, ways to feel like people look up to you, ways to feel like you have some standing in your city. "Like Michael Jordan, he gets power through basketball," Napoleon said. "You don't let nothing get in the way of getting that power . . . It's the fear that make people respect you. I used to love people shutting their doors when they see me coming. Hey, Jim-mie, I loved carrying your guns. I loved that power. I couldn't get it anywhere else."

It was getting late, and so we said our goodbyes. Jimmie smiled and cautioned me, "Alex, you're gonna bust your head trying to fig-ure this all out." Napoleon chimed in, "Take a person like me. How can a guy be so sweet and have a dark side?" Napoleon is married now, to an accountant, and he tells me he wants to find time for simple things, like baking, mostly peanut butter and chocolate chip cookies. Both still try to defuse disputes when they can, but they're at an age where they realize, given all that they were involved in, they're just lucky to have made it through. At the end of the bar, a laptop open in front of him, there's an older man in a Dr. Seuss T-shirt watching a video of a friend's funeral. He's half listening to our conversation. "Dinosaurs," he mutters of Jimmie and Napo-leon, loud enough for us to hear.

A couple days later I text Jimmie and Napoleon to thank them for their time. I don't hear back from Napoleon, and so I call. He apologizes. "I was driving and didn't want to text while driving," he tells me.

Chapter 4

The Tightrope, part two

I first met Marcelo at a second bond hearing, in a courtroom attached to a South Side police station. Some in county government had become outraged by the unusually high bonds handed down by judges, often arbitrarily, without reason, and Marcelo's case popped out to them because Marcelo had no previous criminal record and yet had no chance of bonding out of prison while he awaited his trial. Prosecutors—along with the police—had come to believe that robberies were a gateway crime to more violent acts, and so they requested exceptionally high bonds. Marcelo, unable to come up with the necessary 10 percent, or $30,000, found himself in the county jail, locked in his cell much of the day because he was so much younger than everyone else on the tier. He was so terrified that he refused to take a shower.

At 10:15 that morning Marcelo shuffled into the courtroom, a deputy sheriff by his side. Dressed in the drab tan uniform of jail inmates, which hung off his scrawny frame like sheets on a clothesline, Marcelo had in his couple of weeks in detention grown a wisp of a mustache and goatee, but he looked unusually young and jittery—so much so that two years later the court reporter would tell me that she couldn't get him out of her mind, that she always wondered what had become of him. Marcelo's eyes darted around the courtroom, briefly catching the gaze of his mom, who sat toward the rear, a hand wiping away a tear. He was represented by a public defender, Bob Dwyer, who with his closely cropped hair and chiseled features looked like he could be ex-military. Hearings to reconsider bonds are unusual, but Marcelo had an unusual bevy of supporters, many of whom were present, something which the judge noticed. There was his family: his mother, his older brother, Elio, Elio's wife, and their young daughter. There were also four people from Mercy Home for Boys & Girls, where Marcelo lived, along with an investigator who had been looking into the inequities of bond court and stumbled across Marcelo's case. Of Marcelo's bond, the investigator told me, "It's fuckin' crazy."

This in many ways is what makes Marcelo's story unusual, and in large part what drew me to spend time with him. Marcelo had a lot of people in his corner, so many, in fact, that it took me a while to sort everyone out. Marcelo, who had just turned seventeen, had straddled two worlds, and it now appeared that maintaining that highwire balancing act had proved perilous.

A little backstory is necessary here. When Marcelo was three, his father went to prison on charges of kidnapping a young man for double-crossing him on a drug deal. Marcelo, who knows the details of the case through his dad, insists that he was innocent, that the alleged kidnapping was really a misunderstanding. Marcelo and his two brothers were raised by their mother, Blanca, who spoke little English but was determined to keep her kids on track. They lived in a garden apartment on the city's South Side. Blanca, who emigrated from Mexico when she was eighteen, worked twelve-hour overnight shifts at a factory that made plastic utensils; she would get home in time to take the children to school. On weekends she made tamales, which she loaded into a large ice chest and fit on the back of a baby stroller, along with Omar, the youngest. Blanca would go from house to house, Elio and Marcelo ringing doorbells (and translating when needed), selling the tamales for seven dollars a dozen, extra money which she put aside for her boys' education. Blanca pleaded with the principal at St. Gall, a local Catholic school, to enroll the boys, even though she didn't have money for full tuition. Sister Erica Jordan, the principal, told me, "Her life was so hard and she had to be so focused on keeping a roof over their head and food on the table, she didn't have time for friends." Sister Erica arranged for all three boys to attend.

Since Blanca worked the night shift, Elio was often in charge. He wandered. At thirteen he joined the Latin Kings. He told me, "I wanted to be known so that they wouldn't mess with my little brothers." He earned a reputation as a wild kid and fearless. He once tried to burn down a garage of someone he was feuding with. At thirteen he was shot, in the back. When he was young, everyone in the neighborhood called him Little Elmo, but as he made a reputation for himself, his sobriquet changed to Terror. Trouble followed him. Marcelo can remember bricks being thrown through their front window. Heather Kelsey, Elio's eighth-grade teacher, recalls Elio drawing gang signs on his notebooks. "He could put on that tough-guy face," she said. "He felt like he always had something to prove." In eighth grade, after numerous incidents, he got expelled from St. Gall. And so when Kelsey got Marcelo as a student, she was apprehensive. When he first arrived, she recalled, he was scrappy, always ready to fight. "But he was different," she said. "He wanted to make his mom proud." At one parent-teacher conference, Marcelo apologized to his mom for his grades, which were B's and C's. "He seemed so easily swayed. I worried he'd fall into Elio's mess," Kelsey told me. "I knew he wanted to do well, but I worried he didn't have the self-discipline to stay on track." She paused. "I loved Marcelo."

Marcelo, like Elio, joined the Latin Kings, the gang that ruled his southwest-side neighborhood, a collection of small wood frame homes in this mostly Latino neighborhood. Marcelo earned the nickname Little Terror, a homage, obviously, to his brother, and a tribute to his scrappiness. Marcelo, despite his small stature, seemed unafraid. One time, when he was fifteen, he went to get a haircut in the neighborhood of a rival gang, an act that, if not foolish, was naive. But there's a bravado about Marcelo, and for him it was a challenge. "A macho kind of thing," he told me. "I thought, they ain't gonna do shit." He had gone with a friend, a girl named Ashley. As he exited the barbershop after getting a fade, he saw four boys from the rival gang across the street. They recognized each other from Facebook posts, where they would taunt each other's gang. One of them declared to Marcelo, *Whassup, bitch? King killer,* and contorted his fingers to resemble an upside-down crown, a sign of disrespect. Marcelo ran into the middle of 59th Street, thinking they might not follow him with witnesses around, but they chased him, and one boy pulled a knife from his pants pocket and began jousting, trying to stab Marcelo in the stomach. Ashley pepper-sprayed him, but the assailant didn't back down. Marcelo waved his arms around his torso to defend himself when he felt the sharp pain, and as he backed away, he noticed the blade protruding from his left biceps. As he yanked out the knife, a beer bottle slammed into his wrist. He began wildly throwing punches, none of which landed. Blood spilled down his arm. He heard sirens, and his assailants ran, his *Fuck you*s emptily echoing down the street, cars honking, swerving to avoid the boy with the bloody arm. He needed ten stitches.

A few months later, in February, as Marcelo walked back to his house with his friend Javier, they noticed a black Jeep motoring down the street; a young man in the passenger seat rolled down his tinted window and, like the assailant outside the barbershop, contorted his fingers into an upside-down crown. He wore a ski mask to conceal his identity. Marcelo and Javier, both of whom showed great loyalty to the Kings, each picked up a brick and hurled it at the car. Marcelo's brick smashed into one of the car doors. Javier's cracked the windshield. The passenger in the ski mask pointed a semiautomatic weapon at the two boys and began shooting. They ran. Marcelo, as he'd learned from the older boys, ran in a zigzag fashion, trying to dodge the bullets. He felt lightheaded, and then sharp pain in both legs. He collapsed by a parked car and tried to crawl toward the sidewalk to find some protection. He looked up, and the shooter stood above him, taking aim. Marcelo knew this was it. He knows it sounds clichéd, but it was as if he were watching a movie trailer about his life. First communion. Graduation from eighth grade. Omar, his younger brother, playing video games. *God, please take care of my mother,* he thought to himself. *I'm sorry for all that I did.* Out of the corner of his eye, Marcelo caught Javier hiding behind a nearby car, his eyes wide and pleading. The gun jammed. Marcelo heard police sirens in the distance. The shooter ran back to the Jeep, and it took off. Javier rushed to Marcelo, cupped his head in his hands, and implored him, *Don't pass. Don't close your eyes. Get up. Get up. Come on. Get up.* Marcelo, when he recounts this moment, allows that he was crying, afraid that this was it. He had been shot in both legs, a bullet entering and exiting his left thigh, another bullet lodging in his left calf. Blood from the thigh wound gushed onto the sidewalk until a squad car pulled up; a woman police officer took Marcelo's sweater and tied it around his left leg to stanch the bleeding.

In a good year in Chicago, roughly 2,000 people get wounded by gunfire, or five people a day, give or take. Some years the number has risen to over 4,000, or roughly one person every two hours. These are the survivors, the ones still standing, more or less. Every victim has their own reckoning. For some, getting shot is an affront to their manhood. To their vigor. To their pride.

And so that wound festers; the desire for vengeance and payback burns until it eventually erupts. I've met some who have held on to that fury for years. On the first day of spring in 2006, Jimmy Allen, who was then thirty-seven, spent the morning enjoying the sun in Veterans Memorial Park on the city's far South Side. He was there with his mom and friends, many of whom were drinking even at this early hour. Nearby, a gaggle of men shot dice. Allen had $900 in his pocket, wrapped in a rubber band, money he had made selling marijuana. Allen saw three young men enter the park and saunter up to the dice game. Each pulled out a gun, and one yelled, *Man, stick up.* Another ordered, *Lower it like you owe it.* They seemed impatient, and Allen pulled the bundle of cash out of his pocket and held it aloft. An offering. But one of his friends who'd had too much to drink defiantly declared, *Get the fuck out of here. We ain't giving y'all shit.* The three men started shooting. Allen got hit just above the heart, in the collarbone. "It felt like someone hit me with a bat," he told me. With blood squirting from his chest, he took off running, and as he tried to hoist himself over a fence, he got shot twice more, both times in the buttocks. He flipped over the fence and fell to the other side. A friend rushed him to the hospital, where the staff stopped the bleeding before transferring him to a trauma unit so they could perform surgery. Four other people were shot along with him, including his mother, who was shot in the lower back. Everyone survived.

Allen became fixated on getting revenge. In the following weeks, he drove around the neighborhood for hours, looking for the person who he heard had driven the shooters to the park. He purchased a beanbag to sit on because of the pain in his buttocks; his chest wound still leaked blood. He carried a Tec-9 and wore a bulletproof vest. "I wanted to kill everyone out there," he told me. They'd nicked his pride, his ability to protect himself—and his mom. He considered killing the person's grandmother, and observed her comings and goings. At one point he paid a friend $700 to confront someone he suspected of being involved in the incident, hoping the person might confess to it. He couldn't sleep. People close to him, including his mom, goaded him for not finding the assailants. *Man, you need to get him,* one friend told him. *You got shot. Your mom got shot. They shouldn't even be here.* Every day for nearly a decade Allen thought about vengeance. "I couldn't stand them being here with me at the same time," he told me. "I just wanted them off this earth." It so consumed Allen that there were mornings he woke up crying in frustration. "I was messed up for a long time," he said.

I sat with Allen in his small second-floor apartment on a wintry day so cold that he had the stove burners on to help boost the heat. Allen, who has a rangy build and has lost a number of teeth to diabetes, looks older than his forty-seven years. He told me that one of his brothers, who had served time in prison not long ago, "turned his life over to the Lord." That brother convinced Allen to let it go. "Just let the Lord handle it," his brother told him. "Keep it in his hands." Allen was so astonished by his brother's transformation that he felt he owed it to him to honor his pleas. "I just had to let a lot of demons go," he told me. "It's scary living with wanting that revenge." I asked him what would happen if he ran into one of the people he suspected of being involved in the shooting. "It burns in me, right now today," he conceded. He grinned, the gap in his teeth visible, and I'm unsure if that was a smile of relief or one of knowing, of knowing something I didn't.

For others, getting shot feels like a twist of fate that's not so much bad luck as it is a deserved exclamation point to their life up to then. Roel Villarreal, at the age of twenty-five, worked in shipping and receiving at a small company that built backdrops for photographers. Roel figured he'd invest his earnings, buying crack cocaine and on weekends selling it for a hefty profit. One Friday night he'd purchased an eight ball for $100 and cut it into twenty-one dime bags, hoping to double his investment. He drank some Coronas to loosen up, to muster the pluck to sell his wares. Around three in the morning a pickup truck pulled to the curb a few feet ahead of him, and the passenger stuck his head out to beckon Roel, who trotted over. He heard the shots before he saw the gun, and instinctively hit the ground. A friend ran toward him. *You're bleeding from the head!* his friend yelled. Roel remembers his hands felt cold. He'd been shot in the neck, and in the coming days doctors determined he had lost all movement from the neck down. He was a quadriplegic.

Roel couldn't move in with his mother, because she lived in the neighborhood of a rival gang. He tried living with his girlfriend of three years, but her son had also been shot recently and was paralyzed from the waist down, so she was spent from taking care of him. The only option for Roel was a nursing home, and once he was there, the only available room was on the third floor, in the dementia ward. Now his only visitors are his mother, his brother, and his aunt. His friends have stopped coming by. For a stretch, an elderly woman of Italian descent suffering from Alzheimer's often came by his room and would compulsively touch objects there, including two crucifixes he had by the window, as if she were making sure they were real. Often the woman would mistake Roel for her son, and Roel so welcomed her company that he would not disabuse her of the notion that they were related. She passed away, and he now spends most of his days watching television, mostly movies and sports, sometimes switching to a Spanish-language station to work his mind. Every morning a nurse comes in to brush his teeth. Another nurse feeds him and changes his position so he doesn't get bedsores. His mother shaves him when she visits. He usually wears a winter cap, as he gets cold easily, and he drinks Ensure to maintain his weight. At five foot ten, he's down to 115 pounds. But he's not bitter or regretful or the least bit melancholy. There's a tranquility about him that belies his situation. "I take it day by day," he told me. "I have more good days than bad days . . . I don't hold a grudge. It was no one's fault but mine. I was the one out in the streets, so who can I get mad at?" A friend of Roel's who shared a room when they were going through rehab said of those like Roel who are confined to nursing homes, "Sometimes these guys think it's payback for what they did, like they somehow deserve it. It's kind of like their own purgatory." Indeed, Roel once told his aunt, *Maybe this is the only way God could stop me.*

I was kind of freaking out, like my life is not a game," Marcelo once told me. "You know what I'm saying? My life could have been gone. I could have been swiped from the earth. I didn't realize that when I was gangbanging. I started thinking, reflecting real hard. Be like, damn, what the fuck, do I really want this?"

After Marcelo got shot, he stayed inside his house, his left leg in a cast and a bullet still lodged in his calf (it was too embedded in the tissue for the doctors to remove). His school, De La Salle, thought it best that he complete the semester by taking classes online, as the administrators didn't want trouble to follow him into the school.

The shooting shook him. He burned with revenge, so much so he couldn't sleep. In his head, he concocted a plan. He knew where the shooter lived and decided that he would have a friend drive him, with another friend following in a second car. He'd get out, yell the name of the shooter, wait for him to come to the front door, and fire. He'd then toss the gun into the first car and hop into the second. Once home, he'd urinate on his hands, which he'd been told would eliminate gunpowder residue. (It doesn't work.) His older brother, Elio, convinced him to let it sit for a few months; Elio warned him that if anything happened to the suspected shooter, the police would quickly know it was him.

Marcelo knew he couldn't stay in the neighborhood. It would happen again—or he'd get charged up and go after the guy who shot him, despite Elio's warnings. A few years back, his mother had placed Elio at Mercy Home for Boys & Girls. Mercy's history has a Dickensian aura about it, a place where wayward children were sent to be whipped into shape. Mercy was founded 126 years ago by two Irish-American priests as a place to house and guide children who, for one reason or another, were living in the streets without a parent in their life. The two priests housed the boys in a dormitory setting, fed them, and gave them vocational training, sometimes employing corporal punishment to keep them in line. But over the years Mercy has changed considerably. Where it used to be that counselors at Mercy would ask, *What the hell is wrong with you?* it's now more, *What the hell has happened to you?* Each child there is provided with therapeutic care, and their parents are often a part of that treatment. In 2009, Mercy renovated a giant warehouse, turning it into the main housing; it purposefully feels open, with 15-foot-high ceilings and floor-to-ceiling windows. It's like a college dorm, with the one hundred boys sharing double rooms (the forty girls are at another site). Though not a part of the archdiocese, Mercy is headed by a priest and is privately funded through donations from individuals, foundations, and corporations. One of the keys to Mercy is that each child must want to be there.

Marcelo, on his own, approached Mercy and asked if it would take him in. It was, he thought, his only chance. He needed to put some physical distance between himself and his neighborhood, especially if he was to concentrate on school. At Mercy, almost all children are referred by a parent or by a school, so Marcelo was unusual, since he came on his own. Impressed by his moxie, Mercy invited Marcelo to shadow another boy for an evening, and instructed him, as it did all applicants, not to mention gang involvement or affiliation. Nonetheless, Marcelo, who can be headstrong, arrived in a baby-blue jogging suit, his gang color. He appeared cocky, at one point slouching in a chair with his feet propped on a coffee table. At another point he boasted to the boy hosting him that he was a Latin King. That, coupled with the fact that he'd just been shot—he was still on crutches—raised red flags. The staff found him personable but brash. At their meeting to consider his application, many asked, *What violence is this kid going to bring with him?* Most simply didn't want him. But after some heated discussion, they invited him back for one last shot. Claire Conway, a program manager, told me, "When Marcelo came through the admissions process, I did not want to work with him. I did not believe him when he said he wanted to get out of the gang. I fought him coming for months." Marcelo apologized. He pleaded. He cajoled. He pleaded some more. Clearly he knew what he needed and what he wanted. She'd never seen a kid so determined to get into Mercy. "I had a moment of clarity," Claire told me. "Why are you fighting this kid?" Marcelo won over Claire and the others, and Mercy invited him to move in. Marcelo told his mom to tell others in the neighborhood that he had gone to Mexico.

Mercy helped get him back into De La Salle. The staff got him into therapy. They got him to a psychiatrist, who prescribed the Wellbutrin for his persistent and at times debilitating anxiety. His hands shook. He had racing thoughts, especially when he lay down to go to sleep, reliving the shooting in what he calls "reruns." One time, while he was working in the cafeteria, others found Marcelo staring at the wall as if he were in a trance. A staff person waved her hand in front of his face to get him back. His left leg continued to ache, especially in the winter, but he begrudgingly appreciated carrying around the bullet. He didn't want to forget. He found his footing. His grades soared. He became a mentor to younger boys at Mercy, and the Mercy staff thought so much of him that they had him address potential donors. "I've just never seen a kid work so hard," his advocate at Mercy, Britney Kummerer, told me. "We felt like jerks for not wanting him." He got a tattoo across his chest: *Success is the best revenge.* Then he went home one weekend, as he often did, and with his friends went on the robbery spree.

n court, Marcelo is beckoned to stand before the judge. He shifts from foot to foot. He pivots to get the attention of his mother, to catch her smile. His hands, which he holds behind his back, quiver as if he has palsy. He looks like he has the kinetic energy of a greyhound waiting to take off after a mechanical rabbit. His heart races. He has trouble focusing on what's being said. The portly deputy sheriff standing behind him senses Marcelo's unease, leans in, and whispers into his ear, *The court likes you.* Marcelo looks bewildered. *What does that mean?* he asks. *Shhh,* the deputy sheriff replies.

Marcelo's therapist at Mercy, Jennifer Shully, tells the judge that Marcelo, on his own, got himself into Mercy, that "I can honestly say, Marcelo is a model resident." She tells the judge that in its 126-year history Mercy has never posted bond before, but that it is willing to do so for Marcelo—though it can't afford $30,000. "Mercy is an unlocked facility," she explains. "He could walk out anytime he wanted to. He's never done so. He's repeatedly stated over and over again how much he wants to be there, how much he wants to change. We believe in him. We believe he made a bad decision." It's her hope and the hope of the others at Mercy that they can get Marcelo's bond lowered. Three teachers at De La Salle have submitted letters of support as well. Jaclin McGuire, his American literature instructor, wrote, "I teach a majority of the students as juniors; with this said, I can confidently say Marcelo was at the top of his class . . . During class discussion it was evident that Marcelo was thinking beyond just the literal, which is a rarity among High School students . . . He is the type of student every teacher wants in his/her classroom."

Anita Alvarez, the elected state's attorney, had made a reputation as an unbending and sometimes overreaching prosecutor in the city's response to the violence, and her rigidity had filtered down the ranks. The assistant state's attorney assigned to this courtroom asks rhetorically of Marcelo's therapist, "Is this an isolated incident? Are you aware that he was the one who got out of the vehicle and led the attack on these three separate victims with a group of thugs?" Marcelo's public defender denies that Marcelo was the leader. The assistant state's attorney then briefly recounts what occurred that morning, the brutality of the three robberies. "In the defense's own words," he tells the judge, "he's an exceptional young man. He's a leader. His behavior is that of a thug and thug leader. He's not going to college. He is going to prison. We're going to ask the court to raise his bond to $500,000." Someone in the courtroom gasps. To his family and to those at Mercy, it felt like an act of vengeance, as if to say, "We're going to teach you a lesson for being uppity." Not only shouldn't the bond be reduced, the assistant state's attorney declares, it should be raised.

Marcelo looks around, his head swiveling like he's a sparrow on a telephone wire. The deputy sheriff gently taps him, gesturing for him to direct his attention to the judge. The judge mentions Marcelo's age—he had turned seventeen a few days earlier—and the fact that he's at Mercy and clearly has support. He reduces the bond to $10,000, which means Mercy needs to come up with $1,000. "You're not only getting the sun and the moon today, you're getting the sun, the moon, and the stars today," the judge tells Marcelo, whose whole body appears to be shuddering. "Now, young man, don't let down all the people who have come here. You're about to start the fight of your life."

When Marcelo gets back to Mercy, he holes up in his room to study for the ACT, which he is scheduled to take the next weekend.

Chapter 5

The Tweets

JUNE 13 . . . JUNE 14 . . . JUNE 15 . . .

THURSDAY, JUNE 13

9:35 p.m. Two men shot, 1700 E. 71st Place, M/23 +
M/Unk age, both to Jackson Park Hospital #chicago

9:54 p.m. The night begins.

Peter Nickeas, who's twenty-seven and the overnight reporter at the *Chicago Tribune,* tweets all hours of the night and early morning. One hundred and forty characters. Short, staccato bursts describing the wailing, the crying, the bleeding, the saves and near-saves. He uses shorthand for locations, borrows from the police lingo (M/Unk for male/unknown, for instance), quotes people on the police scanner, quotes people at the scene, sometimes adds a short video, six seconds in length. It's the unadorned facts salted with keen observations, details others might miss. He's a crime reporter on overdrive who's developed his own personal flair. When I first met Pete, he was in the Tribune tower at his cubicle, square-jawed, his hair closely cropped. Between his clipped speech and his appearance, he could be mistaken for a police officer. He was dressed in a red T-shirt, blue jeans, and hiking boots, sitting ramrod straight at a desk piled high with reporter notebooks, three police scanners rattling in the background. Three Kevlar vests lay on the floor.

He heads out in one of the *Tribune*'s cars, carrying a portable scanner, which he had appropriated from the newspaper after it had purchased a number of them to cover the recent NATO summit and the accompanying protests.

10:57 p.m. The breeze outside work tonight was perfect.
I would have liked to not come to work, and instead, just
enjoy the weather.

11:02 p.m. There's a group of people fighting, no shit, a block
from the south side overtime initiative HQ (old Englewood
district, 61/Racine)

Pete often cites the various tactics employed by the police, since they are trying pretty much everything. Extra overtime so they can put more police on the streets. Using data to identify hot spots where they can send more police. Using algorithms to identify the four hundred young men they believe most likely to shoot someone or get shot. Requiring ex-felons to meet with police and social workers. Periodically the police tout the numbers, but just when they're looking good. Other times, when the homicide numbers inch up, they chastise the press for keeping count as if there were some contest at hand. Before Pete arrived, the *Tribune* often rewrote police statements, and would pick and choose which crime scenes to go to, sometimes a handful in one night. Pete is in some ways a throwback. He employs good old-fashioned shoe-leather reporting. He's rarely in the office and instead drives from crime scene to crime scene, listening for the next shooting on his portable scanner. He doesn't have the time for pronouncements from public officials. In fact, he gets angry at what he sees as the city's cynicism. Last year the police superintendent, Garry McCarthy, released a statement celebrating a twenty-four-hour period without a shooting as if that were a great accomplishment. "This is clearly the result of the tremendous police work of the men and women of the Chicago Police Department," McCarthy declared. Another time the mayor, Rahm Emanuel, suggested the shooters stay away from the young kids. "Take your stuff away to the alley," he said. On the streets around many schools, the city has begun erecting signs that read SAFE PASSAGE, a suggestion that these signs act as a kind of shield for the city's school-age children. "They're a joke," Pete told me, speaking of the signs. "What about the rest of the fuckin' city? It's not safe there? Are you ceding the rest of the city?"

11:27 p.m. Cops on two different South Side radio zones calling in gunfire now, 79th/Drexel, 1400 W. 66th.

11:29 p.m. This neighborhood is hot right now. Shots fired in the area.

When Pete began this work, in 2011, he found it gripping, heart-racing. Because he's white, he was usually an outsider in the neighborhoods he covered. He flew from crime scene to crime scene, often with a photographer in tow. He witnessed an arson fire where a family was killed and on another occasion stood over the body of a young man who had been beaten to death with a cinder block, half his face depressed like it was made of clay. But he also saw a kind of grace. He remembers one particular murder, of a nineteen-year-old boy, on the city's far West Side. When he arrived at the scene, the body was still on the sidewalk. A middle-aged man approached him and, realizing that Pete wasn't a police officer, apologized: *You're not the person I need to talk to.* He found an officer and told him that he was the boy's dad and that he wanted to see his son. The sergeant pleaded with him: *You don't want to remember your son like this.* But the father waited. He seemed almost serene, while his daughter, the victim's sister, dry-heaved in his white van, parked nearby. When the body removal service arrived (the "body snatchers," Pete calls them), the father walked to the body before anyone could stop him. He stood over his son and looked to the heavens, offering a short prayer. The boy, it turned out, wasn't involved in the streets. He worked at Sears and just happened to be in front of the building where the shooter's intended target lived. In that one moment, Pete felt he witnessed something deeply personal, something deeply private. He thought to himself, *I shouldn't be here. It's not my place.*

FRIDAY, JUNE 14

1:42 a.m. Setting up the scene, 4400 N. Mulligan. Police shot a young man. #chicago. [accompanied by a short video of police putting up yellow tape]

3:00 a.m. "Be advised, we are in a backlog on the South Side." @chicagoscanner

3:58 a.m. 7 people shot tonight, plus police shot someone up in Jefferson Park.

Pete reported that a boy, maybe fourteen or fifteen, swung a two-by-four at a police officer, and the officer shot the boy in self-defense. The boy lived. "There was a time when I was doing the job and I didn't know what I was soaking up," Pete told me. "You don't know what you don't know. And then when I knew, I thought, *Oh, shit.*" It took a toll. By this summer, two years into his overnight reporting, Pete has begun to grow weary of the bloodletting. He has tried taking melatonin or Nyquil to help him sleep. He lies in bed, "a perpetual half-sleep" he calls it, hearing scanners in his head. He is easy to anger, even with friends. Often when he gets off his shift in the early morning, he goes home and drinks a six-pack of Corona, or he'll head to a bar for something stronger, something to counteract the adrenaline, to dull the agitation.

> 10:03 a.m. (Spotnews tweets) "They fuck up, they get beat. We fuck up, they give us pensions."–Ellis Carver. #TheWire

> 10:36 a.m. @spotnews "Count be wrong, they fuck you up." #season1

Pete has a thing for *The Wire,* and he and others exchange lines from the TV series. He feels it's true to what he sees. It's a touchstone and, with some irony, kind of evidence to others that what he's telling them is real. There's constant chatter on Twitter, between those at home listening to police scanners (there are more than you might expect) and Pete. He also has exchanges with a cadre of freelance videographers and photographers who sprint from one crime scene to the next, selling their footage and photos to the local news stations. They often meet at an all-night diner, Huck Finn, where they take the corner booth and set up their computers and scanners. Pete admires the video guys, but it irks him that many of them wear flak jackets and make no effort to hide them. One wears a military-grade vest which has an extension to cover his privates. Pete refuses to wear one. "It's disrespectful," he says, "like saying, *I don't feel safe here.*"

> 9:21 p.m. @Spotnews @PeterNickeas 2 early for Peter & Huck Finn

> 9:25 p.m. Too early indeed. I'm just settling in here at the tower.

9:49 p.m. Tonight is starting to feel like the night where
I throw this fucking computer from the fourth floor
window of the tower

SATURDAY, JUNE 15

12:09 a.m. 5500 W. Quincy. 2 people shot. #chicago
[accompanied by a short video of a man who can't get to
his home because of the police tape]

12:45 a.m. Two people shot a couple blocks from this scene
we were at. Ambos not here yet.

Pete learns a lesson here. He gets to the scene before the medic
and stumbles on a man bleeding from his neck, gurgling, trying
to ask for help. He doesn't know what to do. He feels useless.
And he can't get the sound out of his head, the desperation, the
inability to make the simplest of requests: *Help me.* From then on
Pete makes a point of arriving at a scene *after* the ambulances.
There's something to be said for being the second one on the
scene.

2:36 a.m. At least 9 shot since Friday afternoon. Total does
not reflect a recent shooting on Central Avenue, for which
we lack details. #chicago

3:52 a.m. Guy calls 911, asking for a supervisor: "Said he
was stopped by a unit, made to exit his vehicle, then he
took it." #chicagoscanner

5:02 a.m. A man walked into Stroger Hospital this
morning with a gunshot wound. He wouldn't tell police
where he had been shot. #chicago

6:13 a.m. Did a guy just get shot at 76th/Ashland? I think
so. #chicago

7:05 a.m. It's glass-of-whiskey time, once I get my shit done
here, which I'm struggling to do.

He and the photographer who's ridden shotgun all night go to
the Billy Goat Tavern, a watering hole for generations of reporters, from Mike Royko to Studs Terkel. There he orders a Jameson,
straight up. This was an unusually difficult shift, and though he
doesn't know it yet, it will change him. In the early-morning hours
he had heard a call over the scanner about someone shot, and when
he arrived at the scene, he began shooting a video on his phone.
A young shirtless man approached him, clearly high and drunk, a
blunt tucked behind one ear, wanting to know if his friend was alive
or dead. Pete makes it a point not to engage with people who are
inebriated, and so he tried to avoid him, which only further irritated the man. *Go back to your neighborhood!* he bellowed. *You're
not from around here!* He started jogging back to his house, yelling
at his girlfriend, who stood on the front porch, *Get my gun.* The
young man entered his house and emerged with his hand behind
his back. Pete told the photographer, *Junior, we need to get the fuck
out of here.* They jumped into their separate cars. The man ran in
front of Pete's car, his hands nearly touching the hood. Pete veered
around him and peeled off, running a red light. He didn't look back
to see if the guy had a gun. He just floored it, realizing that was one
close call. After stopping for the whiskey, he heads home via Lake
Shore Drive and has this inexplicable urge to drive fast, real fast.
At home, his wife, Erin, greets him. He looks shaken, wide-eyed.
Erin hugs him. "Do you think this is safe? Do you think this is
smart?" Pete asks her. Three weeks later he starts wearing a Kevlar vest. "The city became real that weekend," he tells me weeks
later.

5:23 p.m. Sun's out, guns out, as they say. 3 shot, two
critically, in Marquette Park.

9:22 p.m. So this shooting out on Artesian tonight—
mutual combatants. Working on updating the story now.
#chicago

10:50 p.m. 2 people shot here, 77th/homan. #chicago
[accompanied by a short video that shows Dooley Park,
and a sign that reads PARK CLOSES 11 P.M.]

11:50 p.m. Homicide. 26/Ridgeway. #chicago [accompanied
by a short video of a police officer photographing the pool of
blood on the sidewalk]

SUNDAY, JUNE 16

1:15 a.m. Police shot, killed a man here. 1600 S.
Springfield in the alley.

1:25 a.m. Crime scene cat, where police shot a man.
[accompanied by a short video of a blond cat prancing along
the alleyway]

Pete would take videos of cats at crime scenes and post them as
short videos. He thought it was different, that it felt whimsical, but
he eventually stopped because it felt like it diminished what was
going on.

1:35 a.m. 1600 S. Springfield. Tense scene. #chicago
[accompanied by a video of a man yelling at the police, "Yo.
What don't you understand, man? Fuck that! He's dead,
bitch!"]

@PeterNickeas Why is that guy yelling?

@bennyblades22 Cops shot his brother.

@PeterNickeas Ah makes sense. Thanks for all you do, love the info.

3:50 a.m. 2 people shot here. 31/Pulaski, In this car [accompanied by a short video of the car, the doors open, a passenger window with two large bullet holes]

4:12 a.m. Second time tonight hearing gunfire at a scene.

6:09 a.m. That was a bad night.

8:03 a.m. It didn't stop all night, we visited seven scenes between me and the photog. Gone from 10-6a.

9:53 a.m. 5 dead, 18 wounded overnight. Shootings from North Avenue south to 94th Street. #Chicago

Reading Pete Nickeas's tweets, you absorb the relentlessness of the city's violence. It doesn't seem to let up. Over time Pete did more than just take in the moment. He began to talk with people, and began to realize that "the violence isn't in a vacuum. Gang members aren't helicoptered in. They're part of the neighborhood." He soon feels a need to do more than just record the aftermath and spends time talking with family and friends of victims. He befriends two outreach workers who are former gang members and writes a moving profile of them and their work. "I don't think I'm biased by saying Benny and Jorge [the two outreach workers] are doing good work," he tells me. "They're the most beautiful thing I've seen in the city."

There's a no-nonsense quality to Pete, and people seem to appreciate that. I was with him once after a shooting, and people milled about on the street, sitting on stoops, leaning against a cyclone fence. Virtually everyone talked to Pete, even giving him their phone numbers. One middle-aged man thanked him for being there, for bearing witness. "I'm just doing my job," Pete told him. He also has a good rapport with the police. Many of them are fans. Once, as the police investigated a shooting at a low-rise housing project, a plainclothes officer came up to Pete. "I enjoy reading your work," he told Pete. "It makes me feel like I'm there." Pete's seen the police curse at gawkers and at him, but he understands the quick temper: "The violence damages cops just like it damages anyone else who has to watch it day in, day out." He comes to see how the violence has dented everyone it touches.

One time he responds to an incident where three people have been shot, including a seventy-three-year-old grandmother. Two hundred people press against the yellow crime tape. The police point Tasers at a gaggle of agitated young men, the red lasers lighting up their white T-shirts like it's an arcade game. They shout back, *Fuck the police.* A construction worker who lives in the neighborhood tells a sergeant that it wasn't always like this and that he does what he can to talk to the youth. Three boys who look to be maybe fifteen hurl insults at the sergeant, and though the sergeant tries to be patient, he eventually approaches one of the boys, twirls him around, and handcuffs him. A man in his thirties, a golden retriever at his side, embraces a police officer, turns around, and mutters, *Too much violence. It's too much,* and then collapses on the sidewalk and has a seizure. "It was one of those moments when I realized everyone was damaged," Pete told me.

As the summer progresses, Pete continues to record the numbers, but his senses feel heightened, like he can hear and see things that used to feel out of reach. He begins to offer commentary as well.

It's about the gun laws, Sup McCarthy says. So far no other mention of other factors.

In the Austin neighborhood: "All these people wanna grab guns and nobody got target practice," she said.

Someone just dropped off a woman at a hospital, GSW [gunshot wound] to the buttocks. She doesn't know how it happened.

Sleep all day, to wake up for night life.

"He doesn't know he's dead yet." A police supervisor.

Crime fighting strategy: Cold front, storms to break heat wave today.

A man with (what appears to be) an AK-47 tattooed on his forehead was charged with a shooting in Uptown. Story soon. #chicago

Safe Passage crime scene. 6100 S Indiana. 2 people shot, 10 casings (at least) on the ground.

Heavy rain begins to fall on Bridgeport. What I wouldn't give to be home, in bed, with a window open right now.

Geez, what a night.

He tells Erin, "Next summer I'm going to plan it better and take a break." He makes a list of the things he wants to do: watch *Lord of the Rings,* ride a bike through a forest preserve, cook and spend more time with friends and with Erin, go ice fishing. He's gained weight. His right eye twitches. Erin tells him he looks mean even when he's resting. He needs a break. But he can't look away. In fact, the longer he spends chasing the violence, the more he needs to linger, to hear from those still standing. He knows how they feel. He knows their anguish, their fury, their fear, their will to go on. The violence, the trauma, he realizes, has this paradoxical narrative. It isolates people. He knows that, all too well. It especially used to unnerve Erin when she'd find him in the living room after a shift, with six opened Coronas, the TV on, Pete asleep on the couch. She urged him to spend time with his friends, but he wouldn't. He couldn't, really. But he found comfort in talking to people in the streets, people who had seen what he's seen, people who had a lot more at stake than he does. The violence, he tells me, also pushes people together. He gets a tattoo on his left forearm, a quote from Cormac McCarthy's *All the Pretty Horses:* "The closest bonds we will ever know are bonds of grief. The deepest community one of sorrow."

Sitting outside Christ Hospital (second time in two weeks I'm writing on a 5-year-old boy shot) and I met another GSW victim, from last year.

July 4th weekend: 67 people shot this long weekend, 11 dead. Ages 5-72.

I love this city but it can be tiring.

Chapter 6

Father's Day

JUNE 15 . . . **JUNE 16** . . . JUNE 17 . . .

Mike Kelly, who's forty-four, lives on the twenty-first floor in a high-end high-rise along the lake called the New York, a nod to its exclusiveness and to Chicago's Second City insecurity. It's a two-bedroom apartment, which Mike keeps pristine. It's been a long day, not because he's done much but rather because he's feeling somewhat sorry for himself. He just ended a five-year relationship, the longest he's ever had, and he can't quite figure out why it didn't work. He's been napping and is now cleaning: refolding clothes in his closet, scrubbing dishes, washing the windows and the mirrors with Windex. His overweight six-year-old Lab, Lucky, lies on his bed in the living room, and Mike coaxes him up to take him for a short walk. At 8:30 Mike's son is coming by, once he gets off work, and it's the one thing Mike is looking forward to. It's a tradition. Every Father's Day the two of them get together for pizza, and sit on the small balcony which overlooks both Lake Michigan and the downtown skyline, and there they talk about things they don't talk about with anyone else. Mike calls his patio their "dome of silence." For both, their lives have been shaped by secrets, secrets from each other, secrets from others, secrets from themselves. For both, holding on to those secrets have left them floating, alone, with only each other to hold to. They are each enshrouded in silence, silence about what really matters.

After returning from walking Lucky, Mike puts on some freshly pressed shorts, a polo shirt, and boat shoes and sits on his living room couch and waits.

I t's 1993, and Mike, who's twenty-four, is living hard. He sells real estate, making money hand over fist, and during lunch he goes out with the boys, usually to what they call "the chink place" or "the spic place," where they boast of their sexual exploits. On occasion they head to Heavenly Bodies, a nearby strip club, where Mike always brings a wad of cash and pays for a lap dance the moment he walks through the door, which he follows with a couple of vodka tonics. And then he goes back to the office.

On the weekends Mike sees his favorite uncle, Mike, whom he's named after. Like Mike, his uncle is short, but stockier and muscular. He's a brawler and had been a heavy drinker until he gave it up—the drinking, that is. Sometimes Uncle Mike would take Mike out on Lake Michigan in his 34-foot power boat. There they'd smoke cheap cigars—Macanudos—which his Uncle first gave Mike when he was fourteen, instructing him, *Don't inhale it like an idiot.* On the boat Mike's uncle would regale him with stories of his past. The green scar on his forehead? He'd gotten into a barroom fight, and they held him down on the floor and burned cigarettes into his skin. Or Uncle Mike would offer lessons on women. *The definition of confidence,* he informed Mike, *is that you rent the room first and then you go look for the girl.* He taught Mike how to play poker, not to be an "ace kicker," that is, not to blindly hold on to your aces. And together they'd watch John Wayne movies. To Mike, Uncle Mike was like a god. Mike wanted to be like him, to have everyone afraid of him, as they were of Uncle Mike. And Mike knew that he was Uncle Mike's favorite. Uncle Mike didn't even have a relationship with his own kids.

Mike is baby-faced, with blond hair, well coiffed, parted on the side. Were it not for the bags under his eyes, he could pass for a high school student. He wears shirts buttoned at the collar. When he isn't partying, he's selling homes, seven days a week, sometimes twelve hours a day. He made $75,000 the previous year, good money for someone in his early twenties. One day his boss pulls him aside, tells him he needs to slow down. In fact, he demands it. Mike resists, but his boss won't budge. He tells Mike he needs to take a day off from work each week, just chill or volunteer somewhere. Mike's not the type to sit still, so he volunteers at an orphanage which he's learned about through his church. He thinks to himself, *I'll go there one day a week, satisfy my boss, and then, well, drop it.* When he tells his boss his plans, his boss seems surprised. Mike laughs. *I'm gonna teach those buggers how to drink,* Mike tells him.

The orphanage was situated in the western suburbs, and when Mike got there, he didn't like what he saw. The staff called the kids names, like "retard" and "fat," sometimes prefacing them with racial slurs. The staff hijacked the one television and watched the shows they wanted to. They seemed arbitrary in their punishment, one time marching the kids around like they were convicts, their hands on each other's shoulders. One boy in particular returned the verbal lances hurled by the staff. Victor was a wiry nine-year-old African-American boy. He had a coffee-colored complexion. An uneven haircut. A grin that was notable for the overbite and for the cheeks that expanded as if he was hoarding nuts. He was cute but temperamental. Mike asked about him, and learned from the staff that Victor had a lot swirling inside him. His mother had abandoned him and his five siblings. Victor, who was the oldest, would steal food from local bodegas to feed his brothers and sisters. Mike also learned that Victor had been in and out of ten foster homes, mainly because he kept running away or because his temper scared those around him. But it was clear that Victor had much to be angry about. This center was a place of last resort, and given his age and his behavioral issues, it seemed unlikely that he'd find a home. Mike saw something of himself in Victor—hotheaded and stubborn, someone who had a storm raging inside, a storm no one could see. "He was a handful," Mike recalls. "But as long as you would talk to him like a human being, he would listen. He just wanted to be treated fair, like any kid would, and the staff, that wasn't their way." Mike and Victor became close, and the reason Mike kept going back week after week was to see Victor. They would play video games or watch movies, or Mike would watch Victor ride his bike or play basketball. One time Mike had to break up a fight on the basketball court between Victor and an older girl. Victor seemed so angry, Mike thought.

Once, Victor told Mike that a staff person had stabbed him in the wrist with a pen, and he showed Mike the wound. At a game of King of the Hill, out of sight of the other staff, Mike grabbed the offender by the neck and wrestled him to the ground, in front of the kids. Mike and Victor had this in common: they didn't take kindly to perceived injustices—and they both often reacted out of proportion to the offense in question. After the second time the staff led the kids around like prison inmates, hands on each other's shoulders, Victor lost it. It was degrading, to him and the others, so he trashed the cafeteria, flipping over tables and throwing chairs. As punishment, the staff took away for three months the most important thing to Victor: his visits with Mike. But before they did, they let Mike see him one last time. Victor seemed cold and distant, unwilling to make eye contact. Mike assured him, *Don't worry, I'll be back in three months.* Victor snarled, *No you won't.* It wouldn't be the first time he'd been abandoned. Mike felt Victor's fury along with his resignation, as if he were saying, *Look, they can do anything they want to me here. There's nothing you or I can do about it.* Victor thought to himself, *Here's yet one more person in my life who's going to disappear.*

On the way home that day, Mike chain-smoked a pack of Marlboro Lights, one after the other in the span of ten minutes, and on that drive, he made a decision that he was going to adopt—or at least try to adopt—Victor. He knew it would mean a change of lifestyle. He knew that he'd have to dispel notions people might have: What's a single man doing adopting a boy? He knew that he'd have to grow up quickly—learn to cook, quit the partying and smoking, pull back on the swearing and drinking, knuckle down at work. But mostly he worried whether it made sense for a white man to adopt a black boy. Whatever it took, he thought to himself, he needed to get Victor out of that environment. He called twenty or so agencies, looking for someone to help him with the adoption, and only one person called back: Jerry Harris, a caseworker at Maryville Academy, a home for abused children. "It was," Jerry recalled, "one of the most unusual phone calls that I ever received." Mike introduced himself and told Jerry that he was interested in getting this boy from a program into his home.

He's black, Mike declared.

Okay, Jerry replied.

And I'm white.

Okay.

Is that a problem?

Not unless you think it's one. Will you care for this kid?

Absolutely.

Color is nothing, then. Don't worry about it.

Jerry Harris, it turns out, was black as well.

Mike underwent a background check, got approval to take Victor in as a foster child. So Mike went to get him, and when he got to the facility, he couldn't find him. He was in a time-out, which meant the staff had him facing a concrete wall, hands behind his back. Periodically a staff person would walk by and knock Victor's head against the wall. Mike found him, put his arm around him, and whispered, *This is your last ten minutes here. You're done. You're coming home with me.* Victor smiled, barely. When Victor finished his punishment, he told Mike, *Let's just go.* He took nothing with him except for the clothes he was wearing.

At his two-bedroom apartment, Mike had decorated Victor's new room. Posters of Victor's favorite Power Ranger, the green Ranger, and one of Michael Jordan. X-Men toys everywhere. A couple of stuffed animals. A new Schwinn. A comforter with an image of the Wolverine from X-Men. *This is my room?* Victor asked, his eyes wide with excitement. *I don't have to share this with anybody?* Mike turned to the side to wipe away tears. All Victor wanted to know was whether this was permanent, whether they'd be able to stay together.

Immediately Mike started getting pushback from family and friends. Victor would come to his office after school to do homework, and one day one of Mike's coworkers, a woman, came by his desk, and offered advice: *Puppies belong with puppies and kittens belong with kittens.* And then there was his family. Mike's mother, whom he was close to, chastised him: *You're not ready. What do you know about being a parent? You can't even cook. What about the drinking?* "It scared the heck out of me," she told me. Others in his family couldn't stand the idea of Mike adopting a black boy. One family member asked Mike to stop referring to him as "my son" and instead to call him "my foster son." The hardest blow came from Mike's uncle, whom Mike idolized. His Uncle Mike told others, *He better not bring that nigger around. If he does, I'll kill both of 'em. He's not family anymore.* One day Mike's mother asked Mike to pick up two cousins who were visiting from Ireland. When Mike pulled up at his uncle's, the two cousins ran to his car, yelling, *He's getting his gun. He's getting his gun.* Mike drove off, and cut off contact with his uncle. *Fuck him,* he thought.

And then in adoption court the judge wondered aloud whether

Victor wouldn't be better off with a black family. *That would be great, but that's not an option for him,* Mike told the judge at one point. *Nobody wants this kid, and I do, and I don't know what else to say.* Jerry, his caseworker, was so concerned that Mike would unravel in court that he carried cash should he be held in contempt and need to get bailed out.

For four years the case dragged on. And then one day the judge was out ill and his substitute told Mike he had two minutes to plead his case. *No, that's okay. This is a waste of time,* Mike sneered. She looked at her watch. *You now have a minute and a half.*

Mike ranted. *This is a joke. It's been four years. The kid was on medication when he first moved in. He's off medication now. He was flunking all his classes. Now he's an A student. The kid is phenomenal. What else are we supposed to do? And he wants it.* As he ramped up, the judge smacked her gavel down. *This is ridiculous,* the judge told Mike who interpreted her remarks as meaning the case would continue to drag on. *Come back in two weeks,* she continued. *The adoption will be finalized.*

At the ceremony, Mike beamed with pride when Victor stood before the judge, his thin chest pushed out, and announced his new name to the court: *I'm Victor Lee Kelly.*

And so Mike and Victor Kelly began to carve out a life together. Mike bought a home in a northwest suburb, Schaumburg, mainly for the schools and for its distance from the city's street gangs. A stickler for cleanliness, Mike badgered Victor about the mess in his room, his fingerprints on the windows and mirrors. He set a curfew. Victor pushed back, but no more or less than any teen. When Victor got in trouble with a teacher for clowning in class, Mike took off from work and sat in the back of the classroom for the day. Mike didn't cook, so they went out—a lot, so much that at TGI Friday's, their go-to restaurant, they eventually amassed 50,000 points, having spent $5,000 there. Every night before bed, they each told the other, *I love you.* Even when Victor left the house to go to school or to visit friends, Mike insisted. Mike's mother, who immediately took a liking to Victor, still didn't think her son was up to being a father, but when she complimented one of Mike's coworkers for volunteering in the Big Brother program, Mike interrupted. *Mom, what do you think I'm doing? I get nothing from you but this idiot friend does it for one day and you're going to build a statue to him.* That did it. "It hit me like a rock," Mike's mother, Cathy, told me. "I'm not giving my son credit for what he's done or what he's accomplished." She got more involved in their lives. She babysat for Victor. She went to Disney World with them. She would have them both over for dinner. She insisted that Victor call her grandma. She and her husband, Mike's stepfather, were the only ones in his family to embrace Victor.

Victor at first thrived in Schaumburg, excelling at school, but as one of the few African-American students, he got pigeonholed by others as the go-to guy for drugs. And Victor, who'd never really had friends before, didn't want to disappoint. As he entered adolescence, he fell—and fell fast. He sold marijuana. He got into fights. He connected with a street gang that had reached into the suburbs. Mike would call Jerry Harris, the caseworker who had helped him with the adoption, and Jerry in turn would talk with Victor. So did his grandmother. And his teachers. But it didn't let up. Victor continued to sell weed, hiding it in one of the floor vents at home. He got into an altercation and threw a cookie jar at another boy; it shattered in his face. The police would come by, looking to question Victor about one incident or another.

Mike was beside himself. Scared. Irate. Anxious. It got to a point that he dreaded getting phone calls, worried that Victor might be shot, or worse. Some in his family called. One told him, *See, I told you how those people are. Why did you have to adopt him? Why'd you have to ruin our family name?* Mike shot back, *We're not fuckin' Rockefellers. For shit's sake, we're Kellys.* And hung up the phone. Privately, though, he had run out of patience with Victor, and when

Victor turned eighteen, Mike thought, *He's an adult now, he needs to find his own way.* Mike kicked Victor out of the house, sold the Schaumburg home, and moved to the city.

To hear it from Victor's side, well, it's much the same story. He loved his dad. He loved that he had a home. He loved that he had something that was his. At times he felt as if it was the two of them against the world. Once, when visiting Disney World, as they were walking along, arguing about something, a black couple approached Victor to ask if he was okay. *Okay?* He was more than okay. This was his dad. He didn't care that he was white. He didn't care that his foul-mouthed dad yelled at him for cursing. He shrugged off the family members who behind his back used racial slurs, who couldn't stand the idea of a black Kelly—and he quietly admired the way his dad stood up to them. But he and his dad argued over everything, arguments of little substance but of such rancor. Once Victor got shot in the eye with a paintball gun, and on the way to the doctor's they argued so loudly and so heatedly (they can't recall what it was over) that at a stoplight Victor jumped out of the car and ran off.

Victor had a lot roiling inside him. He felt as if he didn't belong anywhere or to anyone. That was his fate in life, he thought. The white kids at his high school thought he was cool. He spoke street slang. He had a swagger about him. At one point he thought to himself, *I just want to be normal. I don't want people to know I'm adopted. I don't belong here.* Truth is, he felt like a misfit. He desperately wanted to feel that he had a place, that he had a history. He knew little about his past, other than that his mom had one day dropped him off at his grandmother's, in the Robert Taylor Homes, a forbidding public housing complex. He doesn't know why his mother gave him away, or why he was so short-tempered, or why he had found a permanent home in the end and his five younger siblings hadn't.

They ended up in foster care. He tried tracking down his mother once, found her through Facebook, and then talked with her by phone. But she started asking him for money, and he just stopped returning her calls. Outside of his dad, he'd never talked with anyone about this. "No one knows my life," he told me once. "Maybe I'm ashamed about it. I keep it to myself."

After Mike kicked him out, Victor lived from couch to couch, first in the suburbs, then in the city. Sometimes he slept in a park. He looked to belong somewhere and began hanging out with a gang, the Latin Counts. He got high with them, drank beer and Barcardi rum. It felt right. It felt like who he was, or at least who people expected him to be. For $200 he bought a .38 special at a house he'd been directed to by fellow gang members. And then one day he and a friend, another Latin Count, took the Metra from the city to Streamwood, a suburb, to meet a couple of girls he'd met at a party a few nights before. They strolled through a park, and when they reached the sidewalk a car drove by filled with four young men who contorted their fingers to resemble pitchforks, the symbol of a rival gang. The car pulled a U-turn and three boys sprang from the car. One wielded a bat. Another yelled, *Count Killer!* Still another threw an empty beer bottle at them. One of the girls started to cry. Victor reached into his waistband and pushed the girls aside. He held the pistol with two hands, shaking. One of the rivals taunted Victor: *You ain't gonna shoot. Pull it. What you gonna do?* Victor purposefully aimed low. He didn't want to kill him. He pulled the trigger. The boy kept coming. He shot two more times, and the boy reached for him, grabbing his wrist before falling. Victor stood over him, the anger welling. It felt like the times at the orphanage when the staff would bark at him and insult him. He felt like nothing mattered at this point. Victor shot one more time, aiming at the boy's stomach.

Victor took off with one of the girls, his friend with the other. They split up into couples so they could pretend they were just out on a date. Victor took the girl's hand in his. But an unmarked police car screeched to a halt in front of them. Victor ran, tossed the gun into someone's backyard, and tried to scale a fence before the police caught up with him, threw him to the ground, and cuffed him. He was nineteen, and they asked him if he wanted to make a phone call. He declined. The only person he knew to call was his dad, and he wanted nothing to do with him.

A couple of days later, a relative called Mike to tell him he had read about the shooting in the *Daily Herald*. Mike asked him to read him the article. The only relief Mike felt was that Victor's victim lived. His relative's wife got on the phone and berated Mike. *Why'd you adopt him? He's an embarrassment to the family. We all told you not to do this.* Mike just took it. He'd known it was coming. Eventually. But once he'd composed himself, hours later, he called back and his relative answered. *I need to speak to your wife.* He refused to put her on. *Tell the cunt not to kick me when I'm down. Fuck you. I don't need this shit right now.* But Mike's vitriol was really directed at Victor. *I didn't raise a criminal. Shooting someone? Where'd this come from?*

Mike drank. Screwdrivers. Jack Daniel's and Coke. Vodka tonics. He'd go on binges. One night he got so drunk at a bar—ten vodka tonics—he goaded a well-known rock musician, someone he's asked me not to name, and threw a punch at him. At a friend's wedding, again drunk, he hit on a pregnant woman. *I'm married,* she told him.

Happily?

I'm pregnant!

So is oral an option?

He told Victor he wouldn't visit him in prison. *You fuckin' chose that life,* he told him. *You deal with the consequences.* He didn't even attend the trial where Victor got sentenced to five years. (Victor would serve half that if he didn't get into trouble in prison.)

Mike felt like a failure. He was embarrassed. A son convicted of attempted murder? He felt dirtied by it. He felt alone. What's more, he'd been holding on to a secret, something he hadn't shared with anyone. It gnawed at him. It isolated him. It led him to drink even more. *No one knows the real Mike,* he thought. That's how Victor felt about himself, too. *No one knows the real Victor.*

M ike never visited Victor during his two and half years in prison. They talked regularly, though, every Sunday on the phone, but those were awkward conversations. What Mike would never concede to Victor is that he looked forward to those Sunday calls, so much so that he wouldn't make any plans for fear he'd miss it. Mike wanted to know Victor was okay. As for Victor, he had no one else to talk to. What's more, he wanted to make things right with his dad, and his dad could make him laugh, which didn't come easy for him in prison.

When Victor got out, he asked his dad if he could live with him while he was on house arrest. They had him wearing an ankle bracelet, and he needed a stable address. Mike relented, and eventually got Victor a job at his real estate firm. The day after Victor got off parole, he visited some friends in the suburbs, and they climbed a fence to swim in someone's backyard pool. When the owner came home, rather than fleeing, Victor stood his ground and told him to fuck off. When Mike heard that Victor had gotten into trouble yet again, he started drinking margaritas at a local Mexican restaurant, at noon. Three hours later the restaurant cut him off, and he headed to a birthday party for a friend, and announced his entry by shouting, *Where are the whores?* At one point he playfully put two friends, one of whom was black and the other Hispanic, in headlocks. He yelled a racial epithet at each, thinking he was being funny. But he later realized he'd become his uncle that night. It was the last drink he ever took.

The police came to Mike's building, knocking on doors, looking for Victor, for the trespassing offense. (The pool's owner ended up not pressing charges.) Mike was humiliated, and at a coffee shop he told Victor he wanted his name back and offered him $1,000. He knew Victor was desperate for money, so he figured he'd take him up on it. *I don't want you to be Kelly anymore,* he told him. *I don't want to know you. I don't want to see you. I'm done with this.* Mike's friends told him it felt coldhearted, that it's what his relatives ultimately wanted, but Mike felt betrayed and was bone-tired. To Mike, Victor seemed to be weighing his decision whether to take the money, but really Victor was thinking to himself, *This is all I have. If I lose my dad, I'm gonna end up in the streets for good. I wouldn't have anyone.* Without saying a word, Victor got up and walked out, slowly, like he was letting his dad know who was in control.

That was it. They stopped seeing each other. Or talking. Six months later Victor got a job busing tables at a nightclub, and he came by to show his dad his paycheck, to let him know that he wasn't hanging out with the same people anymore, that he was moving in a different direction. But Mike didn't buy it. Mike didn't trust him—nor did he trust himself.

Mike had known since third grade. Once in elementary school he told his mom he was worried something was wrong with him because he was attracted to other boys. She sloughed it off and told him, *Everyone has those feelings. They'll go away.* In his thirties, he came out to a friend, who then warned him he needed to keep it to himself, that he'd lose friends and family over it.

He heeded this advice. He didn't tell anyone else. He had a tough enough time admitting it to himself. All that crassness toward women? The lap dances? It was all a front, a mask. The drinking? Mike had no doubt it was because pretending he was someone he wasn't wore on him. In recent years he'd put on nearly seventy-five pounds. Mike had always told Victor that he had to be true to himself, and he felt like he'd been hypocritical. He needed to tell Victor before anyone else. But he also knew that doing so would further alienate Victor, that Victor would walk away, that he'd tell Mike, *I'm done. This is why I'm so screwed up . . . because you're so screwed up.* This wasn't an effort to get Victor back but rather an act of necessity, an effort to get himself back.

They'd barely spoken in over a year, and when Mike called and told Victor, who was now twenty-four, *We need to get together for coffee. I've got something really important to talk about,* Victor imagined he had cancer, or worse yet, that he was dying. They agreed to meet the next day. Along with the drinking, Mike had quit cigarettes, but he was so nervous he bought a pack, smoking as he paced in front of the neighborhood Starbucks. He thought to himself, *I can't do this,* and started back to his apartment before spotting Victor coming down the block. Tall. Lanky. Handsome. His hair worn in long braids. Still some swagger in his step. Mike went inside and found a table near the back. He ordered a coffee, but Victor, who clearly had no intent on lingering, didn't order anything and just sat down. Mike skipped the small talk and spoke fast, his words running together, a tic he has when he gets nervous. *Here'sthethingIgottotellyou.* He breathed in. *I'mgay.* Once he said it, he felt some relief. *I feel like this is right for me. This is the way I am.* He closed his eyes. Victor stiffened. He muttered, *Okay. So what are we here to talk about? What's the problem?* At that moment Mike thought to himself, *I raised a damn good kid. I really did.*

It happened slowly, but the two started checking in on each other. Victor knew all too well the burden of carrying secrets, of not knowing yourself, of knowing that a part of you is missing. Wanting to find out about his childhood ate at him, and he was too ashamed to share what little he knew with anyone else. And he was deeply ashamed of what had landed him in prison, that he had in an act of fury shot someone. He knew what keeping all that inside did to one's soul. On one level he envied his dad, that he was being true to himself, but he also worried about him. Mike was thirty-nine and for the first time had a steady partner and was asking his son for relationship advice. Mike was concerned because he and his partner argued a lot over petty stuff, and Victor assured him, *That's normal. You're going to love each other. You're going to hate each other. That's what a relationship is about.* Of course, he knew. He'd been through it in his relationship with his dad. Victor felt he had something to prove, that he was more than that moment when he shot another boy, that he wasn't a thug. He got a job working at the front desk of a high-end fitness club, and when he was promoted to manager, he stopped by his dad's apartment to show off his new shirt, a white polo with the club's insignia stitched on the pocket. Of course, Mike couldn't help himself, and he told Victor he needed a haircut.

F ive years later, Father's Day, Victor arrives just as the sun's setting, at 8:30 as he promised, fresh from work at the fitness club. He's twenty-nine now, dressed in a polo shirt so large he seems lost in it. His jeans sag off his hips, the pants seemingly held up by threads. *You've got to get clothes that fit,* Mike tells Victor. Victor laughs and gives him a hug. Mike has been feeling down lately. He broke up with his boyfriend last December, and though he knows it was the right thing, he is feeling lonely, anxious that he won't find someone else. Victor hands his dad a card on which he's written *Another great year with me and you being together. You're the best ever. Love, Vic.* He's also brought two cigars—the Macanudos Mike used to smoke with his uncle. It's tradition. Mike never reconciled with his uncle, though he visited him in the hospital when he was dying from a stroke. His uncle was in and out of sleep, and Mike, rather than trying to work through their differences, just reminisced about *The Searchers,* their favorite John Wayne movie. Victor knows Mike's uncle hated the fact that he'd become a part of the family, but he also knows that when Mike was younger his uncle had been his mentor, his friend, and so he brought these cigars to honor that.

They order pizza from a place up the street, and Mike, who has been sober for six years, hands Victor a beer which he kept in the fridge for his visits. They wander out to the balcony and sit across from each other in metal deck chairs, relishing the breeze blowing in off the lake. *Are you going to get back with Dan?* Victor asks. Mike shakes his head. *He never really liked me,* Victor says. Mike tries to brush it off, but he knows Victor is right. His boyfriend never took to Victor, didn't like it that Victor never attended college, that he didn't speak the king's English. *If it's going to make you happy, you should . . . ,* Victor suggests, trailing off. Mike shakes his head and smiles.

When Mike came out, most of his friends embraced him. But there were those who pushed him aside. One of his former coworkers, one of the guys whom he would party with at lunch every day, wrote him, *Good luck in your new life. Sorry I can't be a part of it.* Mike seemed okay with it. He had Victor.

Victor, puffing on his cigar, confides that his girlfriend, with whom he's been having trouble, has threatened to tell his boss about his criminal past. Victor has kept it hidden from the fitness club, knowing that if they had known, they probably wouldn't have hired him. Victor has long had a fear that people will learn what he's done, and he often lets his worries unfurl, imagining the worst thing that could happen. (Indeed, at his and Mike's request, I changed their last name in this story.) He tells his dad that if the fitness club finds out, he'll lose his job and end up homeless, back living in parks and on friends' couches. It feels too real for Victor. Mike assures him that if things don't work out, he always has the extra bedroom. *It ruined my life,* Victor muses, and then corrects himself. *I ruined my life. I'm a felon. I have to work twice as hard. I have to lie.* Mike laughs. *Not with me.* Mike, too, knows what it is to lie, to lie about who you are. He knows the churning stomach, the effort it takes to pretend you're someone else, the unceasing sense of humiliation.

Mike has tried to encourage Victor to open up with others, to talk with young people about his journey, but Victor thinks it would feel too much like bragging. Besides, he tells his dad, *It really messed me up.* Mike leans back in his chair. *Everyone makes mistakes,* he says. *Some are worse than others.* Mike pauses. *When are you gonna start wearing clothes that fit you? You're twenty-nine. It's time you look it.* Victor rolls his eyes and takes another draw of the cigar.

Chapter 7

The Witnesses, part one

The sun had just set, and before heading home, Ramaine Hill kissed his girlfriend, Kaprice, and hugged his two-year-old son, RJ. He hopped on his nephew's BMX bike, which was too small for his five-foot-eleven frame, and so he had to ride it standing up. He always listened to music, mostly Lil Wayne these days, and so he put in his earbuds. This was when Ramaine felt most at peace. By himself, with his music. He pedaled the three blocks home, his head bobbing, singing along to Lil Wayne's "Swag Surfin."

> ... *You think we gon' do our thing?*
> *Well ain't it sunny in the summer?* ...

Ramaine, a sleepy-eyed, open-faced twenty-two-year-old, wears his hair in braids and has a quiet demeanor about him, a shyness really. He doesn't feel comfortable around people he doesn't know well, which includes just about everyone except for his family and Kaprice. Not long ago his grandfather, whom he'd never met, visited, and when he arrived Ramaine disappeared upstairs, accessed the roof, and descended through another staircase, exiting through the mailroom. Anything to avoid having a conversation. Anything to avoid having to explain himself. Anything to avoid contact. He always has his earbuds in, listening to music, as much an escape as it is a way to keep the world at bay. Mostly R&B and rap. When his aunt asks him to take out the garbage or clean his room, he seems to ignore her, often sitting on the couch, rocking to his music, oblivious to his aunt's entreaties. He sometimes falls asleep at night with his earbuds in. Kaprice remembers when they started hanging out together, in their early teens, Ramaine didn't want to come inside her apartment, didn't want to have to talk with her mom, and so he would sit with her outside, on a park bench. He was old school. When at the age of fourteen he decided he wanted to date Kaprice, he asked her mom for permission. He told Kaprice's mom, *I'm really feeling her. I want her to be my girlfriend.* Kaprice's mom laughed and gave him the okay.

On this summer evening Ramaine pedals toward his apartment, invigorated by a late-night summer breeze, his body dancing to the lively beat of Lil Wayne. Ramaine lives with his aunt and older sister and younger brother. As he arrives at the row of townhomes with its manicured midway, a van screeches to a stop in front of him. The side door slides open and a man jumps out. He has a gun. He demands that Ramaine get into the van, but Ramaine, who is strong and agile, throws down the bike and sprints for his home, fifty feet away. As he pounds on the front door, pleading to be let in, he turns and sees the van pull a U-turn before taking off. He recognized the man who accosted him. He knows what he wanted. He knows they'll try again. Standing in his apartment's vestibule, trying to catch his breath, shaking, he tells his aunt, Joyce, *They're after me. They're after me.* Joyce doesn't know what or who he is talking about.

n Chicago, the vast majority of murders and shootings go unsolved. Murder someone, and chances are only one in four that you'll get caught. Shoot someone and injure them, it's only a one in ten possibility that you'll get charged. That's not a misprint. You have an awfully good chance of shooting someone in the city and getting away with it. The police will tell you that much of the reason for the low closure rates is that a street culture discourages cooperation with law enforcement. Which makes the story of Ramaine somewhat remarkable—and challenges the conventional wisdom that when people refuse to assist the police they're acting out of defiance. It's more often than not an act of self-preservation.

Ramaine Hill and his two siblings lived with their aunt in a newly constructed townhome in a neighborhood called Old Town, just north of the city's downtown. The family has been witness to and a part of an astonishing transformation in recent years. Until recently the neighborhood had been the site of the infamous Cabrini-Green public housing complex, a medley of drab-looking concrete high-rises and row houses, a place which served as a marker for the city's brutal history—as well as the city's legacy of gross neglect of those most in need.

The litany of violence at Cabrini unnerved the city. It threw the city off-balance. In July of 1970, a sniper in a sixth-floor apartment shot and killed two police officers walking across a baseball field. In 1981, on the heels of a two-month period during which eleven people were murdered and another thirty-seven wounded by gunfire, Mayor Jane Byrne, angered by the shootings, moved into an apartment in Cabrini for three weeks. It was a move that highlighted the isolation of Cabrini; it sat barely eight blocks from Byrne's posh Gold Coast apartment, and yet she required an around-the-clock full security detail. In October of 1992, seven-year-old Dantrell Davis, while holding his mother's hand on the way to school, was shot and killed by a stray bullet from a sniper on the tenth floor of one building who was aiming for rival gang members. That same year, the horror film *Candyman* was released. It was set at Cabrini, and the film's director, Bernard Rose, said he chose the location "because it was a place of such palpable fear." Cabrini became a symbol of life run amok among the poor, but what few talked about or acknowledged was the abandonment—mistreatment, really—of the most vulnerable by the city and federal authorities. Conditions were appalling: frequent flooding, elevators that didn't work, caged terraces. Cabrini, which sat just a mile from downtown, served as a demarcation between *us* and *them*. It almost felt like an internment camp for blacks set amid the white neighborhoods surrounding it.

Ramaine spent his early years in a fifth-floor apartment in Cabrini with his aunt, who had already raised five children of her own. She had taken custody of her two nephews and niece when they were quite young.

In 1999 the city announced a plan to raze all of its eighty-two public housing high-rises. They housed 200,000 people, equivalent to a city the size of Des Moines, Iowa. One longtime housing advocate, referring to the scope of the plan, told me, "It takes your breath away." Ever since I set foot in public housing thirty years ago, I believed these buildings should be torn down. They served as a bulwark to segregation; they were built on the edge of existing black ghettoes because white politicians didn't want them built in their neighborhoods. They were constructed on the cheap and then ruled for nineteen years by Charlie Swibel, the head of the Chicago Housing Authority, who used them as a patronage fiefdom and whose neglect bordered on the criminal.

The Plan for Transformation, as it came to be called, was a bold, if not flawed effort. Much of public housing, especially Cabrini-Green, sat on valuable real estate, so the idea was to invite private developers to build on these sites if they would set aside units for former public housing residents. The idea was that you'd have people from different economic strata mixing (though the city steered clear of using this moment to reverse decades of racial segregation). On the Cabrini site, you'd have the very rich living next to the very poor. At one point the *Chicago Tribune* reported that many former Cabrini families didn't want to move back into these mixed-income developments because they feared that if anything happened, if anything went wrong, they'd get blamed. But Joyce relished the opportunity. In 2003 she and the three kids moved into a three-story, three-bedroom townhome, one in a row of eight. Three families in her section were former Cabrini residents. The rest were mostly professionals. Their neighbor, a single woman whom they became close to, was a social worker. The neighborhood felt so safe, Joyce and the kids didn't even lock their front door. "I thought we had it made," Joyce told me.

Three years ago, on the evening of August 13, 2010, a Friday night, Ramaine, who was nineteen at the time, met Kaprice in front of Wayman AME Church, a 124-year-old red-brick structure which resembles an apartment building more than it does a place of worship. Ramaine and Kaprice had met in third grade. "He was quiet," Kaprice told me. "He was to himself. In order to see the real him, you had to get to know him. He was quiet as a church mouse." On this particular night they met a friend of theirs by the church and helped him clean up the mess in his car, a four-door white Buick Regal, so there would be room for all of them. They were planning to drive to a party nearby. Ramaine was leaning into the backseat, clearing it out, when a boy rode by on a bicycle, pedaling so fast his hoodie flew off. The boy had a pistol and started shooting, his apparent intended target the young man who owned the car, Ramaine and Kaprice's friend. The boy shot six times and then sped away. Ramaine felt a burning sensation in his back, so he stood, and then hobbled into the driver's seat. "I'm shot," he told Kaprice. He could be a prankster, and so Kaprice thought he was joking until he leaned forward and she lifted his bloodstained white T-shirt. She saw the bullet lodged in his back, inches from his spine. Ramaine insisted on getting out of the car, tried to stand, and then leaned against the hood, bending over for support. There, Kaprice and her mother, who had arrived on the scene after hearing the shots, told him not to move. Ramaine could hear people talking, saying that the bullet was in a dangerous location, and he started to shake from fright. Kaprice's mom tried to calm him, rubbing his shoulders. She asked if he knew who had shot him. Ramaine replied, "Pinkie." When the police arrived, Ramaine gave them the same name, as well as a physical description. The police knew right away who he was talking about, a fifteen-year-old boy named Deantonio Agee who belonged to a local gang, a remnant from the projects.

It's one thing to identify someone who shoots you. It's another thing to then be willing to press charges and to testify. It doesn't happen often. The state's attorney charged Agee with attempted murder, and because of the severity of the offense, Agee's case was transferred to adult court. Before the trial Agee's defense attorney, Nathaniel Niesen, stopped by Ramaine's home, hoping to talk with him, to find out what he knew, to discover what kind of witness he would be. Niesen knew it was a long shot. Most of the time witnesses would turn him away, angry and scared. And he knew Ramaine still had the bullet lodged in his back, a daily reminder of his encounter. But Ramaine invited Niesen in, and along with his aunt, Joyce, they sat down at the kitchen table, where Ramaine, unflustered and undeterred, recounted the shooting while Niesen took notes. His aunt was surprised, mostly because Ramaine so assiduously avoided talking with strangers. "I was struck by the fact that he was so forthcoming," Niesen recalled. "He seemed just very calm and Zen about the whole thing." Ramaine appeared so certain about what had transpired that night and so straightforward that Niesen thought his client, Agee, would never survive a trial with Ramaine as the key witness. A judge or a jury, he had no doubt, would completely trust Ramaine—and convict Agee, who faced a minimum of thirty years. At that point, sitting at the kitchen table, listening to Ramaine recount the evening, Niesen knew that he would urge Agee to seek a plea deal. It was, he thought, really the only option.

On July 6, 2012, Agee entered a plea of guilty in exchange for lesser charges: aggravated battery with a firearm. The judge sentenced him to fifteen years. That's when everything changed. For Ramaine. First there were the phone calls, a voice on the other end telling Ramaine he needed to tell the court that he had been wrong, that he couldn't in fact identify his shooter. As time went on, the calls got more heated. *You snitchin'*, Ramaine was told. On another occasion, *We're gonna get you.* One afternoon, walking to Jewel, a local grocery store, where he worked in the meat department, two men stopped him and offered him $5,000 to recant. Then, a few weeks later, when he was strolling with Kaprice, a man approached them and told Kaprice he needed to speak with Ramaine by himself. She didn't stand down. *Whatever you got to say to Ramaine, you can say to the both of us,* she told him. So the man told Ramaine, *Pinkie's my nephew. I heard about what happened to you. So how much money you want?* He wanted Ramaine to agree to tell the police he couldn't in fact identify the boy who had shot him. Ramaine looked away. *I don't want no money,* he muttered. *I ain't going to court. I just want you to leave me alone.*

Ramaine never told his aunt about the threats, only his brother and sister. One time two young men jumped out of a passing car, one with a gun. *Pop his ass,* the other instructed as Ramaine ran, taking cover in the shadow of a local elementary school. Kaprice tried to get him to stop listening to music as he walked through the neighborhood. She worried that he wouldn't hear anyone approaching. But he insisted, and she said that after the kidnapping attempt he walked with his head dropped, like he didn't care anymore. "It messed with his mind," she told me. But Ramaine, who could be stubborn, went about his life, walking to and from his job. He continued to don his earbuds, drowning out everything around him. He refused to go to the police. Jeremiah, his younger brother (by a year), said he felt too humiliated, too embarrassed. Plus he worried that going to the police would only escalate things. Maybe, too, he also felt reasonably safe, because with each week the neighborhood seemed to grow whiter and more prosperous, a more and more unlikely place for a street assault. Also, it had now been a year since Agee got sentenced. At some point, Ramaine figured, Agee's friends would move on.

And so Ramaine, who kept to himself anyway, went about his life, mostly staying inside except when he walked to and from work or visited Kaprice, with whom he had started bickering a lot. It was, all in all, a reasonably good summer. Ramaine especially took pleasure in hanging out with his son. He so wanted him to start walking, and one afternoon Jeremiah had an idea. He got two oversized remote-control cars their aunt had given them years ago, and in Ramaine's downstairs bedroom he placed RJ against one of the cars, letting him use it as kind of a crutch. He tottered and then let go. Jeremiah burst out laughing, boasting to Ramaine that he, not his dad, had taught RJ to walk. Jeremiah spent much of the summer with Ramaine, and since Jeremiah was at school, at Trinity Christian College, Ramaine, who was working, would treat him to meals at Subway or Mr. Gyro's. Ramaine slowly began to seem like his old self, but Jeremiah and his sister worried about him. Ramaine wouldn't talk about it, but Jeremiah says, "He may not have showed it, but he was scared. I could see it in his eyes."

Chapter 8

The (Annotated) Eulogy

JULY 4 . . . **JULY 5** . . . JULY 6 . . .

The funeral was held on the far South Side at Shiloh Missionary Baptist Church, but it was arranged by Leak and Sons Funeral Home, one of the oldest and busiest African-American-owned funeral homes in the city. Mr. Leak estimated that already this year he had performed over forty services for victims of violence.

At the service, the women wore white dresses, the men white suits or white T-shirts with a photo of the deceased, Robert Douglas, who was thirty-one and had been shot and killed in his car nine days earlier. Robert, too, lying in the powder-blue casket, was dressed in a white suit and a white Kangol cap.

My name is Erin, for those of you who don't know me.

Erin Wells is dressed in a sleeveless, form-fitting white dress, and because she is short, a deacon of the church comes to lower the microphone at the lectern. Erin, the daughter of a white man and a black woman, is light-skinned, with high cheekbones and knowing eyes. She and Robert have five children together, three girls and two boys. They first met in grade school; Robert was on a tumbling team with Erin's older brother. When Robert was a freshman in high school and Erin in eighth grade, they ran into each other at a dance. There, Robert declared, *You're going to be my girlfriend.* They started dating a few months later.

The church is packed, standing room only, so many that a gaggle of men stand outside the sanctuary, peering in through the doorway. A police officer in a Kevlar vest stands in the rear as well. Erin looks around and realizes she doesn't know everyone. Not even close. Robert had a life separate from hers, and that was part of what came between them. With one hand on her hip and the other on the podium, she seems remarkably composed. This is her goodbye, and she is brutally honest about her battle for Robert—which she ultimately lost.

> I've known Robert for almost twenty years now—fifteen of which we were together, back and forth, like a roller-coaster ride. And we weren't together at the moment because the streets had come between me and Robert. But that did not stop Robert from seeing me constantly and seeing his kids constantly. And they say that if you love something you should let it go and if it comes back then it's yours. And I truly know what people mean by that because even though Robert and I were not together, we were with each other every day.

Robert and Erin were very much a couple through high school and in the years after. Erin went to college, briefly, before taking a job at JPMorgan Chase, working her way up to her position as a personal banker. Robert, according to Erin, aspired to be a rap artist, though to make money he apparently sold cocaine. He went by the name Rob Dob, and some of his music still lives on YouTube. During one period when the two were apart, Erin had a set of twins by another man. Then she had five children, all with Robert. He could be a very attentive father. He'd come by Erin's apartment and play Monopoly or Uno with the children, or watch television with them snuggled on the couch, or take them out for a meal. "He truly had a big heart," she told me, "but then he had to be all tough outside. I'd say to him, *Why do you feel like everyone got to be afraid of you?* She knew she was in a tug-of-war with the streets when one late night Robert showed up at her apartment with his arm bleeding, a hole in his sleeve. *What the hell is going on?* Erin demanded. *We got into a shootout,* Robert explained. She looked out the window and couldn't find their van. *Where the hell is your car?*

The police got it, Robert replied sheepishly.

Who were you in a shootout with?

Robert paused.

Robert!

The police.

And you brought your dumb ass to my house, with your kids here. If the police kick in my door, I swear, you get the fuck out, 'cause I'm gonna tell them everything.

Robert told Erin that after he'd been shot he ditched the van and had a relative call the police to tell them that she'd just been robbed and that the van had been stolen. A short while later, Robert left to visit his cousin, who was a medical assistant and who sewed up his wound so he could avoid going to the emergency room, where his injury would undoubtedly be reported to the police.

Erin was under no illusions. Their relationship seemed to be as unpredictable as the weather, sun mixed with clouds. She told stories with a playfulness, marveling at Robert's persistence and mischievousness.

I would come home from work and Robert would be at my house. I would come home from my mother's house and Robert would be there. I moved on Robert's birthday and I did

not tell him where and I just remember Robert shouting my name at the top of his lungs to my window and I asked him, how did you find me? He looked at me like, you know the face he makes, "You thought I couldn't find you?"

A month before he was killed, Erin moved. She had been living in a small house behind her mom's but felt she needed to get away from Robert. She didn't want his troubles seeping into her and her kids' lives. When Robert found out she had relocated, he got her cousin Tevin to point out the apartment building where she was now staying, and at midnight Erin was roused from her bed by someone yelling, "Eeerin! Eeerin!" She raised her bedroom window, and Robert was standing on the street, three stories below. *You just gonna move without telling me?* he yelled. *I gotta go to work tomorrow,* Erin hollered back. When Robert threatened to climb the gate, Erin buzzed him in. He wandered through the rooms and muttered, *I like this apartment.* He then left. *He just wanted to know where I was,* Erin told me. *And that I was okay.*

And I still remember when Robert went to jail a few weeks ago. Tevin came over screaming and I called his mom to find out what happened and she said he would be out and sure enough that Saturday he was out and he was at my house. And we had a long, long talk and Bobby, my son, was really upset and he asked his dad: "Daddy, please don't go to jail anymore. I thought I wasn't going to see you at my eighth-grade graduation." And Robert just cried and cried on my couch about it. And I told him: "Your son means what he say, he wants you to be at his eighth-grade graduation." And so Robert promised he wouldn't go to jail anymore.

Two months before he was killed, Robert, along with another young man and a woman, was stopped by the police and strip-searched on the street, in front of passersby. A neighbor videotaped it from her second-floor apartment and uploaded it to the Internet. The police handcuffed Robert to burglar bars on a first-floor window and pulled his pants down and performed a body cavity search. He was humiliated. Robert and his two friends ended up filing a lawsuit against the police. He told Erin he wanted to leave the city and wanted her to join him. *We got to get out of here,* he told her. *Why you in such a rush now?* she asked. *When I was ready to go, you weren't. I'm not going anywhere with you, not if you're gonna be doing this. I don't want to go anywhere if I got to worry about you going to jail.* He talked about going to Iowa, where some of Erin's relatives had migrated and where they'd found good-paying jobs at a Kraft Heinz factory. The couple stayed up much of the night, talking. Robert pleaded with Erin to leave with him. What he didn't tell her is that a few days earlier, he'd been shot at, and he was afraid.

The last memory that I have of Robert, it was Nani's last day of school. They were having a party and they asked us to get some snacks and so we went to the store. And then we snuck back to my house, and, uh . . .

Erin looks towards the ceiling, shaking her head, as if she's sharing this inside joke with everyone, as if to say, *You know Robert.* She laughs awkwardly.

Robert was just holding me so close—telling me how tired he was and how he wanted to just leave Chicago and he wanted me to pack my stuff and go with him. And I told him no. And he said he wanted to come home and I told him no, because the streets was just torn between us. And I told him I liked my plain life, and he just couldn't understand that, that money didn't make me happy. And then I was sitting in my car and my friend just texted me and Robert just flared up

and jumped up out his car. He told me I couldn't have nobody playing with me and I said, "Robert, you're not my man," and he said, "I'm always your man." We laughed. That was the last time I saw Robert or spoke to Robert.

Robert was killed the next day. While he was sitting in his car with a friend, someone walked up and shot him through the window. Erin insists that a friend set up Robert. After Erin delivered the eulogy, she walked from the podium, and her legs gave out from under her. A friend had to hold her up to keep her from folding over. She went out into the hot, humid air, where some men had unbuttoned their shirts to cool off. In the church's parking lot, police officers made their presence felt as a police helicopter hovered overhead, not uncommon at funerals when they expect trouble. In the gaggle of people milling about, Erin noticed the friend who she believed had had something to do with Robert's death, and so did Robert's uncle, who is in his fifties. The uncle punched the friend, which led to a melee. The police dispersed the crowd before things escalated and then escorted Erin and her children to a waiting car. They headed to Mount Hope Cemetery, where—because so many murder victims are buried there—police search cars before they enter.

Erin told me that the last time she saw Robert, just the day before his death, she told him, *I'm not one of those girls who gets excited* [*by this life*]. *I buried enough friends already.* Her cousin had been killed just a year earlier. *I like my boring life,* she told him. Robert shot back, *All you do is work, work, work.* To which Erin replied, *What else am I suppose to do?*

Chapter 9

I Ain't Going Nowhere, part one

JULY 8 . . . JULY 9 . . . JULY 10 . . .

This morning Anita Stewart pulled up in front of Thomas's house shortly before nine. Thomas's house appeared to wobble as the blue tarp which covered a gap in the roof rustled in the morning breeze. It was hard for Anita to keep track of the abandoned properties up and down the block, sometimes as many as half a dozen, staggering like punch-drunk boxers, downstairs windows covered by sheets of warped plywood, upstairs windows knocked out, open to the elements. It felt like she was witnessing the remnants of a brawl; even the intact homes looked tired and worn. Add the residents and it was, to put it politely, a rowdy street. Earlier this month Thomas had told Anita to stop coming by. He forbid her, really. Though he wouldn't say why, he clearly feared for her safety. Just a few weeks earlier, a forty-two-year-old man, Dwayne Duckworth, whom everyone called Duck, had been shot thirteen times coming out of his house. Thomas ran down the street to see why there was all this commotion. "I ain't never seen so many holes," he told me. "And when they put him on the stretcher, he was still breathing and he had a cigarette hanging from his mouth." Duck didn't make it. People whispered that it was over drugs. I'd been there once when three shots rang out nearby; they're such everyday sounds that the postman paused for a moment and then continued along his route. Thomas liked to tell stories of the block's waywardness. Once, he recalled, a drug dealer offered money or drugs to anyone who would dismantle a police camera that had been erected at the top of a lamppost. Thomas and others doubled over in laughter as a desperate addict rammed his pickup into the lamppost, knocking the camera down and doing untold damage to his truck. Thomas was amazed that the driver emerged unscathed.

Thomas had just completed his junior year at Harper High School, where Anita was one of two social workers. He had failed Spanish and English, and so Anita helped enroll him in summer school, paying the $50 fee. But he had already missed the first week of classes, and Anita knew that if he was to graduate, he needed to complete this summer session. She tried calling Thomas on his cell phone, but he refused to answer. Thomas could be petulant, so much so that Anita and her colleague at Harper had taken to calling him "Big Baby." As in *Hey, Big Baby, get over here* or *Big Baby, I hear you're giving your math teacher trouble.*

As Anita trudged up the rickety front stairs of Thomas's grandmother's house, she laughed to herself. Too early for Thomas or his brothers, she thought. She relished the quiet. Often when she came by in the afternoons or evenings, Thomas's older brothers, twins Leon and Deon, would be on the porch with him. Like Thomas, they didn't talk much. Their faces revealed little. Leon, who was in a wheelchair after being shot two years earlier, looked angry, but it could just as easily have been well-earned sadness. He had recently lost his left leg to an infection. They had a lift installed outside so that he didn't need to be carried down the stairs every time he went out. But this morning the porch was empty. Anita knocked, and Thomas's sister, Stella, answered. Thomas, she said, was still sleeping. She went upstairs to his attic bedroom to rouse him.

Anita could hear Thomas lumbering down the stairs. She smiled. His jeans and shirt were rumpled, his long dreads hanging over his face like a beaded curtain. She suspected he'd slept in his clothes. *Where you been?* she asked.

I ain't going nowhere. His voice rang with a defiance hard to square with the early hour.

Yes, you are.

I ain't going. You hear me. I already told you, man. The pitch of his voice rose, as it always did when he got agitated.

I'm not a man, Anita replied.

I already told you I'm not going.

Anita had learned to remain firm with Thomas. And patient.

You are going. I'll wait in the car—and you can put some new clothes on.

I told you I ain't going. He paused in resignation. *You get on my nerves.*

Anita chuckled to herself and returned to her car to wait.

When Anita first met Thomas three years earlier, she thought he might be a little off. Maybe, she thought, he heard voices. Her first day at Harper —a struggling and deeply proud school in Englewood—she had stepped into a freshman algebra class and noticed Thomas right away. A broad-shouldered, sad-looking boy, he seemed on edge. His head bowed, he was slowly pacing, while class was in session, from an open window to his desk and back again, as if he were contemplating jumping. Back and forth. Back and forth, muttering to himself, *Motherfucker. Motherfucker. Motherfucker.* Anita, who had just been hired as the school's second social worker, reached out to him like she was trying to touch a ghost, her fingers trying to find a place to land. *Don't touch me,* he warned, brushing aside her hand.

Come away from the window, she urged gently. *Come sit with me.* She had at least got his attention. *What's your name?* she asked. He told her, and silently followed Anita to a nearby desk, where they sat across from each other.

Where d'ya live? Anita asked.

Seventieth Place.

I grew up in Englewood, Anita said.

You did?

Anita thought she might not be able to engage him. He seemed to move and talk slowly, his voice distant and garbled, as if he were speaking from deep within a cave.

What school did you go to? she continued.

Vernon Johns.

A connection, Anita thought.

Guess what, I went to Vernon Johns! Do you know Cheap Charlie's? Thomas nodded. Cheap Charlie owned the corner store by the school. *Do you know the reason he's called Cheap Charlie? If you were a penny short, he wouldn't let you go. You'd have to return the candy.* Anita barely made out Thomas's smile, his head bowed so low his chin touched his chest.

Anita went on to share stories of Vernon Johns and of the neighborhood, including the time she stole candy from a local grocery store. Thomas kept his head down, responding to Anita with grunts and groans. He seemed perturbed, but more than anything, she thought, he appeared to be hurting. She just sat there and talked, nothing of substance. She just wanted to connect with him, to pull him out of his state. As she left him that day, she thought to herself, *I know something happened to him. I just know.*

Anita, too, had had her share of hardship. When she was young, an uncle molested her. He would grope her, grabbing her rear and her breasts, and threatened to hurt her if she told anyone. He once forced Anita to grip the chain holding his powerful pit bull, King, and had King drag her through the house, crashing into the walls and furniture. When she was twenty, Anita's anger so consumed her that she confronted him. *I remember everything you did,* she told him. *I'm going to kill you.* (He died a few years later of a heart attack.) Anita doesn't like talking about her uncle, but that experience profoundly shaped her, and the memories have so stayed with her that as an adult she's joined a support group of women who were abused as children. She knows firsthand how in the wake of trauma all hell can break loose in your heart, so that love and fury and sadness get so stirred together it can be hard to figure out how you're really feeling, hard to figure out who you really are. She saw that in Thomas, too.

In the following weeks Anita would stop by that algebra class, usually just to say hello, to ask Thomas how he was doing, and then soon she began to follow him from class to class. She didn't really have the time for this, but she saw much of herself in Thomas. *That was me when I was younger,* she thought. Thomas didn't get into fights at school, but he could be belligerent toward his teachers or simply refuse to attend class. *I ain't doing shit,* he told Anita once. *I ain't doing a motherfuckin' thing.* Soon Anita had to split her time between Harper and another high school—a common practice in the cash-strapped Chicago schools—and when she'd return to Harper for her three days every week, Thomas would throw a tantrum. *Where you been? You don't care 'bout nobody. You don't know nothing 'bout me.* Anita would laugh at these small outbursts, and began calling him Big Baby. The name stuck, and that's how Anita and her colleague, Crystal Smith, would refer to Thomas. "That's like her son," Crystal told me. "Her love for Thomas is like the love she has for her own kids. Thomas would always tell Anita, 'Like, c'mon, don't talk to them [the other kids].'" He wanted Anita to himself.

Anita and Crystal shared an office, a windowless cinder-block room the size of a large walk-in closet which was tucked away in the center of the building, symbolic, I suppose, of where social workers fit into the hierarchy of our schools. The two met as undergraduates at Chicago State University, and they made an unlikely pair. Anita is serious and restrained. Sometimes she can seem judgmental, if not downright irritated. She's a straight shooter, her smile often a mixture of pleasure and sarcasm. Where Anita is short and given to jeans and sweaters, Crystal is statuesque, often in pant-suits and dangling earrings. "I'm heels, Anita's flats," Crystal once told me. Crystal, who's deeply religious, is persistently upbeat; it's hard not to feel good in her presence. When she sees students in the hall, she'll hug them and tell them, *I appreciate you in advance,* her signature phrase, which inevitably makes everyone around her smile. But here's the paradox. Where Anita appears closed and dis-approving, she's the more optimistic of the two.

The two are so close that when Crystal got pregnant—she was divorced and already had two children, but this was unplanned—Anita promised that she'd help raise this new child, and so when Christopher was born, Anita took him home with her every other weekend, an arrangement which exists to this day. Anita and her husband, Virgil, have three daughters, all of whom are whip-smart and attend selective-enrollment public schools.

Anita and Crystal are assigned students who for emotional or learning reasons have an Individualized Educational Program, or IEP, and they're usually students who are struggling with forces that originate well beyond the school walls. One girl refused to leave the side of her drug-addicted mom, even if that meant she had to sleep in a crack house or on the street. One boy had been passed from foster home to foster home and brought order into his life by joining the ROTC. Another had accidentally shot and killed his brother. And then there was Thomas. It was clear from the out-set that Thomas didn't like to talk much. He was incredibly private. Anita learned about him in dribs and drabs, collecting stories as if she had her hands cupped under a dripping faucet.

Once when Anita visited him in his math class, Thomas joined her on the side, and there, in a muffled voice, told Anita about his childhood friend Siretha White, or Nugget. Anita knew right away who he was talking about, since her sister had grown up with Nugget's mom. Moreover, Nugget's death had made front-page news. *You knew Nugget?* Anita said. *Yeah, she live down the block,* Thomas replied, uninterested in the connection. Thomas then went on to recount Nugget's surprise birthday party just a few houses down from his; they were celebrating her eleventh birthday. He was ten at the time. He told Anita that they were dancing in the living room—well, the girls were dancing; the boys were all piled on the couch, goading each other and laughing—when they heard gunfire, which wasn't all that unusual in the neighborhood. The adults yelled for them to run into the kitchen, which they did, but when they looked around, Thomas didn't see Nugget. Thomas told Anita he sensed something wasn't right. When the gunfire subsided, he heard screams, and then the sounds of sirens. His memory from that afternoon exists in small bursts, like a photographer's roll of film. Lying on the kitchen floor to take cover. The police guiding the children through the apartment. Stepping around Nugget, who lay on the living room floor, her brain matter oozing out of her skull onto her braids. He recalls that Nugget had different colored barrettes in her hair. It looked like she was trying to say something, he told Anita. Once outside, he was swallowed by hordes of neighbors who had gathered, soon joined by photographers and reporters. All he can remember about the aftermath was that it was raining— and overhearing a police officer telling another, *Fuck, another kid got killed.* Only two weeks earlier, just six blocks away, a fourteen-year-old girl had been fatally shot, so this seemed like an unusual sequence of events, and after Nugget's death there were marches and cries from city officials demanding more police and tighter gun regulations. But Thomas, a quiet ten-year-old boy, needed to push on. And to do so he needed to shove away the images. He recounted this day for Anita in a flat, distant tone that made it feel like he was talking about someone else. He told Anita he no longer went to parties.

You don't understand or know your own strength, Anita assured

Thomas, who was so withdrawn Anita wondered how he navigated school. *I don't let it get to me,* he mumbled.

Not long afterward she learned that the previous summer Thomas had been with one of his older brothers, Leon, when he was shot across the street from their home. Thomas comforted Leon as he lay on the sidewalk, unable to move his legs. Thomas kept assuring him that the ambulance was on the way. *Just hold on, man. Just hold on,* Thomas told his brother. His brother, it turns out, was paralyzed from the waist down. Anita wondered if Thomas felt guilty for not doing more.

During those high school years, the stories just kept coming. Thomas was like the Zelig of Englewood's violence. There was Nugget. And the time he saw a boy shot in the face in a nearby park. And his friend who was shot in the leg. And his brother. And coming upon two men who'd been shot and killed still sitting in their car, one of them with his head leaning out the window as if he were trying to get some air. "I seen some crazy things," Thomas once told Anita. The thing about Chicago's violence is it's public—very public—and so each shooting or its aftermath is witnessed by many, children and adults alike. I've met kids who have flashbacks or are easily startled or have trouble sleeping. I once visited Lawndale Community Christian Academy shortly after two of its students had been killed in separate incidents. The school's principal, Myra Sampson, told me that students would stop her in the hall, and tell her, *I'm going to be next.* She told me that the kids were in such a heightened state of arousal they were unable to learn. One boy had to be hospitalized after experiencing auditory hallucinations that one of the deceased students was talking to him. "What's going to be the impact of having a group of young adults who shut off?" she asked me, somewhat rhetorically. This was Anita's concern as well.

Anita began visiting Thomas at his home, just stopping by to check on him. The house, which sat near the corner, was immediately recognizable because of the blue tarp and because of the metal lift by the front porch. As taciturn as Thomas was, Leon was even more so. Their other brother, Deon, was in and out of jail. Anita began to learn bits and pieces about Thomas's home life. His mother wrestled with drugs, and his father had virtually disappeared from his life. Thomas lived with his grandmother, whom he was especially close to, as well as his older sister, Stella, and his twin brothers. Sometimes an uncle would stay with them, too. Along with cousins. It was enough of a flow that often when Anita came by, whoever answered the door was someone she hadn't met before. Anita knew. This was her house growing up. Everyone depended on her mother. Two uncles came to live with them, one of whom drank and cursed at people, almost as a manner of affection. A mentally unbalanced neighbor whom everyone called Crazy Stan would hang out on their porch. Anita would disappear into her room, and everyone thought she was stuck up, that she thought she was better than everyone else, when really she couldn't handle the crowds. "I just didn't trust people," she said, by way of explaining that she understood Thomas's reticence.

The young people on Thomas's street, 70th Place, had formed a clique or crew which they called 7-0. They hung together, watched each other's back. It was hard to grow up in Englewood and not be identified with a gang, given that the cliques were organized block to block. You needed to belong, if for no other reason than because you needed protection. A reporter once asked the police officer assigned to Harper, Aaron Washington, how a boy at the school could avoid becoming a member of a clique. He replied, "You can't. It's not going to happen ... There is no neutrons anymore. It used to be if you played sports or you were academically better than the average kid, they didn't bother you. Now it's different. It doesn't matter. If you live here, you're a part of them. You live on that block or you live in that area, you're one of them ... They don't have a choice." Virtually every boy at Harper identified with one crew or another, and the names seemed a statement of both place and intent: S-Dubs. Blockheadz. The St. Lawrence Boys. The 7-0s were in a long-standing dispute with the S-Dubs, who were from the area just south. Thomas couldn't tell me what it was over. No one seemed to know. *We just into it,* he'd say, as if that was all anyone needed to know. Some of the adults at Harper believed that Thomas was a leader of his small band, but Anita scoffed at that. Once, administration and staff gathered to talk about tensions in the school, and there an administrator claimed that Thomas had forty people under his command. When Anita and Crystal returned to their office, they found Thomas waiting for them. They bristled at the allegations, and so they couldn't help but tease Thomas.

"Hey, did you know that you lead the 7-0s?" Crystal asked Thomas.

"No, I didn't," Thomas replied.

"Every time they say you've got forty people under your command."

"Every time y'all have a meeting?" Thomas asked.

"How do you get people to listen to you?" Anita inquired, the sarcasm I'm not sure apparent to Thomas.

"I don't know," he replied.

"You don't know, and you sitting here covering your face and you won't even talk to me," Anita said, as Thomas sat with his head in his hands, as he often did, his dreads hanging over his eyes. There was no way this kid could be telling others what to do, she'd say. Though sometimes blustery, he was fairly passive. He hardly spoke. He kept to himself.

As the months went by, Thomas retreated more and more. He found refuge in Anita's and Crystal's office. He'd be there, it seemed, all the time, sitting on a chair pressed up against the wall as other students wandered in and out. "He seemed deeply sad," Anita recalls. He made friends with some of the other kids who came through. He gravitated toward Devonte, the boy who accidentally shot and killed his fourteen-year-old brother, mostly because he, like Thomas, seemed so alone. Devonte had been handling a revolver his brother had found, and it went off, instantly killing his brother. Devonte told Thomas that he had trouble sleeping at night and so took Nyquil to help him rest. Devonte asked Anita and Crystal if they could ask his mom not to throw away his brother's bed; he needed it to fall asleep. Thomas told Anita, "I don't think nobody know what Devonte be going through."

But the friendship that provided Thomas real ballast was with a girl, Shakaki Asphy, who was a year younger. She could give as well as she could take. She usually wore a baseball cap turned backward, her hair done in French braids. Her pants sagged low off her hips, and she walked with a swagger. "She held her own," Anita recalled, "like she was one of the boys." Shakaki and Thomas adored each other, referring to each other as "cuz." Shakaki memorized Thomas's class schedule and would come to his classroom window, smile, and mouth the words "Let's go. Get some candy." She'd beckon him to join her in Anita's office, and Thomas would find a reason to leave his class to join her. Thomas would walk Shakaki home after school, and sometimes they would sit outside, on a stoop or an abandoned porch, just to talk. Shakaki had a 7 p.m. curfew, so on weekend nights Thomas and a friend would sneak through a window into her basement, where they'd hang out and play video games. Thomas attended Shakaki's basketball games at Harper and razzed her from the stands. Thomas seemed protective of her. She could go off on people, and Thomas would urge her to chill. Sitting in Anita's office one day, Thomas told her, *Girl, you need to watch your mouth.*

Shut up, you don't tell me what to do, she shot back.

Girl, you be tripping. You got to stop tripping. You got to stop going off on folks.

How you gonna tell me not go off on people?

And so it went, back and forth. Anita would sit at her desk, amused by the exchange, amused by the irony that Thomas, a boy prone to his own outbursts, was trying to keep Shakaki in check. One time Shakaki rebuked Thomas because he hadn't told her that a girl she liked was flirting with one of the school's football players. *I hate you,* she yelled at him. *I hope your grandma dies.* Thomas stormed down to Anita's office and told her, *You better talk to that girl. I'm gonna hurt her. I'm for real. I'm gonna hurt her.* Anita had never seen Thomas so agitated. He was trembling, his hands balled into fists. Anita found Shakaki later that day and chastised her. She told her she needed to apologize, that you didn't disparage Thomas's grandmother. Anita was worried he'd strike her. Shakaki laughed. *Thomas ain't gonna do nothing to me. That's my cuz.* And he didn't. Anita says this was the moment she knew how much Thomas cared about Shakaki. He didn't forgive easily, but with Shakaki, well, things were different.

Anita had grown close to both kids. They were like her children. In fact, in Thomas's case, many staff referred to her as his "school mom." Anita refused to let their churlishness get to her. Once, Shakaki lit into Anita, and so Anita demanded that she join her in a room on the fourth floor which had been set aside as a place for students to cool down. There the two sat on rocking chairs, and Shakaki confided in Anita that she was having trouble with some of her family. They spent much time in this room, the two of them together, talking, sharing, confiding. Once, seemingly out of nowhere, Shakaki asked, *Miss Stewart, if I die, will you write a note and put it in my casket?* Anita shook her head. *Little girl, stop playing. No! Nothing's going to happen to you. Besides, if something happens to you and I'm fiddling around trying to put something in your casket, your family's gonna think I'm crazy.* Together they laughed. But Shakaki persisted. *Miss Stewart, but will you write that note?* Anita relented. *Okay, I'll write a note.*

Thomas and Shakaki helped Anita stay erect through what by most measures was a horrific year. The shootings, the deaths, seemed to come so regularly the staff and students were always bracing for the next one. Whenever a student was shot, the principal would page all support staff, including Anita and Crystal, to attend an AAR (After Action Review) meeting. There they'd decide how best to respond to the incident's fallout, which students they needed to keep an eye on, who needed comforting, whether they needed to dismiss certain students early. Chicago public school officials adopted AAR from the military after a visit to Fort Leavenworth in Kansas, when they were researching training tools which they might use in the city's roughest schools.

Early into the school year, Harper's principal, Leonetta Sanders, began collecting photos and tidbits about each victim, assembling them in a notebook binder which she kept on her desk, an assemblage of the dead and the wounded. By the end of the school year, her binder had virtually filled up; in those nine months, twenty-one current students and recent graduates had been wounded by gunfire and another seven shot and killed. Shakaki would become the eighth.

O n a Saturday evening, June 16, 2012, Anita's and Thomas's world shifted, and their lives would become forever entwined, tangled together in a knot so tight that barely a day now goes by that they don't speak.

It was a beautiful summer evening, the temperature in the mid-eighties, and Shakaki had come by Thomas's just to hang. She had gotten permission to stay out past her 7 p.m. curfew. The two wandered over to the porch of a house just two doors down from his home. Many thought the house was unoccupied, but actually a family lived on the second floor. Shakaki perched on the porch's railing. Thomas sat on the top step. Thomas's brother Leon rolled onto the front lawn in his wheelchair and planted himself just beneath Shakaki. For Thomas, there's before and then there's after.

And of those moments before he remembers little, only that they were smoking marijuana and talking, not about much. Shakaki told Thomas she'd gone shopping for clothes with her grandma that day, and that she had purchased a new T-Mobile cell phone. Thomas spotted a hooded figure running from the side of the house to the front lawn. A boy, maybe fifteen or sixteen. Thomas recognized him, mainly because of his acne. Everyone knew him as Monkey Man; he was from a part of the neighborhood belonging to a rival clique. With two hands he raised a gun, a semiautomatic with a clip. Thomas pleaded, *Don't shoot that gun. I tole you, don't shoot that gun.* As Monkey Man shot, Thomas scooted back and then leapt off the porch, sprinting across the street through a vacant lot into the alley. When he looked back, the boy was gone, and so was Shakaki. He thought she had followed him. He ran back across the street and found Shakaki lying on the wooden slats of the porch. Holding her stomach, she told Thomas, *It burns, it burns.*

And then there's after. Two ambulances arrived. EMTs lifted Shakaki onto a gurney and carried her down the stairs. Another set of EMTs lifted Leon into the second ambulance; he'd been shot in the knee, though because he didn't have any feeling there, he didn't realize it until he saw the blood pooling beneath him. By this time, though, Thomas had wandered off in a daze, feeling a kind of fury that felt like it belonged to someone else. He remembers getting a gun, a .38-caliber revolver—from whom he won't say—and going to the gas station around the corner, waiting, hoping that someone from the shooter's crew would wander by. He seethed, the anger welling up like a tsunami about to hit land. He waited.

The next morning Crystal called Anita and asked if she was sitting down. *Why do I need to be sitting down?* Anita demanded. But she knew. It had to be either Thomas or Shakaki, her two favorites, the two who never left her side, the two who would fight for her attention. Crystal told her: Shakaki had died eight hours after the shooting, in the hospital. It was Anita's weekend with Christopher, Crystal's son, so she scooped him up and, along with her oldest daughter, Brianna, picked up Crystal. They then drove to Thomas's. He was sitting on the porch of the abandoned property next to his house. Anita approached him, and before she reached him, she burst into tears. Thomas dropped his head, as if he couldn't bear the sight of what he thought was Anita's disappointment in him. It was, Anita recalls, like he felt this deep shame. When he looked up, it was as if he was looking through her. Speaking in a monotone, he told her what had happened.

"In one day I could have lost two of my students," Anita later told me. "But looking at it another way, at least one of them did make it out. Then I asked myself, did he really make it out? . . . I looked at his face. He just dropped his head and walked real slow and I asked myself, 'Did he really make it out?' One more burden for this kid to carry. I don't know how much more this kid can take."

Anita and Crystal took Thomas to Rainbow's, an ice cream parlor, but as they sat there outside he played with his ice cream, poking it with his spoon as it melted. He had no appetite. He couldn't look at Anita, who kept telling him, *I'm just glad you're okay.* Later, Crystal said to Anita, *We weren't trained for this. We weren't taught how to bury a child.* To which Anita replied, *I can't make sense of it. Can you?*

Hundreds packed a small church on the city's South Side, Shakaki's casket in the front, covered with flowers, a basketball to one side. Her teammates all wore their red jerseys. Anita and Crystal stood toward the back. Anita remembered her conversation in the spring with Shakaki and her request for Anita to place a note in her casket should anything happen to her. *What'd she know that I didn't?* Anita asked herself. Anita did indeed write a two-page letter, which read in part:

> Shakaki, I guess you know I am devastated because I did not think I would ever have to write this letter. My heart is broken

but I am trying to follow through with your wishes. Words cannot express how much I will miss you and forever value our time together. I thank God and I am so very humble and honored that I had the opportunity to cross your path. I will treasure and hold each and every minute of our time together to my heart . . . I love you. Miss Stewart

Anita had it laminated, but when she got to the funeral, Shakaki's mother was so grief-stricken Anita couldn't bring herself to ask for permission to place it in the open casket, so she held on to the note, feeling like she had let Shakaki down. Anita trembled during the service. Crystal felt her legs buckle. One moment deeply unsettled both of them. Shakaki's cousin, who was in her thirties, read a poem. It went like this:

> *If only you had basketball practice or you had to stay in the crib*
> *to watch your little sister*
> *If only you could have left five minutes before*
> *If only you didn't know your so-called friend who ran instead of*
> *jumping in front of those bullets*
> *If only you had something better to . . .*

The "so-called friend," of course, was Thomas. Anita turned to Crystal and they hugged, grateful that Thomas wasn't at the funeral to hear this. In fact, the rumors blowing through the streets blamed Thomas for Shakaki's death. The story passed along from person to person went like this: Thomas had gotten into an altercation and had punched someone so hard that one of the victim's teeth was embedded in his fist. He knew that people would be seeking vengeance. What was he thinking, sitting on a porch, let alone with his best friend, Shakaki, knowing full well that his rivals were looking for him?

As with so much ear hustle, as they call it in the streets, it held a kernel of truth. Thomas had indeed gotten into a fight—and had indeed punched his victim so hard that his tooth was embedded in Thomas's hand. But—and this is important—this fight happened *after* Shakaki's death. After Shakaki was murdered, Thomas couldn't sleep. He tried. But nothing worked. He smoked marijuana. Mindlessly watched TV while sprawled on the couch. Listened to music on his headphones. But his mind raced. The fury. The guilt—that he hadn't been able to keep the boy from shooting. That he had run. He felt like he was losing control. And then one afternoon, a few days after Shakaki's death, an older boy pushed Thomas's six-year-old cousin so hard that his cousin tumbled to the ground. Thomas lost it. He struck the boy. This stupid fight, over nothing, brought Thomas some relief. He could sleep again. His hand, though, got infected, and so he had to go to the emergency room, and they admitted him to place him on antibiotics. He missed the funeral—which in the end Anita felt was for the best. Thomas didn't need to hear that poem or hear the whispers. Thomas was suffering enough.

I first met Thomas that August, two months after Shakaki's death. It was the first week of the school year, and he wouldn't leave Anita's side. In her office—which consisted of two small metal desks, a filing cabinet, and an inoperative paper shredder—Thomas would sit, his back against the baby-blue cinderblock wall, his remoteness morphing into churlishness. One time I asked Thomas why he hung out here so much.

"I just don't know," he told me. "Sometimes I just need to talk to somebody."

Anita started to say something, but Thomas interrupted. "You want me to be quiet?" Anita asked.

"Don't say nothing to me," Thomas snarled.

"What'd I do?" Anita asked.

"Don't say nothing to me!"

"So we're shutting down now?"

"What I say? Don't say nothing to me." Thomas raised his head as if to underscore his point.

"You're not on the block," Anita said, trying to calm him. "We're not the block."

"I don't want to hear nothing no more. Drop me off at home 'fore I hurt somebody."

"After school."

"Now! That's what I'm gonna do, hurt somebody. Watch. Anybody look at me wrong or say something. Watch. I'm telling you that now, I'm gonna hurt somebody."

Anita stopped herself. Her inclination was to chastise him, to tell him, *No, you can't do that.* But "wanting to hurt someone" or "trying to hurt someone," these are notions Thomas had verbalized a lot since Shakaki's death. One time when I asked where he thought he might be in ten years, he said, "Might be in jail. Because I think I'm gonna hurt someone." Another time he told Anita, "I think I might kill someone." She realized in this moment that Thomas was trying as best he could to be honest about some feelings he had, feelings that scared him. He was struggling to let Anita know that he had a lot going on inside, that he was filled with wrath and guilt. Anita realized that he was telling her that if he could hurt someone, he might feel better, that maybe some of the pain would go away, even just temporarily. He knew this because it had worked before.

During the course of the school year, Thomas retreated even more. He shared less. He talked less. He went to class less. Even in his appearance he seemed to be disappearing. He grew his hair longer, so that by winter his dreads fell to his shoulders. When he tossed his head, which he did a lot, the dreads fell across his face and he'd virtually vanish. You couldn't even make out whether he was smiling or frowning. He was there but he wasn't. Sometimes he wore hoodies, which hid him even more. When he did talk, he hung his head, avoiding eye contact, as if he was addressing someone lying on the floor. He mumbled, his mutterings sometimes so sluggish that Anita had to ask him to repeat himself, sometimes two or three times. When the school erected a memorial to Shakaki on one of the stairwells—a glass case with photos, a basketball signed by her teammates, and Anita's laminated letter—Thomas avoided that part of the building. He refused Anita's invitation to view it with her. And he declined Anita's invitation to visit Shakaki's gravesite. It was as if he wanted to push that moment away. But so did Anita. She woke up crying every morning. She and Crystal began seeing counselors themselves. She was under so much stress that the left side of her face went numb and she had trouble seeing out of one eye. At one point she told me that she had a recurring dream in which she grappled with how to tell Shakaki she'd been killed. When she recounted this for me, she said, more to herself than to me, "No, you need to accept it, she's dead."

Thomas still lived just a couple of doors down from where Shakaki had been murdered. He couldn't escape it. He no longer walked in his neighborhood. He'd go out only if he had a ride. When he stepped out of his house, he scanned the gangway next door and the vacant lot across the street, making sure it was safe. He pulled his hoodie over his head so he wouldn't be recognized. Once he told Anita, "If it happens again, I don't think I could stop. If it happens again, nobody's gonna be able to stop me. I know I could hurt a lot of people."

By the time the summer of 2013 came around, Thomas had fallen behind at school. He had trouble concentrating. He had trouble sitting still. Sometimes he'd leave class and head to the social workers' office. There he'd talk with Anita or simply sit in silence, just in need of the company, of knowing he was with someone who knew, or kind of knew, what was boiling inside him.

A few weeks ago, when his block threw a memorial for Shakaki, a year after her death, Thomas kept texting Anita during the day to ask when she was getting there. The street had been cordoned off at both ends with blue tape. Teenage boys played basketball on a rim set up in the middle of the street. Young kids removed their shoes to jump in an inflatable castle. Kids and adults ate hot dogs and hamburgers, trying to talk over the rap and hip-hop playing through three large speakers set up on a neighbor's lawn. Most everyone was dressed in white, and many wore T-shirts which read KAKI WORLD. (Kaki was Shakaki's nickname.) Anita got there early in the evening, and she texted Thomas to let him know she'd arrived. But he didn't respond. She later learned he was off shooting dice and smoking marijuana. Anita guesses that he didn't want her to see him high, but she also sensed his ambivalence about being around her these days. She wondered if he worried that she'd press him to talk about what was going on inside.

When Anita showed up at Thomas's house early this morning, unannounced, she was determined to get him back into summer school. She wanted him to graduate, to taste some success, to sense that there was something ahead of him. She continued to wait for him in her car. She had confidence he'd come.

Five minutes later he trudged down the front steps dressed in his school uniform, khaki pants and a maroon polo, and slid into Anita's seven-year-old Sebring. He reclined the passenger seat all the way back and rested his head on the headrest. He looked defeated, Anita thought to herself. *You okay?* she asked. Thomas told her that their electricity had been knocked out by a weekend storm, and that ComEd had told them it might be a week before it was restored. Anita assured him that she would call. As she pulled into the school's parking lot, she noticed that Thomas had turned away, as if he was admiring the landscape out the window. She noticed tears rolling down his cheeks and so reached over to wipe them away. In the three years she had known him, she had never seen him cry. Not after he told her about Nugget getting killed at her birthday party. Not after he witnessed his brother getting shot and paralyzed. Not in those days after he comforted Shakaki as she lay dying. He seemed so tightly wound at times, he would grunt in place of words. He still talked in threatening tones of hurting one person or another. Anita thought to herself, *Thomas, you should've cried a long time ago.* And what's more, he was now under pressure by the prosecutor to appear at the trial of the boy who shot Shakaki. He was the key witness, one of two people who could identify the shooter, the other being his brother. He kept telling Anita he didn't want to testify. Though he wouldn't admit why, Anita knew. He was afraid.

It's going to be okay, she told him. But she wasn't sure it was.

Chapter 10

Going Home

JULY 13 . . . **JULY 14** . . . JULY 15 . . .

**POSTAL WORKER CHARGED IN FATAL SHOOTING
OF CHICAGO TEEN**

*2nd man is held, could be charged in
Far South Side killing*

By Naomi Nix, *Chicago Tribune* reporter

A U.S. postal worker and another man followed a 16-year-old boy around a Chicago Housing Authority complex before shooting him to death, Cook County prosecutors alleged Saturday.

On July 14, Aries Sanders, the postal worker, and his alleged accomplice drove to the Trumbull Park Homes in the South Shore neighborhood, prosecutors said, citing video footage from the scene.

The video showed Sanders and the other man following Joseph Brewer, of the 10600 block of South Oglesby Avenue, prosecutors said.

The man with Sanders then shot Brewer several times, eventually killing him, prosecutors alleged.

That person is in custody with charges pending, Chicago police said. Sanders, of the 6400 block of South Stony Island Avenue, was charged with murder and held on $1 million bail.

According to police records, Sanders works at the U.S. Post Office at 1300 Northwest Highway in Palatine. He was arrested there Friday.

Ashara Mohammed had wanted out of Chicago, away from the messiness of the city, and so she went away to college and ultimately moved to Philadelphia, where she rented an unadorned, compact third-floor studio apartment. It was there that I first met her. Ashara, who's twenty-six and striking, has big, expressive eyes which hide little. She rolls them when annoyed. They widen when she gets excited. She closes them when she wants to disappear. By her own admission, she's also loud. She likes to talk, to tell stories, to offer her opinion, to reflect, to ask questions. She's a turbine of energy in a rather small, petite body. When I visited, she sat on her queen-sized bed in jeans and white T-shirt, barefoot, her back against the wall, a roll of toilet paper by her side since she was battling a cold, which seemed to have little effect on her stamina. Because there was no other furniture in the apartment, I sat on the floor. We spoke for nearly five hours, with a short break for lunch.

She had a story to tell, really a kind of confession, but it's a narrative which, as I learned, requires a somewhat full wind-up. It's a story that involves Aries Sanders, the postal worker involved in the murder mentioned in the *Tribune* article. Aries and Ashara grew up together, and his arrest rattled Ashara and changed her, in ways she never expected.

Ashara grew up in Auburn Gresham, a working-class neighborhood of single-family homes and small apartment buildings on the city's South Side. Her grandmother, an Egyptologist who taught at Mississippi College, named her. Ashara, her grandmother told her, meant "much light and energy," both of which Ashara had in abundance. Ashara has ambitions to be a writer and a filmmaker, and while in recent years she has swum in darkness, battling depression in part because of events I'll get to shortly, she has emerged with a sense of purpose.

Ashara's sister, who's three years older, is Shema, also named by their grandmother. They were raised by a single mother, Carmen, and though the girls barely knew their dad, they inherited his last name, Mohammed, which he acquired after joining the Nation of Islam. The three lived in a one-bedroom apartment, Ashara and her sister in bunk beds, their mom on a futon in the living room. Ashara reveled in the tight bonds between the three of them. Her sister panicked in thunderstorms, and so when they heard thunder, their mom would corral them into a walk-in closet, where they huddled together under a blanket, safe in each other's arms. When the local Borders bookstore held story night, Carmen would take the girls, in their pajamas, and on weekends she'd take them to the local library or to a museum. They didn't have air conditioning, so during the summer, when their second-floor apartment became thick with humidity and heat, the three rode the bus to the air-conditioned Plaza, a nearby mall, where they bought icies and window-shopped. They were unusually close.

When Ashara was eighteen months old, her mother took a job at a day-care center, but she struggled on her meager salary. They shopped for clothes at a local thrift store. Her great-grandfather bought them a refrigerator, which they otherwise couldn't afford. Their Buick LeSabre, which her great-grandfather had handed down to them, had been in so many fender benders that after all the repairs it was such a mishmash of colors it looked like a child's art project. The gas gauge in the car didn't work, and so while they assiduously kept track of their mileage, they still on occasion ran out of fuel. "I look back on it," Ashara recalled, "and honestly, I don't know how my mom did it."

Though Ashara got into an elementary school for the gifted, her mother sent her to a school near the day-care center so she could get there quickly if needed. At Langston Hughes Elementary, Ashara excelled, often testing in the top of her class and learning Japanese. When she was eleven, she traveled with her school to Japan. Because she was light-skinned and because she was so studious, others would sneer at her, calling her "white," suggesting that she thought she was too good for the rest of them. Her attitude probably didn't help matters. "I think I took the road that I'm better, that I'm not like these other black people," she told me. "I speak better. I work harder. I try harder." She's not proud of it, just matter-of-fact. It's who she was, and her aloofness, as you might imagine, didn't sit well with her classmates. They called her "lame," or they made fun of the discount, off-brand shoes she had purchased at Payless, or they simply ignored her.

Among those who teased her, probably the one who teased her the most was a boy named Aries Sanders. Aries, like Ashara, felt like an outsider. Aries was lively. As an infant he was plump, with what he called "a big boxed head," so his family and friends called him Snub, short for Snubby. He grew to be broad-shouldered and fit, though he was short, shorter than Ashara, something Ashara wouldn't let go unnoticed. He had a stutter, which came and went, and which seemed to do little to button down his self-confidence. His sleepy eyes made him sometimes seem like he wasn't fully in the moment, as if he were drifting away or hiding. The two first met at the day-care center, where Aries's grandmother and mother worked alongside Ashara's mom. Aries and Ashara loved each other. And they hated each other. "They were like magnets," Ashara's mother, Carmen, recalls. "Pull together. Then push apart."

As Ashara remembers it, Aries tormented her. "He was pretty mean to me," she said. "He'd talk about my shoes a lot. Sometimes he'd pinch or punch me because he said I talked a lot." Which of course Ashara did. They were kids, and so they related to each other in ways that masked their affection. One time at the day-care center—Ashara was visiting her mother; Aries was visiting his grandmother—Aries hid her overcoat, and because it was a cold, wintry day, the adults wouldn't let Ashara leave until they found it. A parent ultimately located it hanging on a fence behind the center. Another time, in the crowded school playground, Ashara, who was worried about an upcoming test, squealed, *I'm freaked out.* Aries laughed, taunting her: *Who says that? Freaking out! You're such a white girl.* Ashara had a way of escalating their disputes. When Aries mistreated Ashara, she'd tattle on him to his grandmother. *Aries talked back to a teacher* or *Aries didn't do his homework* or *Aries got into a fight.* It became so regular that when Aries's grandmother saw Ashara, she'd sigh and ask, *What did Aries do today?* Aries would later scold Ashara, saying, *You talk too much, girl. You're always in somebody else's business.* They fought and squabbled as if they were brother and sister, and yet despite Aries's bullying—and in part because she didn't have many friends—Ashara spent time with him. There was another reason, though: Ashara had a crush on Aries's friend TJ. Where Aries seemed hyped-up, TJ appeared smooth, unflustered, self-aware. In fifth grade Ashara sat next to TJ, and they would pass notes back and forth. Ashara, who by her own admission could be "super-bossy," enlisted TJ in school projects. "He was just kind," she recalls. "And patient."

Come ninth grade, Ashara went to the neighborhood high school while Aries attended a vocational school and TJ attended a school in the suburbs. She grew apart from them. At sixteen Aries had a daughter, and he took a job after school, working at a wholesale candy company. Ashara lost touch with TJ, though she remembers running into him in their senior year and thinking he had become incredibly good-looking. He was dark-skinned and self-assured. She remembers his lips were blackened from smoking weed.

By her teens Ashara had become deeply disappointed in the men around her. She wanted nothing to do with them. Her cousin, Kyle, whom she adored, was in and out of jail, and during one visit told Ashara that at fourteen he'd become addicted, though he didn't say whether to heroin or cocaine. Her uncle, too, lived a life shaped by drugs and petty crime. And she quietly raged at her dad for not being a part of her life, so much so that growing up she had periodic temper tantrums over small things, a lost hairbrush or a dinner she didn't like, knowing inside that her fury was really directed at her absent father. Her grandfather, she learned, had died in jail after setting his cell on fire. Her great-grandfather, a community activist, was the only man she looked up to.

Ashara tried to keep everything and everyone at bay by getting absorbed with the notion of getting into college. "I just kept telling myself, those people aren't doing anything with themselves," she explained. "They're not trying to move beyond this community. I just kept focused." By her senior year Ashara had taken four AP classes, all the school had to offer, so in the afternoons she attended classes at Chicago State University. She graduated as salutatorian of her class.

Ashara received a scholarship from Bethune-Cookman University, a historically black college in Daytona Beach, Florida, and once there she cut ties with her friends in Chicago, especially the young men she knew. They continued to let her down or fill her with sorrow. While at college she learned that TJ had been killed, shot in the chest by a friend fiddling with a gun that had jammed. Another friend from high school, George, whom she had befriended while at a summer job building playgrounds, had been arrested for armed robbery. Still another boy, Johnnie, who lived in the apartment above her growing up and had played with Barbies with Ashara and her sister, had been shot and killed by the police. At college she rustled up the courage to call her father, to reconnect, but he seemed uninterested, and so she spent the entire phone call yelling at him for not being there for her and her sister. *Why'd you leave?* she demanded. *We needed you and you weren't there! We made it without you. We're fine without you.* Deep down, she wanted him to be a part of her life, but that anger swirled in her like a spinning top which would knock down anyone who got in the way. Then Aries's older brother, Sheldon, whom he idolized, was convicted of attempted murder. Ashara didn't know Sheldon well, but it was boys like Sheldon who so turned her off. Even Aries had begun dabbling in selling marijuana. Ashara saw too much of this, young black men seeming to play a role, thinking that to be black meant to act tough, to act brutish, to maintain a distance from everyone around them. "I think the way I made sense of it is, I'd tell myself I'm just different, I'm better, I want more out of life," she told me, knowing it sounded snobbish. She would joke with friends that all the good black men were in prison. But it was a half-joke. Of the men she grew up with, she told me, "I couldn't look them in the eye. I'd just ignore them. I was afraid. I was intimidated. These thugs. These criminals." Ashara tried to outrun her world.

Once Ashara went off to college, Aries tried to get in touch through Facebook, once writing by way of introduction "Hey, sexy," but she didn't respond. "I was blocking out everything Chicago, everything South Side, everything in the hood," she told me.

Ashara had aspirations to become a journalist and so began to write, working on an essay she called "Dear Black Man." She wrote:

Growing up on Chicago's south side during the 90s, the inferiority of black women seemed ubiquitous. Almost every woman I knew was alone, left to raise children and take care of the meager tangibles she was able to have. It seemed that the men I saw only cared about getting high, making money and finding another woman to romance and leave hanging. I knew early on I didn't want to be one of those women so I built a mental wall against you, but deep down I wanted a relationship with you so bad. I wanted to enter your circles, partake in the handshakes, and glean from you. I wanted your respect, because I had so much respect to give you, but instead because I was left to see you through the eyes of the masses, dangerous, violent, irresponsible and good for nothing.

After graduating from college, Ashara interned at NPR's *Talk of the Nation* and then settled in Philadelphia. At one point on a weekend visit to Chicago, she briefly ran into Aries, who told her, *I'm so proud of you, you don't understand.* But what she hadn't told Aries—or anyone, for that matter—is that the NPR experience had been debilitating. She was responsible for posting tweets and once used "they're" instead of "their"; her supervisor chewed her out. Another time she admitted not knowing where the United Nations was located, and some colleagues responded in disbelief. She felt humiliated by the gaps in her education—and angry at how she was made to feel. And then, earlier this summer, her cousin, Kyle, had been shot and killed by a friend. Kyle, Ashara told me, went to jail for burglary when she was sixteen. He was in his early twenties. "He was like that wannabe thug guy," she told me. "He always wore baggy clothes, braids. He listened to Ludacris. I think it was like an identity crisis for him." What particularly bothered Ashara was that Kyle grew up in Beverly, a majority-white neighborhood of bungalows on the city's far South Side. "You're this black man who doesn't fit in, and you want to be all things that you think are black," she told me. "I think he was trying to force it."

Ashara spun into a deep depression. It runs in her family, but Kyle's death depleted her. She couldn't get out of bed some mornings. One day, after getting out of the shower, she sat on the corner of her bed wrapped in a towel, unable to move, unable to get dressed. She thought she was dying. And then she learned that Aries had been arrested for murder.

When Aries had graduated from high school, he got a job sorting mail at a postal center in Palatine, a suburb. He earned $16.04 an hour and helped raise his daughter, who was now two. He just wanted to blend in, not stand out in any way. He was still sleepy-eyed, broad-shouldered, but not as skinny. He kept his hair short and braided, his hairline receding even though he was young. He still stuttered. He lived in a one-bedroom apartment, and after his twelve-hour shift at the postal center he would plop in a plush chair in his living room and watch the African cichlids in his 60-gallon aquarium. It soothed him. And often he fell asleep there, smiling, admiring their luminescence, as if they each had swallowed a light bulb, their flashy colors unlike anything outside.

One day a friend asked Aries if he knew where he could get a pole—a gun—not for himself but for some boys in the friend's neighborhood. As it happened, Aries's older brother Sheldon, who had recently been released from prison, had just bought a Tec-9 semiautomatic handgun for $150 from a drug addict desperate for cash, and he was looking to turn a profit. So Aries told his brother about his friend, and Sheldon responded simply, *All right, cool, we can do that.*

Sheldon asked a friend, Brandy, if she would drive them across town to the Trumbull Park Homes, one of the few remaining public housing complexes. It was Brandy's birthday, and she and Sheldon planned to celebrate at the Cheesecake Factory after the transaction. When they got to the housing complex, Sheldon out of habit snapped the magazine into the Tec-9. They were, after all, in an unfamiliar neighborhood, and he knew intuitively that anything could go wrong. He borrowed a shirt from Aries's friend and wrapped it around the gun so that he wouldn't be seen walking in the open with it. He and Aries and their friend—Brandy remained in the car—marched single-file through the project's wide court-yard, much of it caught on videotape by security cameras in the complex. On the videotape we see Sheldon approaching sixteen-year-old Joseph Brewer, who looks as if he has at least one friend with him. A conversation ensues. Aries and Sheldon would later testify that it got heated, that they wanted $450 for the gun and that Brewer didn't want to pay that price. They believed Brewer had intended to rob them all along. They later testified that Brewer pulled a gun from his waistband and began shooting. Sheldon got hit in the hand and he fired back. Aries and Sheldon ran back to their car, where Brandy was waiting for them, but before they could pull out of the parking lot they were surrounded by squad cars. Aries would be charged with first-degree murder; under Illinois law, you can be charged with murder even if you didn't pull the trigger.

I n her Philadelphia apartment where we met, Ashara got up to stretch. She wandered by a window and, with her back to me, said that when she learned of Aries's arrest she thought to her-self, *A murder? A sixteen-year-old boy? This is fucked up.* Ashara had moved here after Aries's arrest, after she was prescribed Celexa for her depression, after she began attending church. She works as an assistant teacher in a kindergarten/first-grade classroom and as an assistant basketball coach in middle school. She also has taken up boxing, and when she goes on her three-mile training runs lis-tens to what had been TJ's favorite song, "Ambition," by the rap artist Wale, a mournful tune about conflicted aspirations.

She told me that when Aries got arrested she had neither the strength nor the interest to return to Chicago and visit him in the county jail, a place that she came to detest when she visited Kyle. "I was trying to shield myself from any more sadness," she explained. But before Aries's trial she spoke with him briefly by phone, and then began a correspondence.

Dear Aries,

Man the news really messed with my head. I know you are strong and you stay positive but this is fucked up!

... That day we talked on the phone really lifted my spirits. You may think I'm helping you, but you are way for me. Your strength inspires me to keep working hard. There are so many days I want to quit work and give up on these kids but because of you I won't... On a silly note do not put Sanders on the end of my name. Boy we will be fighting like when we was 5. LOL!... Sadly it did take you going to jail for us to have a conversation. The truth is I never trusted you and was always scared you were going to insult me in some way. I know I was different because I chose to remove myself from the hood and acted like I was better than what was around me. But there were so many times I wanted to talk to you and TJ. Also, TJ is who I had a crush on. I liked him since 2nd grade. LOL. But I trust you now whether you on the outside working on your business and such or on the inside staying strong I am your friend and I'll never act like a stranger. Bet on that. Take care my friend.

And so began a series of letters between Ashara and her childhood friend Aries, she looking to make sense of what her friend had done, Aries looking to make sense of how he had gotten to this place. Ashara found the letters from Aries refreshingly honest and open, unlike any conversation she'd had before with Aries, or with any man for that matter. At the time she was living with two roommates in a larger apartment, and she would take his missives, written in pencil on a yellow legal pad, close the door to her bedroom, and sit on the floor and read them. Over and over. "Wow, Aries talks about who he is," she recalled. "He's struggling just like me. It was like a load had been lifted."

Ms. Ashara,

☺ *As you can see I started off my letter with a happy face because that's the current emotion I'm feeling right now. Just to receive a letter is the most precious diamond in the world, definitely coming from you!! That's because believe it or not for some odd reason you have been on my mind. Now you asked how am I? Well lets say that I'm a stronger/better Aries than I was before. The old Aries paid so much unnecessary attention to things I didn't have any control over that it became so depressing. Like the girl I was about to marry walked away . . . SO while I was going through this episode I began to conform to what was around me which was negative and I began to give up. Ashara I was thinking no one loved me and all type of crazy nonsense and that made me became such a stoic person . . . You know the crazy part of this whole ordeal is that I really got caught up in someone's mess, but can't give any details before the case is over . . . keep rooting and praying for me Punk. But enough about me cause I'm ok. Ashara I read your letter several times, but before I say what I want to say I'm going to share something I learned since I been here and that is us as people when we have difficulty on our journey of life we tend to focus on what we need at the moment that we forget what we already have . . . Hey maybe one day you can invite me out to Philly for dinner . . .*

Aries,

It's crazy to read your letter and see how much you have matured. We really are not kids anymore. I'm so proud of you . . . Today has been hard. I have been very emotional.

Ashara went on to tell Aries about a new job teaching social justice to sixth-grade students, explaining how the other day her students had opened up about what they contend with day to day. One boy watched someone get shot, a girl's god-brother was shot and killed, still another lost his father to prison. She wrote that two students broke out crying. "I realize that I am up against a lot," Ashara wrote. "Those kids don't even know how amazing they are . . . So right now I am very tired and emotional. Your letter was a gift." She then for the first time revealed to Aries that she battled depression: "My health is MUCH better now and the biggest change is me. I have grown so much wiser and mature now. So it's interesting we both in our own ways have been on journeys that we would not have chose but have shaped us into much better people." Ashara continued,

You said you want to know more about me. Well I'm still loud. I can't lie if someone offered me a million dollars to. I'm so transparent, so honest. I guess it's a blessing. My favorite person on earth is my mother . . . We talk every day at least twice a day. She talks about you pretty often and feels the same way I do . . . What's up with the mobile spa? Why does that interest you? On another note, I'm not sending you a picture cuz you not about to be looking at it thinking that my future wife [drawing of a laughing emoji]. You my homie. Can we leave it at that? But seriously what happened to the girl you wanted to marry? I didn't even know you were planning to get married.

Ashara,

I hope this letter finds you rested with your feet up after a strenuous day at work. As for me I'm still standing strong and optimistic awaiting my trial. Ashara it's still weird to talk to you,

especially after I called you. When I hung up I was like wow!!
I just talked to Ashara, but the odd thing is it felt comfortable,
maybe because you are a familiar person or you have such a
genuine spirit . . . One thing I can say you are very inquisitive, so
Ashara make no limitation to the questions you want to ask . . .
first thing first congratulations on your new job. Ashara by me
having a kid and having conversations with Amoni made me
realize that they do have real life issue in their own lil world. The
things we go through trickle down to them . . . Now far as the
mobile spa, its something I been wanting to do. The idea actually
comes from being around my mother, aunts and other women.
I know you guys love being catered to. So my idea is this. My
team comes to your home and we offer massages, facials, pedi,
mani, etc. . . . I see you gave some thought about being my wifey
lol . . . Mrs. Ashara Sanders do have a nice ring to it. [Drawing]
But honestly I'm only looking for something that is platonic.
Even though I want to be in love again one day because it felt
so good . . . As far as [my daughter's mom] goes, she was a real
team player, my best friend, overall the love of my life. Long story
short she couldn't handle me being here and being lonely so she
left and moved on. I have a suggestion far as dealing with your
older students. I think you should continue giving them sessions
where they can open and share with you the things that's going
on with them. Just remember everyone need an ear to listen . . .
which comes to me wanting to tell you how much I greatly
APPRECIATE you for taking the time out of your day to write
me. Just to be blunt I didn't think people gave a fuck what was
going on with me, so when you told me you and your mom cared
about whats going on with me, it made me feel so much better. It
actually made me smile . . . I'm not going to bore you any longer . . .
Get some rest. I'm pretty sure you had a long work week.

Your Homie Aries

Aries,

I apologize for the delay in getting a letter out. My life has been crazy busy. My students are awful some days and I'm taking two college classes right now so I have been trying hard to keep up with everything . . . How are you doing? Any updates on a trial? My mom is very positive that you will be home soon and she says "Aries is not a criminal. I know that for sure!!!" Just know we really care. Talk to you soon!

Ashara

Hey Punk,

Well I hope this letter reach its destination and bring a smile to your day . . . I've wanted to share something with you because I do see you as my "PERSON." So I have this disease called neurofibromatosis and I'm very insecure about it, and to give you an understanding as to what it is, its fibromes on my nerves system and also they grow outside of my skin which makes me feel ugly, unattracted and undesirable . . . I've been wanting to ask you about your father. I never hear you talking about him. I do want a bond with you where we can share personal things with each other. If you're comfortable of course. On the phone you asked do I think if TJ was still living would I think he would be supporting me? Of course he would! . . . Honest I really miss him. You know after that happened I didn't come around for a long time . . . Look right I remember one time in 5th grade TJ booty ass lit a firecracker in the class and the teachers thought it was me and called my father and his grandfather so we would tell on each other but it didn't work so of course we got suspended and put on punishment but the bad part of it was it was on my bday. Man I had fun times with him . . .

Dear Aries,

*I have planned to write for quite some time but I became
consumed with my own life that I didn't take the time out to write
a letter . . . I think I'm still in denial about this . . . It's crazy that
TJ's gone, and it may seem like that doesn't affect me, but it does.
I'm hoping for the best for you and I am rooting for you to do well
all the way in Philly.*

*As I am sitting here worried about you maybe this time away
has been life changing and meaningful. Has it? . . . I'm your
homie even though you despised me as a child lol. It's all good
now, though. I know you didn't know any better. Take care Aries.*

Ashara

Ashara,

*What's the deal Punk? I just hung up the phone your crazy
self . . . I gotta admit that you are a cool ass person to talk
to. You definitely keep me laughing. I wonder how it's going
to be when I get home and we kick it LOL . . . Ashara, you
really have a good heart, not to get mushy or anything but I
really want to thank you for taking [time] out of your busy
day to deal with me, the lil things that you do for me I will
always adore. It might seem simple to you but something lil as
answering your phone means so much to me . . . Ashara I really
appreciate that wholeheartly, definitely since I was so mean to
you. LOL. Now what's crazy about this whole situation is that
I wonder if I never came to jail I wonder would we ever become
friends? See some good did come out of this situation . . . In the
event that I do gotta go down state you better send pics and
keep writing, and I'm not going to stare at your pics thinking
that's my future wife, but seriously I might flirt . . . I'm going
to end here . . . , its just I gotta lot on my mind where I just need*

to sit back and relax a lil. So once again thank you for taking
time out of your day for me . . . have a good day punk and stay
positive . . .

Until next time your friend Aries

In these letters Ashara saw someone different. It wasn't that
Aries had changed, rather he had discovered who he really was.
He seemed confident yet vulnerable, clearheaded yet searching.
Before these letters Ashara had felt isolated, almost as if she was
barely holding on, and with Aries's surprised openness she found
a portal back, through which she could crawl. Aries pushed her to
face what she had so wanted to put behind her, and in this paradoxical moment, her childhood friend got arrested for murder
and yet she felt closer to him, and to her past, than she ever had
before.

I attended Sheldon and Aries's trial, though Ashara in the end
chose not to come. She couldn't take off time from her job,
and moreover she worried it would be too emotional, too draining,
especially if they got convicted and sentenced to long terms. Aries,
in black-rimmed glasses, with a tailored goatee and his short hair in
cornrows, wore his tan jail-issued outfit, which announced its size
in big, bold letters on the front of the shirt: XL, as if the size of the
defendant was the only thing that mattered. (His brother wore a
3XL.) When he testified, he spoke quickly, in an effort to reduce his
stuttering, and told the judge how he had joined his brother to sell
a gun and how everything had gone terribly wrong. When asked by
his attorney why he sold the gun, Aries replied simply, "Because my
brother asked me to." Aries and his brother's attorneys argued that
Aries and Sheldon acted in self-defense. Both were found guilty of
second-degree murder.

Before sentencing, Judge James Linn lectured Aries and his brother: "I know the amount of street violence that Chicago is going through is beyond horrific. It is appalling, shocking, frightening. With that said, it is not my responsibility nor my task to hold Mr. Smith and Mr. Sanders responsible for everything else that is going on in the world. I can only hold them responsible for themselves. They are two very different young men. They are half-brothers, but . . . it doesn't seem like they are brothers at all because their backgrounds are so dramatically different.

"Mr. Sanders had never been in trouble in his life. I read some letters today that were submitted to me where people truly care about him and actually looked up to him and respected him. How he got in this situation I can't fathom. I don't understand how what seems to be a decent person could make terrible judgments and get involved in something like this."

That, of course, was what Ashara had been asking herself.

The judge then sentenced Sheldon to twenty-eight years and Aries to five years. Since he had already served two and a half years, he would be released in a few days.

Months after Aries came home, Ashara flew to Chicago for a weekend, both so she and I could have more time to talk and so I could sit down with her and Aries together. The way Ashara explains it, Aries's involvement in this murder unnerved her, sickened her, but it also forced her to reconsider her hostility toward him and others she had grown up with. The experience seemed to reveal a part of Aries he'd worked hard at hiding. In his letters to her and in their phone conversations, she sensed his vulnerability, she saw his sensitivity, his thoughtfulness. Aries has confided to Ashara that he can't fully fathom his involvement in this murder. He thinks about Brewer, the victim, because he had a young daughter, too. Ashara says Aries seems subdued, mournful, ashamed. In court at his sentencing, he apologized to Brewer's family: "I know that no amount of words, written letters or tears, or anything else I could think of that would show the magnitude of my grief, remorse and sorry. What has happened has changed me and given me the time to understand how valuable life is and has taught me that I have so much at risk. I realize that something I felt so careful about, violence, has so deeply affected me."

It took this bloodletting for Ashara and Aries to reconnect. Ashara stopped running and for the first time faced what she was running from. I think back on the Cormac McCarthy quote Pete Nickeas, the reporter, had etched into his forearm:

The closest bonds we will ever know are bonds of grief
The deepest community one of sorrow

Ashara began talking with Aries's brother Sheldon as well, and then visited him in prison in downstate Illinois. Sheldon told Ashara he felt like he had let Aries down, and that he has trouble getting past the fact that he killed someone. Ashara relished their conversations, and thought that he, like Aries, seemed exposed and vulnerable. "You think you need to be strong and prove that to people," she told me. "But in jail you've hit rock bottom. It's not about what you're drinking or wearing or how many girls you have." Sheldon and Aries, she told me, "just softened my heart."

We met at the Greenline coffee shop on the South Side. Ashara and I drove together, and as we pulled into a parking space on the street, a car shot past us, honking. Ashara rolled her eyes. "It's Aries," she said. "He thinks he's a hot shot." Aries then pulled a U-turn, sped back, and pulled into a space, wheels screeching. "He's showing off," Ashara declared. She wasn't happy. It was not an auspicious beginning for this gathering.

Inside the coffee shop, I offered to get Aries something to eat, but he declined. "You said you wanted breakfast," Ashara chided.

He replied that just a cup of coffee would do. Ashara didn't let up. "But you told me we'd meet and you could have a good breakfast." They went back and forth like this for a few minutes, and then I steered them to a table by the window. "This is the story of our lives," Ashara told me. "We irritate each other." She then turned toward Aries. "You're irritating," she told him. "You're a bug." He shot back, "She remind me of my little sister. And she's only four."

I both laughed and cringed. It was like they were kids again. I asked them about growing up together, and Ashara said, "We were like a cat and a dog in a cage together. But we love each other." Aries wasn't having any of that. "She talk too much," he retorted. "She had a crush on me."

"I had a crush on you?"

If I were making this all up, if I were writing fiction, I suppose this is where Ashara and Aries would fall in love, but that's not where this goes. It's messier than that. As real life often is. In the wake of Aries's arrest, Ashara had come to realize that she was selling herself and others short. She came to realize that young men like Aries have so much going against them, not the least of which is feeling like they don't fit in. Because of race. Because of class. Because of geography. She had by now experienced it firsthand herself. When Aries got out of prison, he couldn't get his postal job back because of his felony record, and so he landed work at an Italian food market and restaurant, where he buses tables for $6.95 an hour plus tips. He lives with his grandmother, since he can't afford his own apartment. "I felt like Aries was the first black man in my life who really let his guard down," Ashara told me. "Aries really shifted me."

Aries doesn't talk about that day much, but he has confided in Ashara that it haunts him, that he can't get past the fact that he had a part in someone's death, that he got himself into that situation in the first place. But today, at the Greenline coffee shop, he seemed, if not blustery, then chary and in a place that felt, well, too familiar to Ashara. It especially upset Ashara that when Aries talked about his time in the county jail, he did so without any acknowledgment that it had been really tough on him.

She fidgeted in her seat. She leaned into Aries. And then gazed out the window, and then glared at him, as in the moment when he asserted, "I don't remember being mean to her. She always told on me. She cried a lot." *Of course I cried a lot,* Ashara thought to herself. *I had a lot to cry about. My dad bailing on us. TJ's death. Kyle's. You having a kid at sixteen. You and your brother . . .* Her thoughts drifted. *Shit, I still have a lot to cry about.* It irked her that Aries, who had in his letters seemed so open and reflective, now acted as if he had something to prove. When I asked Aries about whether his time in jail had been difficult, he seemed dismissive, telling me that because he'd been associated with a gang, he felt protected. Ashara rolled her eyes. He seemed self-conscious, and at one point said, "The good that came out of it, me and her had a friendship." I'm not sure Ashara heard that. I think she had pretty much checked out by then. From her purse she pulled out a small plastic bag containing two honey buns and dropped them in front of Aries. "From my mom," she said, and then she stood and walked outside.

Aries and I continued to talk for another half an hour, mostly about the details of the shooting, most of which I already knew. I could tell it was exhausting for him. "It is what it is," he said in resignation, knowing there was no way to rewrite that moment. I knew from Ashara that beneath the bluster he had trouble making sense of what had happened, that he thinks about it every night when things are quiet, when there's nothing to distract him, that he wonders how much he's to blame, and wonders about Joseph Brewer, who like him had a young daughter.

We got up to leave, and when we walked outside, I couldn't find Ashara. Aries nodded toward her car. She was sitting behind the wheel, and he went by her window to say goodbye. She stared straight ahead. She was fuming. Aries stood there making faces, trying to get her attention. Finally she rolled down her window a few inches, just enough so Aries could hear her. "See you," she said. She rolled the window back up, and we drove away. I realized she'd been crying.

I asked if she was okay. She shook her head. She wouldn't talk. We turned the corner, headed south on a side street, and in front of us a woman had stopped in her car to back into a parking space. Ashara left her little room to maneuver, and so we sat there in a standoff, the woman in front of us honking, yelling out her window, "Move, bitch!" while Ashara refused to budge, despite my suggestion she back up a few feet. "She can get in," she muttered, her lips pursed, her ire now with a clear target. Soon we had a line of cars behind us, honking as well. Five minutes passed. More epithets were hurled. Finally the woman ahead of us carefully maneuvered into the parking space, and as we passed I could hear, "Fuck'n bitch" hurled at us. Ashara was crying. We rode in silence to her mom's apartment, where my car was parked, and when we got there, I asked if it was something I had said. No, she told me. It was Aries. It was being back in Chicago. It was remembering that she didn't fit in anywhere. She told me that when Aries was in jail, when they exchanged letters, she had felt like herself for the first time. She felt she understood Aries and TJ and Kyle. Even her father. It was, she said, as if Aries had pulled off his mask. And hers fell away as well. She told me that when she'd read those letters in the privacy of her bedroom, it was as if "Aries brought me back to my roots. In a sense, I was wearing a mask, too. Aries was saying, 'You could be Ashara again. You can be just you.' This is me. I'm North Philly. I'm South Side. I didn't feel afraid anymore."

She was gripping the wheel so tight her knuckles had whitened. She looked straight ahead, into the distance. The Aries she had just seen wasn't the Aries she saw in those letters. Vulnerable. Playful.

Thoughtful. Reflective. "I didn't think it would be so hard," she said between tears. "It's crazy, because I love Aries, but I love what's beneath all the extraness. He really is a cool guy. If I could get him outside of him trying to front, then we're good. I think he's still trying to prove himself to people." She paused, shook her head. "I'm on his side."

Chapter 11

Day of Atonement

Eddie Bocanegra, who's thirty-seven, scans the flowers in the floor-to-ceiling cooler: the red, orange, and white roses, the red and yellow tulips, the white lilies. He tells me that he loves the panoply of colors, but as is his wont, he digresses. "I really like trees," he tells me. "Especially willows." He pauses. "They look kind of sad, but they also look so calm. It's like they've seen a lot." *Kind of like you,* I think to myself. With his hair closely cropped and his stylish rectangular glasses, along with his buttoned-up blue shirt and gray slacks, he resembles a prep-school graduate. The look is purposeful, one he's honed in recent years. "I asked myself, *How do I dress in a way that the police don't hassle me and the gang leaders don't recognize me?*" he once told me. In the winters he used to tie a sweater around his neck, but he worried that that looked *too* preppie, that it made him look like a pushover, so he abandoned that touch. He tells me that if he dresses as if he walked out of a J.Crew ad, people won't make assumptions. Or they'll make different assumptions. Maybe they'll think he's a college graduate or a businessman or a professional. They'll take him more seriously.

Women find him quite handsome. He has full, dark eyebrows and a small goatee. He's a wiry five-foot-nine and exceedingly polite—and apologetic. About everything. For being late. For saying the wrong thing. For sounding immodest. His eyes, though, sometimes seem out of sync with his demeanor. Even when he's laughing, his eyes, partially shut, sometimes surrounded by dusky circles, are the eyes of a willow tree: sad and calm and filled with experience. He is clearly someone who has seen a lot. Maybe too much.

The young, fresh-faced florist asks, "What can I get you?" Eddie's unsure. He apologizes for taking so long. "Give me a second," he tells her, lifting his right hand to rub his chin. Nothing comes easily for Eddie. He ruminates on just about everything, from where to eat lunch to what to wear to a meeting. It's his nature. He asks me what he should get, and I shrug my shoulders. "Okay," he tells the florist, pointing at the roses. "I'll take three. One red and two white."

While the florist wraps the flowers—"Separately," Eddie asks—he strays yet again. "The time in prison really fucked me up," he tells me. "Touching and all that." He pauses. "I never really thought I could love, not this way." He's speaking of his four-month-old daughter, Salome, whom he adores and thinks about all the time. "Now when I hold Salome, I hold her so tight I feel like I'm going to break her." He pays for the roses, and the two of us climb into his 2008 Chevy Impala (Salome was born in the backseat) for the first visit of the day.

E ddie did the unimaginable. He took another human life. I suppose for some that might be all you need to know. For others, it may be all you *want* to know about him. And that's what Eddie fears the most, that this moment is him. That there's no other way to view him. That he deserves to be a pariah. That it's shaped him. It is, after all, why I'm writing about him. It's one of the first things you learn *from* Eddie. He can't help himself. He feels that you need to know this about him—to know it from him, not from anyone else.

On this day nineteen years ago, Eddie killed another man. Eddie was eighteen. It was payback. Eddie had joined the Latin Kings to protect his two younger brothers—he reasoned that this way he could keep the gang from recruiting them—and because he wanted to escape the alcoholic rages of his father. He also concedes that the gang had an allure to it. "Walkin' to grammar school, in third grade, I seen this group a people hanging out," he told me. "I was like, *Damn, they seem like they got their things together.* You know, they got a nice car. They got the girls. They were dressed sharply. They distinguished themselves from everybody else who lived in the community. They had so much pride in themselves. And to me, that's what attracted them to me."

Both of Eddie's parents had immigrated from Mexico and carved out a reasonably good life in the city's main Latino neighborhood, Little Village. His father worked as a body man, repairing damaged cars, his mother in a factory that produced calendars and greeting cards. They purchased a wood-framed, two-story home, and when Eddie became a teenager he and his uncle dry-walled and painted the attic so he could have his own space. They laid thick blue carpet and hung curtains on the one window. There Eddie collected baseball cards and other baseball paraphernalia, a hobby encouraged by his dad, who loved the sport. In fact, his fondest memory of his father was of lying in bed with him at the age of nine watching the St. Louis Cardinals in the World Series. By the age of seventeen, Eddie had grown distant from his dad, but he also had collected over 10,000 baseball cards, which he stored in albums and shoeboxes. When his friends visited the attic, they seemed puzzled by Eddie's hobby. One fellow gang member simply blurted out, *You collect this shit?* On the wall he had hung posters of Nolan Ryan and the 1989 Chicago Cubs. He framed baseball cards of Tom Seaver,

Andre Dawson, and Mark Grace. In a bookcase he displayed auto-graphed baseballs. And he hung lots of pennants, mostly from the Cubs, his favorite team. Eddie also was an artist, and on one wall he had painted a mural of Mickey and Minnie Mouse break dancing.

In the streets Eddie earned a reputation as a swift and effective car thief, mostly of American-made cars from the 1980s. With a screwdriver he'd peel the casting from the steering column and reach in to toggle the ignition switch. Because he wasn't all that strong, he'd stand outside the driver's side and put all his weight into turning the steering wheel so that he could break the steering pin. He had another method as well. When he was twelve, his dad lost his key to their Cutlass Ciera, and with a device ordinarily used to pull dents out of cars he popped the ignition open and then with a screwdriver started the car. Eddie, ever observant, utilized that dent puller for his own purposes. He used the cars mostly for joy rides or what was called "ramming," using it to crash into newer cars owned by rival gang members. He would park the stolen cars in the parking lot of the local high school, Farragut, and lend them to friends. Before long he had a nickname: Bandit, shortened by some to B.

Eddie had a fierce sense of loyalty, both to his family and to the gang. One late summer night when he was eighteen, he was in the attic organizing some newly purchased baseball cards when two friends, fellow Latin Kings, drove up in a four-door sedan. Eddie right away noticed the shattered back window and bullet holes in the trunk and on the passenger side. His friends told Eddie that two of his other friends, Ricardo Garcia and Alberto Gonzalez, had been shot. They were known as Rico and Flako (pronounced "flaa-ko"). Rico was a big guy, six years older, muscular, one hundred pounds heavier and half a foot taller than Eddie. He was Eddie's protector. One time Eddie got into a fistfight with another kid and Rico intervened, placing his large hands on the assail-ant's throat and instructing him, *Don't fuck with my guy.* From his friends, Eddie learned that Flako had been shot in the thigh and immediately released from the hospital, but Rico had lost all feeling and movement below his waist.

The next morning Eddie left for his job running a cutting press at a factory that made calendars and greeting cards. Halfway to work he impulsively veered off, picked up some fellow gang members, and drove to the intersection where the shooting had occurred, looking for someone, anyone, from the rival gang they suspected of shooting Rico. They had with them a .357 Magnum, and Eddie insisted on holding it. They couldn't find anyone.

Eddie visited Rico in the hospital and then, after he was released, at his house. "He was depressed," Eddie recalls. He didn't come outside. He didn't laugh anymore. He got around by wheelchair. At one point Eddie asked him, *Hey, man, how long before the doctors find a cure, before they fix your nerves?* Rico glared at him, at his naïveté. *I just want someone to suffer the way he's suffering,* Eddie thought to himself. *I'm feeling this anger. I'm feeling this rage. I'm like, 'Okay, you know what? They shot one of our guys. We're going back.'* About a month after the shooting, Eddie got word that some rival gang members were hanging outside, on a nearby side street, and so he asked his girlfriend at the time to come by and drive him over there in his Caprice station wagon. Eddie had jacked up the car on hydraulics so that it rode high. It was more a practical decision than an aesthetic one. This way if he got rammed from behind, there'd be more damage to the other car than to his. Everyone in the neighborhood referred to it as "the War Wagon" because of the bullet holes in the doors and back panel.

Eddie convinced Flako to lend him his gun, a .380, which Flako did reluctantly, urging Eddie not to do anything stupid. Flako was placid and humble, and Eddie always thought that he seemed out of his element. A year and a half later, Flako reportedly threw himself out of a third-floor window, and Eddie sometimes wonders if his distress didn't find its roots in what Eddie did with that gun.

I've talked about this July day in 1994 numerous times with Eddie, and each time he grows distant, almost as if he's retreating into that evening, still trying to make sense of what he did, still trying to take it back, still thinking of all the signs that he should've heeded. A hesitant Flako. A nearly empty gas tank. An initial pass-through in which the streets were empty. As they rolled down the side street a second time, past a row of modest single-family homes, Eddie spotted a group of seven or eight young men, none of whom he knew, hanging on the curb, and as he pulled up he saw one reach into his waistband. To this day he doesn't know if the man had a gun on him, but Eddie jumped out of the station wagon and shot at him three times, and then shot at the others, who took cover behind a car. He then raced to his car, and he and his girlfriend took off, headed for his house. There he parked the Caprice in his back-yard, on the lawn, so that it was tucked away, out of sight.

The next day a thirteen-year-old boy whom Eddie had recruited for the Latin Kings stood outside Eddie's house whistling. Eddie opened his window and waved him up. The boy had with him an article from the *Sun-Times* which read in part: "William Stuckey, 18, of the 6100 block of North Washtenaw, was critically injured in an apparent drive-by shooting while standing on a porch . . . Six shots, two of which struck Stuckey in the abdomen, were fired from a passing blue station wagon . . . Stuckey was pronounced dead around 5:30 a.m. at Mt. Sinai Hospital Medical Center, said hospital administrative supervisor Betty Gammon."

This is you, the boy said, his voice dripping with pride. *That's not me, man,* Eddie told him, sending him along his way. He sat there on the edge of his bed mulling over the realization: *I killed someone.*

E very July 17, the anniversary of the shooting, Eddie fasts and visits with people who are struggling, often because they've lost a loved one to murder or to prison. He's asking for forgiveness, not from anyone else but rather from himself. He thinks of this as his day of atonement—though honestly, he spends virtually every minute of every day trying to prove himself, that he's worthy, that he's worthy of friends, of lovers, of having children, really of life. I suppose the right thing to do would be to ask forgiveness from his victim's family, but Eddie doesn't feel he's earned that privilege, if you can call it that. At least not yet. He once declared, "I don't feel like I've done enough to honor his life." And so this is what he's doing—raising a family, working with youth in the streets, marking each anniversary of the murder. He knows, somewhere deep down, that it will never feel like enough. The best he can hope for is to get close.

We pull up to a red-brick three-flat and are greeted at the first-floor apartment by a diminutive woman, her hair a deep red. Doris Hernandez gives Eddie a hug. She's dressed in a lime-green pant-suit and orange flip-flops. She's rubbing her eyes as if we've woken her from a nap. She invites us in, and Eddie hands her a white rose. "For you," he says. She seems flustered, but thanks him.

We take a seat in her compact living room, on a green velvet couch. Doris, who had trained as a pharmacist in Colombia, immigrated to the U.S. twenty-four years ago. She now works as a seam-stress; her sewing machine is sitting in the corner. While she reads and writes in English, she prefers to speak Spanish. Eddie has known Doris for a year. She's one of the original members of the group Eddie helped put together, of mothers who have lost a child to the violence. But he's never told her about his past, that he killed a man, and so for the first ten minutes, as we sit on the couch, Doris on a chair, Eddie explains why he's here. He begins by referencing Doris's son, who was shot and killed a year earlier.

"I was in the same thing as Freddy, from a very young age. I fought with my parents every day. A lot of days it had to do with alcohol. My dad. And there was a point where I couldn't take it anymore," he tells Doris. "Although it's hard to believe I felt more relaxed in the streets than in my house." He recounts the story of his friend Rico and how he was shot and paralyzed. And then he chronicles his vengeance. "From that moment on," he says, "I knew my life had ended." He never bows his head, never asks for sympathy. He's not looking for that. From anyone. He just wants her to know. He feels it's only right. "Today is the day nineteen years ago when I took William's life," he says. "He was called William." This is the first time I've heard him refer to his victim by name, and he tells me later that that's progress for him, that it's been really difficult for him to say his name rather than calling him "my victim." He apologizes to Doris for not telling her all this earlier.

"I admire you," Doris assures him. "Because the day they killed my son I didn't feel hate for the kid that killed him . . . I preferred being on the opposite side. That's the truth. Because I think it would be harder on a mother knowing that her son took someone else's life."

Eddie looks away. I don't think Doris meant for Eddie to take this observation personally. But Eddie knows that it's true. His own mother, whom he adored and who adored him, moved to Texas three months after his arrest, in large part because she didn't want to have to explain to others what her son had done. She felt disgraced and embarrassed.

Eddie had something else to tell Doris, too. Something that he'd been carrying like a weight around his neck. The night her son, Freddy, was killed, Eddie had been driving through the neighborhood. At one point he pulled alongside a maroon van. The occupants stared him down, as if they were trying to take measure of him, and Eddie knew then that they weren't from the area. He worried that they were here to inflict damage, to instigate a fight. He had a dilemma. If he told the guys in the neighborhood that there was a maroon van filled with outsiders driving around, he worried they would shoot at the men in the van. When Freddy was killed, no one could identify the shooter, but people described the van they arrived in: it was maroon. It was undoubtedly the same van Eddie had seen earlier.

"You could've called the police," Doris suggested.

"But the thing is, I wanted to follow them," Eddie explained, not that he would've taken them on, just to ensure they didn't cause trouble.

"You never wrote down the license plate?"

Eddie shook his head, wondering now whether he should've shared this at all. But that's Eddie's problem—he shares everything. He can't help himself. Most angle their memories to reflect the best in them. Eddie's too honest for that.

Doris seems unfazed. She opens up in return and shares her son's story. A few years ago her son, Freddy, took a beating to get out of his gang, so he could become a neutron, she explains, meaning that he didn't identify with one gang or another. But then he spent the next three years at home. "Literally like a prison," she explains. "The curtains were drawn and he didn't let anyone open them. He slept with three or four knives under his pillow. Why, I don't know." She tells Eddie that periodically a rival gang spray-painted their garage with slogans she couldn't fully decipher, but she knew that they were meant as threats to her son. "He lost all interest in life," she says. "He didn't want to live." She continues, "That day, it was like five in the afternoon, a Friday. A lady had come by giving me some clothes to repair. I thought Freddy was going to ask me for money, but he would never ask me for anything. If his sneakers were ripped, he wouldn't ask me for a new pair. He told me he was going to some friend's house to watch movies."

She trails off. She doesn't finish the story. She doesn't need to. "You are fortunate," she tells Eddie. "Life gave you that opportunity and you grabbed it. My son did not grab the opportunities. Many people threw their hands out to help him, and he didn't stick out his hand from his pocket." She holds her hands out to Eddie. "I forgave him a long time ago," she says of the person who murdered her son. But in this moment it feels like she is telling Eddie, *It's okay. I forgive you.*

A month after Eddie shot and killed the rival gang member, the police came for him, and Eddie confessed and pled guilty. He was sentenced to twenty-nine years, which with good time meant with any luck Eddie could be out in fourteen and a half. His mother, who felt tarnished by Eddie's crime, was also worried about his younger brothers and sisters; she sold their house and moved the family to Pharr, Texas, just along the Mexican border, first moving in with Eddie's grandmother, then ultimately purchasing a home. She also needed the sale money to pay the lawyer. In those first few years in prison, Eddie by his own admission was a handful. Because he called the shots for his gang in prison, the authorities moved him around, trying to limit his influence.

In the winter of 1996, a month into his time at Menard, a maximum-security prison at the very southern tip of the state, Eddie noticed that the people most feared at the prison were those who signified their gang affiliation, especially his fellow Latin Kings, who had crowns tattooed on their neck or their forehead or the back of their shaved head. So Eddie made an appointment with a prison tattoo artist to get a crown on his neck, along with the name of the street where he grew up, Spaulding. The cost was $30 worth of goods from the commissary. That night before his appointment, as he lay on his top bunk in his cell, the yellow light from the watchtower reflecting along the walls, he thought to himself, *Hey, dumbass, you got an out date. These guys are going to be here forty, fifty years. I'm going to go home.* He couldn't sleep. And the next morning he canceled the tattooing. It's not to say that Eddie didn't continue to associate with the Kings. Over the coming years he got a palm-sized crown tattooed on his back and another on his left biceps. But these could be covered up. He was thinking ahead, looking for a way out.

Eddie saw reasons all around him for vigilance. The story of another inmate, whom everyone called Mingo, was legend inside the prison. Mingo had been sentenced to two years for armed robbery, a sentence short enough that he could look forward to his out date the moment he walked in. As Eddie tells it, Mingo was slow—maybe he had learning disabilities—and one night (this was many years before Eddie entered prison) an inmate who belonged to the Simon City Royals, a white gang, and who continually disrespected the Latin Kings despite warnings not only by rivals but also by members of his own gang, was stabbed by a Latin King member while watching a movie. As he stumbled out, Mingo, who also belonged to the Kings, added to his wounds, allegedly stabbing him one last time. At least that's what Eddie heard. The white inmate died, and Mingo was the only one caught and charged. He was given an additional fifty years. Eddie met Mingo, a fair-skinned, beefy man now in his forties. As the story went, Mingo's two brothers became police officers, and they and his father essentially disowned him. He had nobody—except for his mom, who stood by him. He had a reputation in prison for being able to repair anything electrical, from homemade stingers (devices to heat water) to radios. But he was viewed as a cautionary tale. *You may think you don't have much time. You may think others have your back. You may think you have a future. But in prison things change. And they change quickly, on a dime. So tread carefully—and smartly.*

Eddie had his family, who remained with him and who visited twice a year, driving the twenty-two hours from their new home in Texas. Eddie also had a high-ranking Latin King, Jorge Ruiz, who kept an eye on him from the outside. Ruiz put the word out with other Latin Kings that they were to keep their hands off Eddie, that they weren't to bother him, to try to recruit him into their prison ranks. He told Eddie he needed to get himself an education, and every month or so Ruiz would send Eddie a hundred-dollar money order so he could buy food and art supplies at the commissary. Eddie had taken up painting, mostly oils, and he painted landscapes and cartoon characters and, on commission, portraits of inmates, in which he'd draw them in expensive tailored suits, which he'd copy from *GQ* magazine. He made and sold greeting cards which he would personalize for inmates. He also became a tattoo artist, using guitar strings and a small pin powered by a Walkman radio. For ink, he melted plastic chess pieces.

"The worst enemy I had in prison was myself," Eddie told me. He worried constantly about what lay ahead once he got out. *No one's going to hire me,* he thought. And so he envisioned buying a hot dog cart which he could wheel around his neighborhood. He'd be his own boss. He wouldn't have to rely on anyone else's goodwill. In the first few months he was locked up, his girlfriend broke up with him—and Eddie worried, too, that he'd never find someone to grow close to, that once any right-minded woman learned of his past, she'd run. At night he'd lie on his bed unable to sleep, his headphones on, listening to oldies on the radio. He'd imagine meeting a woman he liked after prison, and then would try to calculate when he would tell her about his crime. He'd want to prove himself first. That he was hardworking. Of sound values. He even imagined how he'd dress when he got out: like a preppie, buttoned up and conservative.

Eddie once shared with me that after he got out, he had lunch with an academic who was hoping he could convince Eddie to appear on a panel with him. *Do you think people in prison have hope?* the scholar had asked. Eddie soon realized this was merely a rhetorical question, that the scholar already knew, or thought he knew, the answer: that prison sapped one of hope, of any sense of future. That prison diminished your sense of self. It's funny, I think Eddie on some level would agree with part of this, but he became agitated, at least inwardly. He tried not to show it. He didn't want the academic to know that he'd gotten to him. Eddie politely but firmly declined the offer to join the man on the panel. I think what so bothered him is that it's only human nature to have hope. Without it, you have nothing. It's about as close to death as one can get without actually dying.

In those early years in prison, Eddie tried to intimidate. He fought. A lot. But, he thought to himself, even that craziness, that desperate urge to survive, is an emblem of hope. At first he wanted to get by. Then, slowly, as he enrolled in classes, as he learned to paint, as he got closer to his family, he wanted to grow. He learned to hold his tongue with correctional officers—though it was hard. He once got caught in the gallery with a guard who didn't like him, who thought he was too slick, too uppity, and the guard told Eddie to put his hands behind his back. Eddie complied, and then looked as the guard craned his neck, left, then right. Eddie later realized he was looking to make sure they were out of sight of any cameras. The guard sucker-punched Eddie in the stomach, so hard that Eddie doubled over. *He folded me,* Eddie recalls. Eddie remembers looking up, and the guard, who the inmates called Vanilla Ice because of his uncanny resemblance to the white rapper, smiled. For Eddie, the messed-up part was that Vanilla Ice took pleasure in it. Eddie held his tongue. He kept his hands behind his back, almost as an act of defiance. And only later, in the privacy of his cell, lying on his upper bunk, did he cry. Not because of the physical pain, but because of the humiliation. He did that many nights—though quietly and in the dark so that no one could see.

Eddie spent many hours trying to figure out who he was. He had killed someone, and to reconcile that with who he imagined himself to be was virtually impossible. He couldn't make sense of it. Not then. Not now. Every July 17 the world seemed to close in on him. In his prison journal, he struggled to make sense of what he did. On one July 17, in 2002, he wrote:

Today marked 8 years since the victim in my case was killed.

Written in the passive voice—he couldn't bring himself at this point to concede what he had done. In another July 17 entry he wrote:

> I'm at a loss of words for my feelings have emotionally drowned me. What do I say? And when I finally bring myself to express what I feel, how do I say it without glorifying, gloating or advocating what I did? And when is saying sorry enough? Or does enough even exist?

For the first few years, on the anniversary, he felt like his victim, or his spirit, had entered his cell. He knows it sounds New Age-y, that it makes him sound off-kilter, but he was deeply distressed by the experience. "You know, I felt like there was somebody else in that cell with me," he told me. "And it wasn't 'cause I was see-ing this shadow, this black shadow, in the form of a human being. I couldn't see the face or anything. It was just black. And it wasn't really a shadow, 'cause a shadow you can see behind it. You couldn't see behind this. And the only thing I remember is just praying and saying, 'Man, you know I'm sorry, bro. I'm sorry. I'm sorry for what happened. I'm sorry for, you know, you know, your mom. But man, just work with me. Be with me. Help me out.'" At the time he was so scared he was trembling. He prayed. "I still remember his face. I still do. That's not something that goes away. I forget sometimes, like, damn, I can't remember how he looked like, but then days later or weeks later, I'm like, damn, his face comes back . . . Some of the events that took place that day have faded away. Some of the details. But the things I actually felt that moment for the most part are still there."

By his third year in prison, Eddie decided he'd devote that day to remembering his victim. He'd fast and do something for others in need, often people he didn't know. In prison he made meals—usually burritos made with dehydrated rice and beans, sliced summer sausage, onions and green peppers swiped from the kitchen, ramen noodles, ketchup, mustard, and mayo—and handed them out to inmates who couldn't afford anything at the commissary. He also made personalized greeting cards fellow inmates could send to a girlfriend or a family member. Sometimes he drew landscapes, which were coveted because of the lack of scenery inside, and gave them away as well.

He took classes. He read. He pulled away from the gang. His brother Gabriel, who served two tours in Iraq with the Army, mostly as the gunner on a Humvee, visited when he could. Eddie asked him to come in his dress greens. He wanted to show him off, and on some level to let the guards know there was more to him than what they saw. Sometimes Gabriel was joined by their youngest brother, Fernando, who was in the Marines. Gabriel, who was soft-spoken and had a gentle demeanor, told Eddie stories of war, stories he couldn't shed. He told Eddie about the time he had come upon a teenaged Iraqi boy raping his twelve-year-old sister and of punching the father, who clearly had sanctioned the assault. He told of the time another soldier killed a farmer for sport and recorded the kill in a notebook. Or the time in Sadr City when they raided the home of a man suspected of manufacturing IEDs. Gabriel could hear a baby crying inside, wailing. And at the doorway the man's wife, a large woman, tried to block Gabriel from entering. Gabriel struck her in the face with the butt of his M16. Or the time his roommate got blown up by an IED, and seeing his body riddled with metal fragments. He was unrecognizable. And the thing about it, he lived, disfigured, his face reconstructed. Or the time the gunner in the Humvee behind him got shot by someone on foot, and Gabriel couldn't shoot back because of the crowds. Gabriel told Eddie it was hard, that he'd been drinking a lot, two bottles of Jack Daniel's a day, that he'd kicked his longtime girlfriend out of the house, that he couldn't stand the sound of babies crying, that he couldn't sleep, that he couldn't tolerate crowds, that when driving he'd sometimes forget where he was headed, that he had tried college—majoring in biology—but had trouble remembering what he'd read. Gabriel explained that he had to keep busy, that if he slowed down, if he was idle, he'd start daydreaming and it would all come back. He told Eddie he'd been diagnosed with PTSD. To Eddie, Gabriel seemed defeated and tired and lost. And he thought to himself, *That's how I feel. I can't sit still either. Or I get flooded with memories, moments I'd long forgotten. So I try to keep busy, not to slow down, not even for a minute.* During one of the visits, Gabriel told Eddie, *I went through my own shit just like you went through your own shit.*

Doris embraces Eddie as we say our goodbyes. In the car, Eddie is unusually subdued, wondering if, given all that he confessed to Doris—about seeing the maroon van and knowing its occupants didn't come from the neighborhood—he'd let her down. "We're going to visit Jorge's mother," he tells me. Jorge Ruiz was the gang chief who watched over Eddie from outside prison. Eddie first became aware of Jorge when he was in his early teens, and would play arcade games—mostly Centipede, Pac-Man, and Galactica—in the rear of a bar. On occasion a group of Latin Kings in their twenties would enter. One would distract the manager while the others would pop the video games open with screwdrivers and empty them of their change. "It was Jorge and his crew," Eddie told me. "I was in awe of him." As Eddie got older, he'd see Jorge driving around in his brown Oldsmobile Delta 88, and then he got to know him once he joined the Kings. Jorge was a ranking Latin King, a "Supreme Inca." Jorge would have the younger Kings practice what to do if interrogated by the police. He told them to be mindful of what they were wearing, especially when in other neighborhoods. Jorge, for reasons Eddie never fully understood, encouraged him and one other boy to pursue college. Eddie got arrested. The other boy graduated from Brown University. It feels self-contradictory, someone so committed to the streets and yet someone so above it. Someone committed to maintaining order through beatings and worse, yet someone committed to seeing some of his protégés move on. Two years before Eddie came home, Jorge got arrested, charged with drug conspiracy. He was convicted and sentenced to twenty years. "I try to make sense of people like Jorge," Eddie told me as we pulled up to a single-family home. "Really good people, someone who would watch after you even though they're caught up in this stupid mess."

Maria, Jorge's mother, invites us in, and we gather at her small kitchen table. Maria has a booming voice, like she's trying to be heard in a noisy restaurant. Her fingernails are painted to resemble the American flag. Eddie hands her the red rose along with $50 which he asks her to send to Jorge. He explains that Jorge protected him while he was in prison, that Jorge told other gang members to leave him be. He tells Maria that Jorge pushed him to continue with school, and he lets her know that since he's been out of prison he got his BA from Northeastern Illinois University and is now working toward his master's at the University of Chicago's School of Social Service Administration.

Maria wipes away tears. "You know, he worries about you," she says. Maria, who seems agitated, tells Eddie that federal agents recently raided her house, presumably looking for guns, and that afterward the neighbors on both sides stopped talking to her. And then they each built a fence. It clearly enraged her. She was speaking so loudly I almost thought it was for the benefit of the neighbors. "What do they know?" she huffs.

Afterward, in the car, I tell Eddie that I can understand why the neighbors might want to distance themselves. The minute this comes out of my mouth, I regret it. "Imagine my neighbors one day realizing they're living next to a murderer," Eddie tells me, clearly seeing the connection. "How do you think that makes me feel?" I wasn't sure whether he was talking about my comment or a scenario in which his neighbors find out what he did nineteen years ago. Either way, I suppose, Eddie was telling me he was marked, that people would make their assumptions about him. He was basically repeating what Maria had said of her neighbors: *What do they know?*

After fourteen years and three months, Eddie was released from prison and moved in with his cousin. On his second night out, his cousin held a homecoming celebration. At one point Eddie retreated into a bedroom to get away from the clamor. As he sat on the bed, playing with a Chicago Cubs bobble-head doll, his six-year-old nephew walked in and grabbed the toy. The head came off. *What the fuck!* Eddie yelled. Eddie wanted to slap him, and after his nephew left, Eddie burst into tears. His cousin came in to comfort him. *Why am I having all of these fuckin' crazy thoughts?* Eddie asked. And to himself he thought, *I don't know if I can do this.*

Eddie had been mandated to meet with a therapist as part of his parole, but he found her judgmental and unhelpful. Once he found someone he trusted and whom he could open up to, he began to steady himself. He sold fireworks which he'd buy in neighboring Indiana and he worked as a tattoo artist, a lot of Rest in Peace etchings along with tombstones and crosses. Finding work as an exfelon is extraordinarily tough, but he got hired by an antiviolence organization, CeaseFire, where his job was to suss out disputes in the street and interrupt them before they erupted into something more. It meant walking the same streets where he'd grown up, running into the same people. It was hard on him. He'd stand outside with gang-affiliated teens, trying to get to know them, and he worried that passersby, his neighbors, would see him and think that he'd returned to his old ways.

He found himself thrust back into the violence he so wanted to leave behind. One nineteen-year-old who Eddie had been mentoring was shot in the side by a rival gang member, and his friends were pushing Adam to seek revenge. Eddie visited Adam in his family's basement apartment, and, standing in his cramped bedroom, Adam pulled his shirt up to show Eddie his wound and the colostomy bag, which he complained about because of the odor. Eddie saw himself in Adam, in his wariness and cockiness, and tried to rein him in by asking questions, by gently prodding. Adam seemed distant, and Eddie worried that Adam's friends' influence would supercede his. When he left Adam's, he seemed unmoored. "Am I really helping?" he asked. "Some people I can't. As much as I want to, they don't want help."

He ran into former gang members. One late evening, under the streetlights by the parking lot at Farragut High School, where Eddie once kept his stolen cars, he came across Rico, the friend who'd been shot and paralyzed and for whom Eddie had sought vengeance nineteen years earlier. Eddie sat on a low concrete wall separating the school from a soccer field, and Rico, who was now in his early forties, rolled up next to him in his wheelchair, caressing a beer. Rico was dressed in a white T-shirt, his jet-black shoulder-length hair combed back. Rico seemed genuinely happy to see Eddie. It soon became clear that Eddie had never asked Rico about the day he got shot, and so Rico told him that he and Flako had run into rivals "and they lit me up, three times under the armpit, point-blank." Eddie cut him off. "I was so angry, bro," Eddie told him, "because I was picturing myself. Damn, I always thought if something happens to me I always knew, you and—rest in peace—Flako, you'd go out and take care of your business, too. And I did what I did, and as messed up as it is, I learned a lot from being locked up. Honestly, bro, it saved my life, the way I look at it. I was out there bad, bro."

"You trying to say it was a blessing you got locked up?" Rico asked skeptically.

"To me it was, bro. The victim of my case, I owe him my life.

Because of him, I'm where I'm at now," Eddie explained. He then asked Rico, "If you were to go back, honestly, bro?"

"If I was to go back?" Rico asked in disbelief.

"If you went back to before you got shot, would you make the same decisions?"

"There's no such thing, man. I don't have no regrets."

"Believe it or not, you got a lot to give. A lot of potential."

Rico seemed anxious to move on. They said their goodbyes, Eddie leaning down to hug him. As Rico rolled away in his wheelchair, a friend alongside him, Eddie seemed genuinely sad, knowing that Rico was still in the streets. "It breaks my heart, honestly," he told me later. "To know that my friend who I admired, who I looked up to, you know, is doing the same thing he was doing . . . But I love this person and there's nothing I wouldn't do for him now." Eddie is a faithful friend, someone you can count on, but there are certain things Eddie wouldn't do for Rico now. He knows that and others, like Rico, know that as well.

On a summer afternoon, Kathryn Saclarides was driving through the streets of Cicero in her Ford Focus when she spotted a friend, Eddie Lopez, an outreach worker who had served time in prison and had recently opened a barbershop to hire people like himself. Kathryn was a therapist for a small nonprofit in Little Village. She stopped to chat with Lopez, and he introduced her to his old friend Eddie Bocanegra, who, he explained, was an outreach worker like himself. Kathryn thought it was a joke. Eddie, in his blue dress shirt and creased jeans, looked both conservative and nerdy. Eddie told Kathryn that he worked in the Little Village neighborhood and that he had been working with some kids who needed professional counseling, and so Kathryn asked for his card. Eddie laughed nervously. He didn't have one, but pretended to fumble through his wallet. He wrote his name on the back of someone else's card he had. Eddie found Kathryn strikingly beautiful, lithe and dark-featured. There was a serenity about her. Her voice was soft and soothing, and she seemed so comfortable with herself, a place Eddie aspired to.

A few weeks later Kathryn began working with a couple of kids from Little Village, so she called Eddie and he went by her office to meet them. He seemed intense. He spent forty minutes talking about how he wanted to set up a support group for grieving mothers. Kathryn just needed help with these kids. They crossed paths again a couple of weeks later, at a local church, and Eddie ended up back at her office, and there Eddie told Kathryn everything. About his youth. About running with a gang. And about the murder. He immediately regretted opening up like this. Kathryn would later laughingly tell me, "He has no filter." Eddie didn't feel judged by Kathryn. She told Eddie about herself. She had spent her high school years in Northfield, a tony North Shore suburb, and attended Vanderbilt and then the University of Chicago for graduate school in social work. Raised Greek Orthodox, she also was deeply religious, which Eddie admired. Kathryn needed help with a teenage girl, Vanessa, who had cradled her older brother, Miguel, in her arms as he bled to death after being shot. Eddie spent time with Vanessa, invited her to art classes he taught, and accompanied her to the cemetery where her parents camped every day, barbecuing hot dogs and burgers and just sitting by Miguel's gravesite, honoring him. Kathryn was moved by Eddie's commitment, by his kindness toward Vanessa and her family. He again told Kathryn that he wanted to start a support group for mothers who had lost a son, and so together they created one.

Eddie was seeing someone at the time, but he fell for Kathryn. I knew Eddie then, and I did what I could to encourage him to ask her out. But he couldn't do it. He couldn't imagine what she'd see in him. And then there was his past. Why would someone so accomplished and so smart and so beautiful want to date someone convicted of murder? "I had to bring myself into reality," he told me. This went on for weeks. They'd have lunch together. They'd sit in his car, talking, sometimes into the early-morning hours. Eddie would tell her everything—overshare, he said. He told her about this one friend, who at fifteen was stabbed at a cotillion and bled to death in the backseat of a car on the way to the hospital. He told her he had trouble retaining things, except for his time in prison. That, he remembered with such clarity it felt like it had all happened last week. He remembered small details, like the cell numbers of his friends.

I'd try to get Eddie to take that leap of faith, to tell Kathryn how he felt—and he'd pass, make excuses, put himself down. "We're not even in the same ballpark," he'd tell me. Once Kathryn asked him, *What does it take for a girl to know if you're interested?* But Eddie totally missed it. He couldn't imagine she was talking about the two of them. As it turned out, Kathryn really liked him, admired his thoughtfulness, his gentleness, his modesty. Sometimes after Eddie would tell her stories of his past, she'd go home and cry, wanting to figure out how to help him. He finally told her how he felt, and once it became clear that Kathryn had feelings for him, too, he went to Kathryn's dad to ask permission to date her. Kathryn is old-fashioned that way. As is Eddie. Eddie and Kathryn's father, Ted, met at a sports bar, and Ted, a colon and rectal surgeon, immediately took to Eddie. "I wanted to make sure my daughter wasn't going to be abused, that there weren't character flaws that would make him violent. But all you have to do is meet him," he told me. He warned Eddie, though. *Eddie, do you know what you're getting into?* he asked rhetorically. *You're asking to date someone more spiritual than Mother Teresa. She spends half a weekend in a monastery.* Eddie smiled and told him, *Love will find a way.* Kathryn's mother, Elena, though, had misgivings. How would Eddie find work? How could he take care of a family? What would he tell their children? What if they got pulled over by the police—would they find out who he was, what he'd done, and take him in? Why not marry another Greek Orthodox? With intention, Eddie would call Kathryn's mom to let her know about any accomplishments. When he received his BA from Northeastern. When he got admitted to the University of Chicago's School of Social Service Administration. When he got invited by the State Department to travel to Spain to talk about violence prevention. When he got invited to cochair the mayor's public safety commission. He wanted her to like him, to trust him. Before he and Kathryn got engaged, he converted from Baptist to Greek Orthodox, something he did as much for Kathryn as for her parents. But Kathryn's mom told her, *We all know this is going nowhere, so you should end it now.*

I t's dusk, and Eddie has one last visit, to the mother of Adam, the boy who'd been shot and who Eddie had mentored. We find Adam's mother, Rita Garcia, sitting in a lawn chair in her backyard, dressed in T-shirt, shorts, and sandals. Her son, aged five, and her grandson, who is two, play nearby. Eddie retrieves a plastic bucket from elsewhere in the yard, turns it over to use as a seat. He hands her his last rose. "I'm really thankful for you letting me into your life," he says. He tells her about the day, about his seeking penance. Rita is a member of the moms group. "I feel conflicted being at those meetings," Eddie tells her. "All these moms looking for the perpetrators, and here I am having taken someone's life." Eddie seems tired at this point, his chin resting on his hand. "I don't see you that way," she tells Eddie. "You're someone who picked himself up and kept moving forward." She pauses. "I feel like I'm on both sides, too." Her oldest, Adam, a year and a half after he'd been shot and after Eddie had intervened, was stabbed multiple times by a rival gang member and died shortly afterward in the hospital. Another son at the age of fifteen was convicted of murder. He was present for a killing and is serving twenty-two years. Rita confides in Eddie that after her son was arrested, two boys came to her house, one armed with a handgun, and told Rita they would kill her youngest children if her son testified against the others in the case. They then cut the electrical wires to her house, just to remind her that they were there. Her five-year-old, she tells Eddie, started peeing in bed at night and was too afraid to go to school. Uncharacteristically, Eddie has little to say. He shakes his head, both in empathy and in disgust, and gives Rita a hug before heading out into the night.

K athryn and Eddie were married in an Orthodox church, and after the two-hour ceremony, on the steps of the church, their friends and family (including his brother Gabriel, the Iraqi-war veteran, who is now married and raising three children) were greeted by a mariachi band. Nine months later, Kathryn gave birth to Salome. Then two years later she had twins, also girls, Melania and Viviana. Eddie loves being a dad. He dances with his daughters, sometimes under a strobe light to the sounds of house music. He reads to them. He has sleepovers, spreading out on their bedroom floor with them. He drives them around in his 1957 Chevy Bel Air, which they love. (Eddie cherishes classic cars.) "Eddie's a phenomenal dad," Kathryn told me. "I'm there for utility purposes."

Eddie's always moving. He has to. If he stops, the memories flood back. He can't let them in. He's tried finding ways to relax, to ease the stress. He loves amusement parks, and so one summer day he spent twelve hours with his cousin at Six Flags, riding every heart-stopping ride there, from the Raging Bull to Batman: The Ride. Kathryn says he was sick for days afterward. "It was not a good way of calming down," he concedes. He loves the casinos, mainly roulette, and while he's quite savvy about it (I've been with him on a few occasions, and he's come out ahead each time), that can get expensive. Sometimes he'll disappear into their attic to shuffle through his 10,000-plus baseball cards. In bed late one night, his heart beating fast, he couldn't sleep. He tried talking to Kathryn, even though she was half asleep. Kathryn says he thinks about death a lot, and that night he talked about what if something happened to his daughters. He worried about his colleagues at work, he worried about Kathryn. He worried about himself. He had worked himself up so that he had a massive headache. He couldn't get back to sleep. He prayed aloud. After that night, at Kathryn's urging, he spoke regularly with a close friend who's a psychologist—and he discovered gardening. Kathryn had suggested he give it a try, but he initially resisted because he felt it fed into the stereotype of Mexicans as landscapers. He planted some lavender and mint and found it so soothing that he went on to spend hours in the backyard, adding rose bushes, tulips, and other flowers. Sometimes he'd be out there until two or three in the morning. The smells. The beauty. The chirping of the crickets. He just felt at peace.

Eddie eventually left CeaseFire to become the executive director of the YMCA's violence prevention efforts, and there he got the idea to connect combat veterans like his brother who struggled with PTSD with gang-involved youth, both to mentor them and to let them know they aren't alone. The flashbacks, the fitful sleep, the anger, the overwhelming sadness, the forgetfulness—they've been there. The program, Urban Warriors, was featured on NPR's *All Things Considered* and on *CBS Sunday Morning.* Other cities have looked to replicate the program. He met with police officials and with the mayor's staff. Eddie replaced his preppie sweaters with tailored suits. He had an effect on people. Kathryn's sister ended up teaching in a prison because of Eddie. Anderson, a boy Eddie had mentored since he was thirteen, told me, "I want to do for other youth what Eddie did for me." My son, who'd gotten to know Eddie, wrote about him in response to a college application question asking him to write about a hero.

The vets Eddie worked with at Urban Warriors seemed indebted to him. One, Alberto Boleres, who suffered a traumatic brain injury after driving over an IED in Iraq, saw himself in the kids he was mentoring. One of the boys talked about how he couldn't hug his mom, how he couldn't show emotions, and Alberto thought to himself, *That's me.* Eddie helped direct Alberto to counseling at the local VA hospital and then encouraged him to go to college, which he did. "When I talk to Eddie, he's like a father figure," Alberto told me. "I know it sounds weird, because we're the same age, but some of the talks I have with him are deep . . . Eddie's the reason I'm in school." Eddie developed this quiet charisma, and people found themselves drawn to him.

But the one person Eddie couldn't seem to win over was Kathryn's mother, Elena. Though she had warmed to Eddie, she didn't share Eddie's past with anyone, and she never asked Eddie about it. Over the years Elena struggled with her weight and her health, and she'd recently been having trouble walking and trouble staying awake. She was diagnosed with pulmonary hypertension and cirrhosis of the liver. She needed a liver transplant. Over the course of the year she spent many weeks in the hospital, until her final visit in the summer of 2015, at Loyola University Hospital, where her husband, Kathryn's father, worked. She went into septic shock. Her organs began to shut down, one after the other. Kathryn and Eddie went to visit her, leaving their five-month-old twin girls and Salome with Kathryn's brother. When they entered Elena's small room in the ICU, much of the floor space occupied by her bed and various medical machines, Eddie shut the door behind him, and as Kathryn stood by the door to block the view of passing nurses, Eddie pulled a paper bag out of the diaper bag he'd been carrying. "Mom," he said, "I got the contraband." She loved the food from Portillo's, a local chain, and she just smiled. She could only manage two bites of the hamburger, but in a tired voice she told Eddie, *Oh, this is so good. Thank you.*

Her head sank back into her pillow. She told Kathryn and Eddie that she was feeling depressed and alone. *The family doesn't understand what I'm going through,* she complained. *This is so hard. I'm feeling claustrophobic. I can't leave this room. All I can do is watch TV. I'm so bored.* Kathryn didn't know what to say. Eddie smiled. *I know what that's like,* he reassured her. Elena looked bemused. Eddie explained, *Mom, that's what it was like to be in prison.* Eddie went on to describe his cell, saying that he knew how wide it was because if he spread his arms (which he performed for her), he could touch both walls.

How'd you survive? she asked.

You just had to. People did things to help me. My family was with me, Eddie told her. Once Elena had told Kathryn she couldn't imagine what kind of parents would raise a child who ended up in prison, so Eddie wanted her to know how loving and loyal his family had been.

It must've been lonely, she said.

You have to have faith.

He described the dinners in prison, always ground turkey and soy, which he detested. (To this day he can't eat ground turkey without getting nauseous.) *That sounds gross,* she said. Eddie wasn't telling her all this to make her think he had it worse. It's just that he had found a connection and was taking full advantage of it. And Elena, for the first time, seemed curious about Eddie's life. She wanted to know how he had managed. Lots of reading and letter writing and studying, Eddie told her. And, of course, his painting. Elena opened up. She told Eddie and Kathryn that she was scared, that at night her heart would sometimes go into shock and they had to use paddles to revive her. She asked them about her grandchildren. The conversation lasted maybe fifteen minutes, but in that time she and Eddie shared more with each other than in all the time before. A nurse came in to change the sheets, and so Eddie and Kathryn each kissed Elena on the cheek and took the remaining hamburger to hide in the diaper bag. *I love you, Mom,* Eddie told her. She died five days later.

At her funeral, Eddie was awed by those who attended. The janitor from Kathryn's grade school; every Christmas Elena had made a Greek holiday meal for the custodial staff. A former grade school teacher of Kathryn's who had gone through a painful divorce; Kathryn's mom had counseled her. Another teacher whose husband traveled a lot; Elena would bring her premade dinners. "I learned a lot at the funeral," Eddie told me. "She gave a lot of herself. She cared about people who were often overlooked . . . I realize now that it wasn't that she didn't want someone like me in the family. I think she simply wanted the best for her daughter. She was anticipating the challenges."

O ne day, after Eddie had given a eulogy at the funeral of one of the Iraq war veterans involved in his program—he was shot and killed driving on the South Side, not in the Middle East—he seemed shaken. We stopped to get something to eat at a tired-looking taqueria, taking a booth near the door. He left his suit jacket in the car and loosened his tie. He leaned over the table, and at first I thought he wanted to tell me something, but I realized he was just fatigued, more so than usual. I asked him how he was doing, if he'd thought about seeing a counselor again. He laughed and told me that just the other week his boss had told him, *You think you're good, Eddie. You're helping everyone else, but who's helping you?* He informed Eddie that he'd arranged for him to see a counselor. *This isn't optional,* he told Eddie. On telling me this, Eddie sighed and muttered, "I hope it's just one time." I laughed, only because of course Eddie's wife is a therapist, and he more than most knew the toll that losing friend after friend can take on one's spirit. And one counseling session, he knew all too well, wasn't going to cure anything.

Sitting there, Eddie told me a story. When he was twelve years old, there was an abandoned two-story brick building, a former state office facility, in his neighborhood, and while it was boarded up, you could enter it by pulling down the fire escape ladder, climbing to the roof, and letting yourself in through an unlocked door. Eddie and his friend Sergio periodically sought refuge here, away from the craziness of the streets. Sometimes they would just lie down on the rooftop and soak in the sun, or Eddie would try to catch the attention of a girl he had a crush on who lived across the street. Sometimes they'd meander through the empty building, spray-painting their names or knocking holes through the walls, though the novelty of that wore off quickly. On this particular occasion, early evening, he and Sergio had climbed the fire escape to the roof, and then, guided by the day's remaining light streaming through the building's windows, made their way to the basement, just poking around, kicking at empty beer bottles and syringes, evidence that they were not the only ones who used the building.

As they clowned around, they heard a rattling of something metal, someone pulling down the fire escape ladder. They froze. Eddie panicked. *No one knows we're here,* he told Sergio. *How the fuck are we going to get out of here?* Sergio told him to be quiet. They tiptoed up the stairs to the first floor and then to the second floor, where they heard voices, two men who were clearly keyed up. Eddie and Sergio stepped into a small room and squatted so they could peer through a hole in the wall. They could make out two Hispanic men, maybe in their twenties, arguing with a skinny black woman. Eddie recognized all of them from the neighborhood. The young woman, everyone said, was a prostitute and a crack addict, and while Eddie didn't know precisely what that meant, he knew from the way people spoke of her that it wasn't something to admire. They couldn't see a lot through the wall, but Eddie remembers one of the men yelling, *Fuck you, bitch.* Eddie then heard the sound of a fist smashing into a face, and he could make out the woman falling.

She yelled, *Help! Help!,* her pleas rising and falling as if she was try-ing to catch her breath. Eddie and Sergio stayed where they were, both of them frightened—for themselves and for her. Because of the angle they had, Eddie couldn't see what happened next, but he could tell from the grunts of the men that they took turns raping her. Eddie worried that they could hear his heart pounding. The boys sat there, their backs to the wall, waiting for it to end, wait-ing for the two men to leave. Eddie was sure they had killed her. Once they heard the men descend the fire escape, Eddie and Sergio stood and began the march to the roof, which meant, Eddie knew, they had to pass the woman, who lay on her back on the floor, com-pletely naked. *I think she's dead,* Eddie told Sergio. *Should we call the police?* She stirred, her small breasts moving with her short breaths, just enough to let Eddie know she was still very much alive. They kept on going, too afraid to call the police, too afraid of the guys they saw. "I knew it was all wrong," Eddie told me as he recounted the evening. "I knew it. This stuff stays with you," he added. "It fucks with you."

This story was a preface to what he was really thinking. "I look at my little girls," he said. He and Kathryn had a fourth on the way. "What would I do if someone were to do something to *my* daugh-ters?" He then told me of a recent dream he had had. Someone—he's not sure who—kidnaps his oldest, Salome, and Eddie stalks the person, eventually catching him. Eddie ends up taking him to his basement and there ties the kidnapper to a chair. Eddie pulls up a chair in front of him and sits down, a pair of wirecutters in hand. *I'm going to ask you the question,* he tells his captive. *And if you don't answer, I'm going to cut off a finger.* He asks the question: *Where's my daughter?* There's no answer, and so Eddie cuts off a finger. He keeps asking, and he keeps cutting, so that in the end he's snipped off three fingers. Blood's everywhere. Eddie woke up sweating, and was so unnerved by the dream he woke Kathryn. He shared it with her, and, ever patient, she listened, nodding her head, rubbing his hands. *This is the price of resiliency,* she told him, trying to reassure him.

He didn't seem to hear her. *Am I capable of doing that?* he asked. *Am I? Here I am asking people to forgive me, but can I forgive others? That's fucked up.*

Chapter 12

The Two Geralds

On the city's near West Side sits one of Chicago's few residences for men coming out of prison. It consists of three low-slung red-brick buildings surrounding a small courtyard where you can usually find a handful of men smoking, each standing alone, lost in thought. The buildings and the men appear tired. The men do what they can to avoid drawing attention to themselves. They don't need trouble.

I came here to meet with some residents, and so we assembled in the basement of one of the structures, five of us: myself, a man from the residence, and three women from a women's halfway house nearby. The women told stories. One, Pam, mentioned that her son had been killed and that the only way she could cope was to write down thoughts and then rip them up, as if that would some-how discard the memories of the day. Another, Alison, told the group, "I don't have any fear. That's my problem. Once my mom was murdered I had nothing else to fear. That shaped me." Another told how she had become a bully. "It was like water to me," she said of the violence she inflicted on others. The women all said they'd been in trauma therapy, which explained why they seemed so self-aware. The man, who was short and slightly built, sported a goatee and an intense expression, as if he were pondering the deepest of philosophical questions. He had deep-set eyes that locked on you when he talked. But he didn't talk much. Early in the conversation he introduced himself as Gerald, and then he seemed to disappear. As the women reflected on their pasts, he folded forward in his chair, his head buried in his hands. He wore a blue hoodie and I couldn't see his face, so at first I thought he might be nodding off, but then I realized he was in some discomfort. At one point he raised his head and asked the women where they found their therapists. He mumbled something about a fire, about four people dead, about not being able to get it out of his head. "I'm always afraid," he told the others in a voice so soft they had to lean in to hear him. "I'm not afraid of dying. What I'm afraid of is losing my mother, of being in prison, of being a failure. I'm afraid of living."

Here's how Gerald remembers that night of the fire, twenty-seven years ago, almost to the day. It was July 24, 1986. Gerald was thirteen, though when he tells the story, he remembers himself as younger, as eleven or twelve. He lived with his mother, Gladys, and his younger brother on the first floor of a small, compact coach house set back from the street, along an alley in a struggling working-class West Side neighborhood. An elderly woman lived in the apartment upstairs. Alongside the coach house, in the alley, his mom had set up a basketball hoop, tying it to a utility pole for stability. She wanted this to be the place neighborhood kids hung out, so she could keep an eye on them. When the kids would gather and play pickup games, she'd make lemonade and Kool-Aid for them. Sometimes Gerald, who liked to tumble, would lug a mattress to the alley, and he and his friends would practice flips, learning moves he could use later when he tried to make money break dancing on Michigan Avenue downtown. Gladys worked as an assistant manager at 16 Plus, a clothing store at a suburban mall, and had chosen this cottage because next door, in a larger home, lived her older sister, Heddie, and her five children. They could help each other out.

One of Gerald's cousins next door, a girl who was a few years older, had been dating a teenage boy who had a twin brother. Gerald remembers this because the twin brothers got into a running dispute with some boys in the neighborhood. Gerald didn't know what it was over, but it escalated rapidly. It started outside a candy store when the twins argued with a local boy, Ken Floyd, who lived just up the street. The verbal exchange turned into an exchange of punches. That was followed by an incident in which one of the twins pulled a Louisville slugger out of his jogging pants and, according to Gerald, knocked Floyd across his head, so hard he required stitches. That was followed by Floyd and a friend retaliating by allegedly kicking in the front door of Gerald's aunt's house and unleashing a German shepherd and a Doberman pinscher on the twins, one of whom was bitten on the chest. Gerald seems to remember the twins getting the better of the dogs and chasing them away. And then one night someone tried, unsuccessfully, to set his aunt's porch on fire. Even at thirteen, Gerald had a sense this wasn't going to end well.

In the thick humidity of the early morning hours of July 24, 1986, Gerald sat with his mother and his aunt, Heddie, on the front porch of the carriage house, chatting and half watching television on a set his mom had placed there using an extension cord. His mother was worried that the conflict with the twins would escalate, so pleaded with her sister to bring her kids to spend the night with them. Gerald recalls his aunt telling his mother, *Girl, I ain't gonna let them run me out of my house.* And so, at three in the morning, his aunt, either in an act of defiance or in a move of resignation, left to go home and walked the twenty feet to her front door, assuring them that she'd be okay. Gerald retreated to his bedroom and lay down while his mother took a bath. He soon fell asleep, sprawled across his blankets, only to be jolted awake an hour later by the sound of glass shattering. He could hear his mother on the phone, panicked, first asking for the police, then for the fire department. Gerald ran onto his porch and saw his aunt's house ablaze, so close he could feel the rising heat. One of his cousins stood on the roof of the back porch, desperately trying to get his younger siblings and cousins to crawl to the window, but the heat was too intense. (Investigators would later find that the refrigerator downstairs had partly melted.) Smoke seemed to be escaping from every pore of the house. Gerald was frozen on his porch, counting in his head who must still be inside. Ten people lived in the house: his aunt and her five children, one of the twin brothers, and his mother's niece and her two children. It was a lot to account for. All he could make out was his sixteen-year-old cousin Homer on the porch roof, along with two other figures; Homer had gotten his mother and his eight-year-old brother out.

What happened next has been etched into Gerald's memory like an ancient cliff painting, the scene still recognizable but the drawing faded in places and in some cases simply erased by years of erosion. But if Gerald closes his eyes, he can feel it—the urgency, the hope, the sheer force of will. He can taste the smoke which seeps into his clothes. Sometimes he can smell the distinct noxious odor of burned flesh. He sees Homer still on the porch's roof, uncertain. Homer's mother is now climbing back in through the window to get the others. Gerald wants to yell at her, *No!* Then he watches as his eight-year-old cousin, Dante, follows. Gerald waits for what seems like hours but of course is maybe a matter of minutes. They don't reemerge. If only he can reach them, lead them downstairs, lead them to the door. Gerald, dressed in jeans and T-shirt, runs to the back door, pulling at it, trying to get it open, thinking maybe he can run inside and find his aunt and cousins and lead them to safety.

Finally he yanks it open, and with the surge of oxygen the kitchen erupts, and he's thrown backward by the force of the fire. Flames leap out the window. Homer jumps from the porch roof to the ground. And in that moment Gerald realizes he'll never reach his aunt or his cousins. Later, after the bodies have been removed, the house still smoldering, the floorboards still hot to the touch, Gerald wanders to the second floor and in his cousin's bedroom sees what he believes to be Dante's flesh seared into the bed board.

Gladys, Gerald's mom, would later testify to what she had witnessed. She had gotten out of the bath and was lying across her bed when she heard the back fence rattling. She looked out her bedroom window and in the backyard of her sister's house she said she saw two figures, both of whom she recognized: Ken Floyd, the boy who had had the dispute with the twins and who lived just up the street, and a sixteen-year-old neighbor, Gerald Rice, who lived across the alley. She says that they had with them what looked like a glass Coca-Cola bottle filled with a liquid, a rag protruding from the mouth. A molotov cocktail. She testified that Floyd handed the firebomb to Gerald, who hurled it, unlit, through the kitchen window. When she spoke with the police at the scene, disoriented and distraught, she identified only one of them. "Junior," she told the police. That was Gerald Rice's nickname. She didn't mention Ken Floyd until later, when she picked him out of a lineup. Gladys would be the prosecution's key witness at their trial.

The four dead—Gerald's aunt, Heddie Johnson, and Gerald's cousins Dante Johnson, who was eleven, Wendell Johnson, who was eight, and Shekita Johnson, who was seven—were completely charred, skin burned off, tendons and muscle exposed, hair singed. One of the children tried to find safety between a mattress and the box springs. While the medical examiner declared that they had died of "acute carbon monoxide toxicity," they were, in layman's terms, burned alive. After the funeral, Gerald's grandmother, who was sixty-four, had dreams that her grandchildren had drowned, a way of trying to find comfort, that in drowning they might not have suffered as much. She kept asking how they had died, and Gladys couldn't bring herself to tell her mother the whole story so would simply say, "Smoke inhalation." But her mother knew. Seven months later, she died of a massive stroke. "My mom," Gladys told me, "grieved herself to death." So did Gerald, or close to it.

When I met Gerald at the halfway house, I learned that he had been clean for a few months. He was clearheaded and thoughtful, a pleasure to be around. We met on numerous occasions after our first encounter with the women. He told me that after the fire had been extinguished, he had walked to a nearby apartment building, curled up by the front door, and sobbed. He had failed his cousins and his aunt. Something—he couldn't fully describe it—bore in on him, like a jackhammer on cement, pounding cracks in his soul. It never went away. And he couldn't—or wouldn't—talk with anyone about it. "I felt like a coward," he told me. It was his burden to carry. A few months after the fire, sitting in a car with an older cousin, he tried heroin for the first time, snorting the powder rather than injecting it. He hated needles. At first he felt nauseous, but then he felt this stillness, an ease he hadn't experienced before. It erased the anguish. It softened the blows he hurled at himself. "I was in heaven," he said. "I fell in love with it." At thirteen years old, Gerald became hooked.

The next year his best friend appeared to fall asleep on the couch after snorting a dose. In the morning Gerald tried to wake him, and when he rolled him over, Gerald flinched. His friend's face was covered in blood, the result of a ruptured blood vessel in his nose. He had overdosed. But it didn't deter Gerald. His habit went from $100 a day to $200 a day. He hustled to make money. He sold drugs. He stole jewelry from his mom and a fur coat from his girlfriend. He once robbed a man who drove up to his corner to buy heroin. Gerald reached through the car window and snatched $1,500 from the buyer's hand and took off running. The next day that same man came back around, and in an alley gunned his car as Gerald tried to evade him. The car slammed into Gerald, hitting him with such force that he flew twenty feet into the air, like a rag doll, and into a utility pole, cracking his skull and fracturing his spine. But Gerald was so in the grip of heroin that he checked himself out of the hospital two days later, against doctor's orders. He was arrested time and again. For possessing and selling heroin and marijuana, for urinating on an El platform, for disrupting a police sting operation, for stealing a car, and eventually for armed robbery; he held up a man with a gun and took a pager, three lottery tickets, and a gold chain. For this crime he was sentenced to six years.

Here's the thing: Gerald is unusually smart and thoughtful. Even with his drug habit, he graduated from high school and attended college, albeit briefly. He learned to play chess in prison, and when he was out he would find games along the city's North Avenue beach. He kept a journal, the only way he knew to articulate what was going on inside, written mostly as missives to God.

> Sometimes it's so difficult to express how I really feel inside because my heart aches so, so much. Death. It's suffering that spoils the spirit . . . I'm afraid. Afraid to love. Afraid to trust. Afraid to care. . . . Help me know what it is to be happy.

Sometimes he expressed a tinge of hope, especially in talking about his mom.

> First day of college at Harold Washington College. It feels good to know that after all my suffering, heartache and pain that I was given another chance to recapture so many lost dreams . . . My mother has always amazed me with her love for me . . . She has been a blessing to me and my life. I pray that you give me the ability to overcome my addiction so I can make her proud. Please Lord help me overcome the burdens of my heart . . . Ma, thank you for loving me.

Or the usual ups and downs of life.

I feel so hurt, angry and yet confused because for the first time in my life I finally realized what it is I want and I'm willing to share it with the only woman I've ever really loved but she's found someone else. It hurts so deeply.

But throughout his writings, he finds his way back to the early-morning hours of July 24, 1986.

I can't help feeling like maybe there was something I could have did to change what happened . . . I watched as my loved ones died . . . That summer night, when only a child, twelve yrs old, four of my loved ones were murdered, right in front of me, something inside of me changed. I felt hurt and betrayed by God . . . but I'm gradually starting to realize that I would've died also [if he had gone into the house]. It happened exactly the way God intended.

Why am I so angry inside? I guess I'm so angry because I feel like I'm a failure . . . I felt abandoned and angry, afraid to trust in anybody, angry that I allowed my environment to suppress me . . . angry for the fact that God took all my beloved friends, family and acquaintances right in front of me. I had to watch them die and there was nothing I could do about it . . . I'm plagued by the spectres of my past. I ask you for forgiveness . . . My mind is filled with self-doubt, fear, loneliness and confusion. I feel that maybe I'm running out of time.

For the longest period, no one knew, not even his mother, about the nightmares or the flashbacks. Sometimes if he smelled something burning, he was right back at the fire, at the door. Helpless—and, in his mind, cowardly. He rarely laughed. He didn't know joy. "I just didn't feel comfortable being in my own skin, and I always wanted to escape what was going on around me," he told me. In 2011, just out of prison, Gerald was placed in a program for ex-offenders at A Safe Haven, where once a week he participated in a therapy group. During one session the counselor asked why he had started using heroin, especially at such a young age, and for the first time Gerald told others about the fire and the guilt and the torment. As he did, it felt like he was there, on his porch, sweating from the heat of the flames, yanking open the door, the fireball, the smell of charred flesh. Tears rolled down his cheeks. Someone in the group, someone he didn't know, seemingly amused by Gerald's outpouring, muttered, *Aw, man, this ole crybaby bitch-ass nigga. This nigga crying like a little bitch, you know what I'm saying?* Gerald jumped from his seat and slugged the man so hard he fractured his hand. He ran from the meeting and later wandered to a CVS, where he stuffed into his jacket two electric hair trimmers and half a dozen electric toothbrush heads, looking for things to sell to get a fix. He got arrested yet again.

When I met Gerald this summer, he was in a good place. He soon moved out of the halfway house into his mother's apartment on the West Side. He got a job driving train conductors to their jobs at the railroad. He seemed determined not to find his way back to the heroin. Gerald's sponsor in Narcotics Anonymous, Otto Brown, told me, "To get the definition of who that cat is, you got to catch him when his mind is clear." I felt lucky, I suppose, to get to know Gerald when his mind was clear. We'd sit around his mom's apartment or meet for coffee or a meal at MacArthur's, a soul-food restaurant just a block from his mom's. We talked about the fire, about his addiction, about his love for writing, about women, about waking up in the middle of the night drenched in sweat, heart pounding, and we talked about forgiveness, really about forgiving oneself. Once over lunch he told me, "I'm sitting here with you, but in my mind I'm there, experiencing everything associated with that moment. The feelings, the smoke, the sirens, the crying." He told me that outside of a couple of therapists, one in prison, one at A Safe Haven, he'd never spoken about the fire in any detail, not even with his mother. In fact, when I spoke with her, she seemed surprised that it still bothered him. "The heroin," he told me, "was the only way to cope." He told me that he worried that he'd only find peace when he died.

Over time, though, he slowly began to slide. His hair appeared unkempt, his usually groomed beard uncombed. He developed dark circles under his eyes. He seemed agitated. One time, as we walked through the gate toward his mother's apartment, a young man and woman stood in the walkway, blocking our path. "Excuse me," Gerald said. The couple, who were talking, seemed not to notice, and so Gerald repeated himself, each time getting louder. The couple were locked in on each other, oblivious of their surroundings, and didn't hear Gerald. Finally I nudged him, nodding, suggesting we step around them, and as we did Gerald purposefully bumped the woman. She turned around, sneering. "I said 'excuse me,'" Gerald muttered sarcastically, and then to me, "What else they want from me?" The next time I came around, Gerald had a black eye. He told me he got jumped, but it seemed odd that he would have been hit for no apparent reason. Then came the requests for money. Five dollars. Ten dollars. Not a lot, but enough—and enough times to make me realize that he was using again. And then he disappeared. He stopped returning my phone calls. I went by his mother's apartment one afternoon, and Gladys confirmed that he had indeed started using heroin again, that he'd been arrested, this time for selling drugs. "I've had it with that boy," she told me.

I thought this might be a good time to talk with her about the fire, and she told me that her son needed to get over it, stop using it as an excuse. She then instructed me: "You need to call the attorneys for Gerald Rice." Gerald Rice was their former neighbor from across the alley, the only one to be convicted of the murder of Gladys's sister and her children, convicted mainly on Gladys's testimony. "Why would he have lawyers after all these years?" I asked. Because, she told me, he didn't do it.

Two years later: I'm in the county's criminal courthouse, in a fourth-floor courtroom so cavernous that spectators sit thirty feet from the judge's bench. It's like sitting in the bleachers. The sound system is so old and neglected that even sitting in the first row, leaning forward, hands cupped to your ears, you have to strain to hear the proceedings. I'm here for the resentencing of Gerald Rice, twenty-seven years after he was convicted of arson and murder. The first witness for the state, Michael Magana, acting deputy commander of the intelligence unit at the Illinois Department of Corrections, testifies that Gerald Rice, who's now forty-six, had admitted to being a member of the Mafia Insane Vice Lords, a street gang that also operates in prison. Magana testified that on October 1, 1992, Gerald fought another inmate, and a staff member who intervened got injured. As a result, Gerald was placed in segregation for a month. Then the following January, Magana testifies, after Gerald had been released back to his cell, guards found a six-inch-long shank made of plexiglass as well as a gallon of homemade hooch there. This time he spent three months in segregation. Again in October 2001 guards found a shank under Gerald's mattress. This time he spent a full year in segregation.

During this testimony, Gerald sat at a long table alongside his lawyers, two women from Northwestern Law School's Children and Family Justice Center. Gerald, who has a shaved head, was dressed in a blue short-sleeved button-up shirt. His hands rested on the table, folded together like a schoolboy's. He was shackled at the ankles. He barely moved, focused on the testimony. What I'd come to learn is that Gerald Rice is cognitively delayed. This is kind of a mushy label. Gerald has trouble with anything layered or at all complex. It's not that he can't interact and laugh and make sense of the immediate world around him, but it's often without any nuance, without a full understanding. And often people with this kind of delay do things that they know are not a part of their moral makeup, but in the moment it seems to make sense, or in the moment it feels like it'll win them a friend. And friends, when you have this condition, can be hard to come by. Gerald is without guile.

Gerald's condition came out at the original trial, in 1988. Gerald, who was sixteen at the time, attended classes for what was then called "the educably mentally handicapped." He couldn't read or write. His math abilities were at a third-grade level. His lawyer told the judge that he was having trouble communicating with Gerald. At one point, he said, Gerald asked him the difference between an attorney and a lawyer. Two psychiatrists testified that Gerald had problems with memory, that he couldn't remember the name of the last school he attended and that he couldn't remember the name of his lawyer. They both testified that Gerald could not understand his Miranda rights.

As I mentioned, at the original trial Gladys Johnson, the other Gerald's mom, testified that she saw Ken Floyd and Gerald Rice, who was known as Junior in the neighborhood, passing back and forth between them a Coca-Cola bottle filled with liquid. She testified that the bottle Gerald hurled through her sister's kitchen window was unlit. (The police found no accelerant on his clothes.) Gladys also said that when she ran out of the house, Gerald Rice and Ken Floyd ran right past her. She knew both boys from the neighborhood, especially because they would frequently come by to play basketball in the alley with her son. (She told me that Floyd and his friends wouldn't let Gerald Rice play, so he would watch from the sidelines.) It was a bench trial, and the judge acquitted Ken Floyd because, he said, Gladys hadn't identified him at the scene as she had Gerald Rice, and only identified him later in a lineup. Gerald had told the police that he wasn't with Ken Floyd, that he was asleep when around four in the morning a friend knocked loudly on his door to alert him to the fire. He said that he and his friend stood in the alley and watched the house burn.

At Gerald's sentencing, the judge, Richard Neville, seemed discomforted by the facts. It was clear to Judge Neville that Gerald had been lured to assist others, that he wasn't acting out of his own volition, that he clearly had developmental issues that made him highly susceptible to others' influence. But because of mandatory sentences set by the state legislature, Judge Neville had no choice in deciding Gerald's fate. In an extraordinary admission, Judge Neville suggested that Gerald wasn't fully at fault. It was clear, he said, "that Ken Floyd was the instigator of this occurrence." He rued the fact that he didn't feel he had the evidence to convict Floyd. He then went on to apologize to Gerald: "I think it is outrageous that I cannot take that into consideration in determining what an appropriate sentence is for Mr. Rice . . . Were I able to, I would not sentence Mr. Rice to mandatory life for these charges. I would find another sentence which I think would be more appropriate . . . I think the legislature has overstepped its bounds and indicated an inappropriate sentence must be given to Mr. Rice and has stripped judges of the ability to consider each defendant individually which was the keystone of our constitution to begin with . . . It is with total reluctance that I enter the sentence and it is only because I believe I have no authority to do anything else that I enter this sentence." Judge Neville, with great reluctance, sentenced Gerald Rice at the age of sixteen to natural life in prison.

In 2012 the U.S. Supreme Court in *Miller v. Alabama* ruled that mandatory natural life sentences for juveniles was unconstitutional, and as a result most of the two thousand inmates around the country who were sentenced to natural life as children were given a new hearing, a chance at resentencing. The ruling came nearly thirty years after Gerald Rice was originally sentenced. The prosecution put on only two witnesses before turning it over to Gerald's lawyers, who pointed out that since 2001, Gerald hadn't received a single ticket for even a small violation while in prison—and that whatever gang affiliation he might have had was long in the past. The former director of the Illinois Department of Corrections testified to Gerald's remarkable record, recalling an incident in which a ladle, a potential weapon, went missing, and Gerald helped the guards find it. He also mentioned that since 1994 Gerald had had 1,101 visits, mostly from his mother, his grandmother, and his sister. "This doesn't happen often with someone who has a life sentence," the former director testified.

Even Judge Neville, the judge in the original trial, weighed in, with a letter to the court. He wrote: "I continue to be troubled by the sentence I was required to impose. When I sentenced Mr. Rice, I never had the opportunity to consider mitigating information regarding Mr. Rice in order to reach an appropriate sentence. I would have wanted to consider his cognitive capacity, his age, the circumstances of his upbringing and family life, his educational and criminal history, the source and strength of support for him in his family and community, and his lesser role in the crime. In that regard, I recall that, based on the evidence I heard at the trial in this matter, I felt that Mr. Rice was being used by the other individuals who perpetrated the crime . . . I do not believe that Mr. Rice deserved the sentence he was given."

Gladys sat in a middle row, leaning into her younger sister, Faye, the two at times holding hands. Gladys can be forceful and direct, and sometimes I imagine that because she says what's on her mind and because she often looks fatigued, people underestimate her. She had considered testifying but chose not to once she learned that the assistant state's attorney might introduce photos of her sister, nephews, and nieces after the fire. She knew she'd fall apart. Instead she submitted a short written statement, which was read into the record:

> Through the years, my mental and physical states have changed both due to age and periods of stress. Shortly after the incident, I took custody of my sister's remaining children

and raised them as my own. Not long after this incident, my mother's health began to fail and she passed away. Through the years, I've grown to the point where I believe that individuals deserve a second chance. Heddie's surviving children have grown to have their own families and have been able to surpass the grief and place forgiveness in their hearts. For whatever it may mean, I have continued my life and accept whatever sentence the judge may place on Gerald. Sincerely, Gladys Johnson

The statement, not surprisingly, was ambiguous. While she testified in his original trial that he'd been partly responsible, she now says he both deserves a second chance *and* that he had nothing to do with igniting the fire. Gladys's memory of the fire and the subsequent trial has shattered and rearranged itself numerous times. Trauma does that. It toys with you. That's the case for Gladys. And if you listen to her stories closely, it's not that she's seeing something completely apart from what she saw before, but rather it feels like with time that moment three decades ago comes into clearer focus. "It was just like yesterday," she told me. "It just is so vivid in my mind." At the original trial she testified that she saw Gerald Rice throw an unlit firebomb through the kitchen window. Years later she told Gerald's lawyers, "I will go to my grave believing Gerald is innocent." She claims the transcript from the trial isn't accurate—which is unlikely. And then she told me that she saw Ken Floyd and two others, close friends of his from the neighborhood, throw Molotov cocktails into her sister's home, and that when they all ran past her toward the alley, Gerald followed them. She assumed he'd been on the side of the house she couldn't see. She's described this to me multiple times. Here's the bottom line: Gladys believes that Gerald, if he had a role in the firebombing, was there only at the instigation of others, that he was bullied into it. Here's where she never wavered: Gerald Rice should be freed.

The judge, after hearing all the testimony, resentenced Gerald so that he would get out in a month. The judge stated, "It's pretty clear for a variety of reasons that Mr. Rice didn't intend for this to happen. Ken Floyd did . . . It is clear from my review of the record . . . Ken Floyd was the moving force in this." Gerald's grandmother, Mary, walked a few rows back and hugged Gladys, told her they'd all get together, both filled with relief. Gladys looked as happy as I'd ever seen her. Gerald, still shackled, shuffled out of the courtroom accompanied by two sheriff deputies, looking bemused, uncertain as to what had just transpired.

Gerald Rice had told one of his lawyers that all he wanted when he got out was pepperoni pizza. It is a chilly day in February, the thermometer hovering around freezing, and we talk and pace in the waiting room at the Stateville Correctional Center. Gerald's brother, Taiwan, who repairs security alarms and runs a small real-estate brokerage firm, tells me he'd gone online to read accounts of men getting out of prison so he would know what to expect. One former inmate, he says, didn't feel free until he went to the beach where he used to go as a child. Another talked about his need for privacy. "If Gerald wants to close his door, that's fine," he explains.

Gerald's family is incredibly close-knit. Warm. Welcoming. Each with wide, open smiles. Gerald's sister, Velinda, remembered that as a kid Gerald loved shoes and Reese's Peanut Butter Cups, so she got him a pair of white sneakers and three Reese's. The family explains that they visited him so often in part because he can't read, and so sending letters was a useless exercise. His grandmother and mother recall the time right after the fire when they were called down to the police station. They weren't allowed to see Gerald, but they caught a glimpse of him through a window, and he pounded his chest, suggesting he'd been hit while in custody. Gerald, a minor, had been questioned by the police without his mother or a lawyer present.

After two hours of waiting, shortly after noon, a guard announces Gerald's being released, and everyone races outside. Across the parking lot, we spot Gerald lugging a cardboard box with his belongings, following another released inmate to the bus stop. One of his lawyers laughs and yells to Gerald, "You don't need to take the bus." Gerald's in a blue skullcap, white T-shirt, and black pants, not dressed for the weather. His brother pulls out a new winter coat he purchased for the occasion, and Gerald wiggles into it, complaining that it's too small, too tight. Taiwan tells him, "That's the style. It looks good." One of the lawyers asks Gerald how he feels. "Nervous," he replies.

At the Golden Corral, a buffet-style restaurant, Gerald eats pepperoni pizza and roasted chicken. He seems lost amid the celebration. Over a dozen family and friends and his lawyers hover around him, hugging him, patting him on the back, urging him to pose for photos. At one point Gerald walks to his grandmother, who's in a wheelchair and who has been quietly sitting at the head of the table. "You awright?" he asks. "I'm all right seeing you," she says, and takes his hand in hers.

I sit with Gladys Johnson on her second-floor back porch, late afternoon, both of us sipping water. We watch as disheveled-looking young men and women enter and exit through a rear door of an apartment building across the alley. "A drug den," she explains. Gladys knows this because she's seen her son, Gerald, enter there. Gerald got out of prison a few months ago, and by her count has been in and out of four rehab centers in that time. He's back using. She knows this because he spends hours in the bathroom and has blood in his stools; heroin use can block one's bowels. He's also lost color and has fallen asleep beneath the kitchen table.

He's tried to hock a pair of her shoes. She has understandably run out of patience with her son, and tires of hearing him talk about the fire and how it's consumed him. "I just think it's an excuse," she tells me. "He's using it as a crutch. It could've played a part then [when he was young], but come on now, you're forty-five years old." Nonetheless, she lets him stay at her apartment. He's her son, after all. She loves him. She had told Gerald I was coming by, but, not surprisingly, he didn't show.

It's hard not to recognize the irony. Her Gerald is a prisoner of his drug habit, and the other Gerald, Gerald Rice, is free. Don't get her wrong, she's glad Gerald Rice is out of prison. "Everybody misinterpreted my story," she insists, explaining that she saw only Ken and his two friends throw lit bottles into her sister's home. When the three of them ran from the burning house toward the alley, she says, Gerald was running with them, pulling up the rear. "Thirty-some years. That wasn't fair at all," she says of his time in prison. She wanted to meet Gerald, to talk to him, to tell him everything's okay, but she never heard from him or his family. She's upset by that. "I would've liked to get together. I just want him to know that I don't have any animosity in my heart toward him. I know he got bullied." The thing is, Gerald still contends that he had nothing to do with the fire, that he was at home asleep when the house across the alley was torched. His lawyers are pursuing a case to clear his name.

Over a quarter of a century ago. A dispute between teenage boys. A fistfight. A baseball bat. Then a firebombing. Four family members burned to death. Of one of the survivors, one of her nieces, Gladys says, "She's lost in her sorrows." It's hard not to think that for Gladys, too, that morning is still very much present. Every year she writes the birthdays of her sister and her sister's children in her calendar. Every July 24, the anniversary of the fire, she hosts a barbecue which the survivors of the fire, her nieces and nephews, attend. She often can't sleep at night because when she closes her eyes, she can see everything like it's right in front of her: her eleven-year-old nephew Dante on the porch roof, panicked, hollering through the window for his mom, Gladys's sister. *Momma, where you at? Momma, where you at?* Gladys yelling at Homer, who's also on the porch roof, *Get Dante! Get Dante!* Dante disappearing, crawling back through the window to find his mom. Then, later, a heavyset white police officer, a woman, taking Gladys in her arms. *Come here, it's going to be okay,* she tells Gladys, who nestles her head in the roundness of the officer's shoulder. Gladys just wants to know what's taking so long to get everyone out. She thinks they're still alive. She can still feel the warm, comforting embrace of the police officer, the softness of the officer's shoulder, a place where in that moment, for just that moment, she feels reassured; it's a feeling she wants again. The visions are too real, too vivid, so much so that she can't keep her eyes closed at night. And so she can't sleep, sometimes for two or three days at a time. Her psychiatrist has prescribed trazodone for the insomnia, and Gladys, who's sixty-two, now goes to the gym three times a week, mostly water aerobics, to burn off the anxiety. "Sometimes," she tells me, "I think I'm going to my grave with this on my mind and in my heart."

Chapter 13

The Tightrope, part three

AUGUST 15 . . . AUGUST 16 . . . AUGUST 17 . . .

In line to enter the city's neoclassically designed criminal courthouse, the same place where Gerald Rice was resentenced, men and women—mostly men—fidget and keep their heads down or look off into the distance. They avoid eye contact. They're preoccupied, subdued, on edge. Many look as if they want to disappear. In front of me is a young Hispanic man, a tattoo on his shaved head which reads *Renegade Killer*. On his neck he has etched *Thug Life*. The man behind me mutters, "I wonder what kind of case he's fighting?" Many of the men wear shorts and T-shirts, a statement of defiance. Whatever status you hold on the streets is stripped from you here. Whatever your history, it's erased. Whatever your aspirations, no one cares. They say it's a place where justice is served. But justice too often feels arbitrary. Like a game of craps. You enter this building, and whatever control you had in your day-to-day existence is lost. The judges, the prosecutors, the deputy sheriffs, the public defenders, are intently focused not necessarily on you but on getting through the day without too much going wrong.

I came here today to meet Marcelo. Bob Dwyer, his public defender, has done two stints in this building, with an interruption of working for an insurance company, and is one of the most respected attorneys in the Cook County public defender's office. Despite his laconic manner, he can be a fierce advocate, and he seems determined to ensure that Marcelo, who along with his friends robbed three people of their cell phones, doesn't get a felony on his record. Marcelo's case has become a priority for his office, partly because of the Mercy connection (there's a kind of Catholic mafia in the city) and partly because Marcelo's case felt as if it represented something more: a way to push back on the inflexibility and unnecessary harshness in applying justice. Dwyer wanted the prosecution to reduce Marcelo's charge to a misdemeanor— or, better yet, get his case sent to juvenile court, anything to keep him from getting a felony on his record. In a nation that likes to see itself as forgiving, we are mulishly unforgiving of those who have committed a felony, which could be anything from selling drugs to street robberies to murder. A felony marks one for life. In some states you lose your right to vote. For certain felonies you can't receive federal loans for college and are barred from federally funded housing. You can't legally buy a firearm. In many states you can't get a license to become a realtor or stockbroker or nurse or teacher. You can't work in child care. Potential employers can lawfully refuse employment if you have a felony on your record. It's permanent. No one was arguing that Marcelo shouldn't receive consequences for his robbery spree, but those around him asked, *Should this singular moment constrict the rest of his life?*

This is the second of sixteen court appearances Marcelo will make over the next two years. The first judge is replaced after becoming ill. An effort to transfer the case to juvenile court—Marcelo turned seventeen just five days before committing the crime—proves unsuccessful. Arguments over whether to reduce the offense to a misdemeanor charge are stymied by dogged prosecutors. For the next two years Marcelo will be on house arrest, an electronic bracelet cinched around his ankle, his movements restricted and tracked by the sheriff's office. He's allowed to go to school and to a job, when he has one, but he can't visit his family on weekends. He can't go to the store or out for dinner. He can't take a walk. He can't leave his third-floor suite at Mercy. He can't play basketball in the gym or lift weights or eat lunch or dinner in the cafeteria.

On this day in court, Marcelo is dressed in a black shirt and black tie. His gray dress slacks, which are too long, gather in a pile of cloth on his shimmering black shoes, the ones he purchased for his junior prom. He's also slipped on a pair of hip-looking rectangular reading glasses. "It makes me look like a good person," he tells me before confiding, "I feel really funny in them." He's a creature of habit (he claims the same shower stall every day at Mercy), and so we sit in the back row of hard-backed wood benches, me on one side, Claire Conway, a program manager at Mercy, on the other. "I feel like we sat here last time," he says. "We should sit here again." His right leg pumping, he's biting his fingernails. There's so much movement, it's almost like he's exercising in place. Bob walks by, stops, places a hand on Marcelo's shoulder, and asks, "Are you okay?"

"Yeah, I'm okay," Marcelo mumbles. "But I'm pretty nervous."

"Just relax," Bob urges him, and then explains to him that he needs to keep doing well at school and he needs to abide by the regulations of electronic monitoring. It's a lecture which, in one form or another, he'll deliver each time after court. "Now mind your p's and q's," Bob will tell him. Or, "I know you're tired of hearing this from me. You're young. It's summer. But you're in school. You have a job. You can't have any violations. You've been really good this year. Keep going. Okay?" Or, simply, "No slip-ups."

The judge continues the case to a date in October, the first in a long string of delays. Marcelo groans. In the hallway outside the courtroom, he presses his forehead against the wall, slapping it with one hand, more to make a statement than anything else.

De La Salle, it turns out, won't take him back, and it appears his only option is an alternative school. "I Googled myself and my mug shot popped up," he says. "I felt horrible." He's angry. And most of that wrath points inward, at his own bad decisions. He tells me later that he has trouble trusting people, including himself. "I don't know how," he says. "My mom forgave me. Mercy forgave me. But I'm having trouble forgiving myself."

Bob tells him, "It's going to take grit to get through this."

Marcelo shrugs. "I don't even know what grit is." It's hard to tell whether he's being sarcastic or is honestly expressing what he doesn't know.

"Think about what your brother's been through," Bob says, referring to Marcelo's older brother, Elio, who has a felony conviction. "Think of the ball and chain he has around him. You're looking too short-term. Don't give up. Everyone's in your corner fighting for you. Hang in there. Please, hang in there."

"All I can do is try," Marcelo mutters before walking on ahead of us, one hand tugging at his beltless pants, careful not to put too much weight on his left leg, which still holds the bullet and which bothers him from time to time.

Claire playfully scolds him, "Your pants are a little low on your happy little ass."

Marcelo defiantly lets his pants drop to his hips, his walk turning into a slow trot, wanting to put distance between him and everyone else.

Chapter 14

Artifacts

AUGUST 16 . . . **AUGUST 17** . . . AUGUST 18 . . .

GeORGE Spivey purposefully kept his room bare. A twin bed pushed up against one wall. A dog-eared Bible resting on a bedside table. A portable color television and a radio, along with three cans of pop and a bag of potato chips, sitting atop a scratched wood desk. A white plastic chair. And a Fender bass guitar leaning against a wall. He had no desire to make this home. He wanted to do nothing to alter its impermanence. Five months earlier, George had been released from a federal prison in West Virginia after serving ten years for possession of a handgun while guarding a heroin sale. As part of his release, the authorities required him to stay six months at this halfway house run by the Salvation Army, a decaying three-story red-brick building on the city's near West Side. The constant noise, mostly men arguing and complaining in abundantly loud voices, was a vestige from their time in prison. The odor of perspiring men. The strangers. The rules. It felt less like a celebration of what could be than a reminder of what was.

George, who was thirty-nine, had put on weight in prison and was a bear of a man, the extra pounds piling around his center. He had a shaved head and a light beard and seemed preternaturally calm, almost sphinxlike. It was hard to read him, especially given his reticence. Yet while it may not have come across in his demeanor, he was determined to remake his life. He had just started an entry-level woodworking program. One of the counselors at the program told me that they were reluctant to admit George because of his limited work experience. "But," she told me, "he impressed us with something else: his character and the way he presented himself." They came to so admire his purposefulness, they later nominated him for student of the year among a national network of job reentry programs.

Though George didn't work on Saturdays, he had a pass for the day to attend his church, where he was the choir director. He awoke at 6 a.m. without an alarm; he was accustomed to getting up early from his years incarcerated. He headed downstairs for breakfast and ended up at a table of newcomers, men just out of prison. He didn't say much, as was his custom, and ate his pancakes and sausage in silence. He returned to his room, made his bed, and showered. He then hopped on a city bus to the Christian Greater Rock Baptist Church, a small storefront house of worship two miles west.

George most looked forward to the afternoon. He had planned a visit to his ex-wife and his two children, twins, a boy and a girl. When he went away to prison, they were seven. They were now eighteen. He had remained close to his son, Daquan, despite their distance, but their relationship was complicated. Early on, they had written to each other virtually every week. The letters spoke to how much Daquan missed his dad.

Dear Daddy

Hello how are you doing in there. I hope you doing alright. I miss you so much. I wish you was home I'm dying to see you home with my mom in person, but you are in that dump I only could see you on the picture or hear you on the phone. Dad don't you know I

*love you so much I want you to see how much I've grown and how
I look.*

  I MISS YOU DAD!!!

From: your son Daquan Spivey

When Daquan was eleven, he drew a likeness of Dino the Dino-
saur and wrote:

*I love you and miss you. You are the best dad that I ever know.
Kiss. Kiss. Draw me something back soon. Love you with all my
heart.*

Soon the letters had more serious inquiries. When Daquan had
problems with girls, he'd ask for guidance. When he thought of
getting his name tattooed on his arm, he asked his dad for permission. In prison George learned to play bass guitar, and occasionally he'd send home videos of his makeshift prison band. Daquan
took immense pride in the fact that he had a father in his life, even
if he wasn't accessible. But there were moments when he seemed
upset, if not resentful that on a fundamental level his father had
failed him. Daquan joined a mentoring program at his high school,
VOISE. Early on, he scolded his mentor, John Robinson: *You're
not my dad. I'm actually one of the students who has a positive male
role model in his life.* Robinson thought it unusually direct. *What
do you mean by that?* he asked. Daquan replied, *Most of these kids
don't have a dad in their life, but mine's in mine.* Robinson says there
was a boastful yet defensive quality about it. On Facebook, Daquan
once posted,

I Had To Teach Myself . . . #Self-Made

Daquan, one of his teachers told me, "carried himself differently than a lot of the kids." He was, she said, shy among teach-

ers, but very thoughtful, careful about what he said. He was like his dad in this regard. He struggled at school but held his own, and like many of the students at VOISE had plans to attend college.

Daquan, his teachers said, sometimes seemed bored, like he didn't care, but those close to him knew it was just an affectation. One teacher told me that some thought him "cold," but she said it was insecurity, not distance. Once at a dress rehearsal for a talent show, he got stage fright and tripped over the lyrics of a rap song he had written. Students heckled him, and he stormed off the stage, refusing to perform in the show. "He was usually so confident," his music teacher, Candice Davenport, told me. "And onstage you saw this little boy trapped inside this little man. He seemed so vulnerable." Daquan, Davenport said, was different from the other students. He had two piercings in his lower lip and wore large glasses that made him look unusually hip. On his Facebook page, he posted about girls and smoking weed, but he also posted pithy reflections which read almost like haikus of daily living:

Headphones In . . . Volume All The Way Up . . . I Can't Hear Shit, . . . Good Moment

Dont Push Someone Away & Then Expect Them To Still Be There When You're Ready.

Respect My Elders? Ummmm No, . . . I Respect Whoever Respects Me, Regardless Of Age

Missing Someone Is "A Part" Of Loving Them, Because When You're "Apart," . . . You Realize How Strong

When George came home from prison, he visited the school to thank Robinson for watching over his son. *I will do everything pos-*

AN AMERICAN SUMMER **207**

sible to make sure he doesn't make the mistakes I made, George told Robinson. Daquan refused to visit his dad at the halfway house because, he said, it felt too much like prison. George felt the distance, the tentativeness. He got on Daquan, wanted to know if he was in a gang. *I'm gonna whip you if I find out,* George told him at one point. *I'm too old to get whupped,* Daquan shot back. Daquan in fact didn't belong to a gang, but George worried nonetheless. George told Daquan he needed to remove his piercings. Daquan refused. They were cautiously circling each other, trying to figure each other out.

After choir practice at his church, George still had a few hours before he needed to be back at the halfway house, so he caught a bus to his ex-wife's house, where there was a neighborhood party. Daquan had been after him to come by, and so he was excited to go. In shorts and a button-up shirt, George hung out in the backyard, where his ex-wife's family was barbecuing. Daquan popped in periodically, one time cajoling his dad to play him one-on-one in basketball. *Come on, old man,* Daquan urged. *Think you can beat me?* George laughed, and told him another time. *You scared? Too old?* Daquan shot back. Daquan disappeared with one of his best friends, Lomeck Johnson, and returned an hour later and sank into a couch near the kitchen. He asked his dad to fix him something to eat. *Who you talking to?* George replied lightheartedly.

I'm talking to you, Pops. Fix me up a plate.

You better get up and fix it yourself, George told him.

Daquan got up, and his dad smiled. *This feels good,* George thought to himself. *It feels, well, normal.*

Daquan ate a plate of ribs and spaghetti, and as he prepared to leave, he took the red-and-white Chicago Bulls cap off his head and handed it to his dad. *Matches your shoes,* he said. George smiled. His son was paying more attention than he thought. Then Daquan and Lomeck hopped on their bikes to pedal to a neighborhood street festival nearby. George left as well, since he needed to return by his six o'clock curfew. When he got back to the Salvation Army, he placed his son's Bulls cap on his dresser, washed up, and wandered the halls for a while, catching up with some of the others there. Tired from the day, he was in bed by nine.

A couple of hours later, he was awoken by his cell phone. It was his daughter, Daquanta. She seemed out of breath. Something about Daquan.

He's lying there, not moving, she said, her voice becoming slurred by her hysteria.

What do you mean, he's just lying there?

He won't move.

George got out of bed, and with his daughter still on the phone, he found one of the officers in the hallway and told her he needed to find out what was going on, what had happened to his son. And then his daughter told him, *Daquan's been shot.* George, ordinarily restrained, started crying. A guard gave him a hug. Another man on probation put his arm on George's shoulder and walked him up and down the hallway, trying to help him catch his breath. Word came down that he could leave for a few hours, more if it was needed, and so he called a friend, a fellow student at the trade school, who picked him up and drove him to the West Side.

There, on a street of three-story apartment buildings and single-family homes, the police had blocked off the alley with yellow tape strung from utility pole to utility pole, a sight so familiar in parts of Chicago that there are times you can see pieces of yellow tape fluttering from a phone pole like remnants of party decorations. When George got there, people were milling about, the shrill wails of women piercing the summer night. A detective told him that his son had been shot by two guys who rode up on bicycles, asking his son and his friend who they were with, meaning what gang did they belong to. They apparently mistook Daquan and his friend for rival gang members. Daquan's friend was shot in the side but lived. George remembers so little of those hours, as the body of his son, covered by a white sheet, his sneakers peeking out, lay in the alley. He alternately pleaded with the police to let him see his son and to have his son's body removed. The body lay out there for five hours, so long it made the newspapers. The police said they were just following procedure. But to George and others it felt disrespectful. Who leaves a dead boy lying in an alley through the night? (Pete Nickeas, the *Chicago Tribune* reporter, happened to be there that night and told me, "They didn't need to keep that body out. It wasn't right.") At 4 a.m. the police let George and his ex-wife under the yellow tape to visit their son's body, and as George walked down the alley the police pulled the sheet back. George was disoriented, and he hollered at his son, *Stop playing. Get up.*

A couple of hours later, in the early-morning light, George sat on the front stoop of a nearby home, dressed in a red, button-up shirt with an American flag sewn on the front pocket, a *Chicago Tribune* reporter filming him. He seemed neither sad nor tired. He seemed wistful, his voice, as usual, quiet and soothing, like a slow jazz number. "I guess some guys rode up on a bike and started shooting at him. I mean, I really don't know why. I don't understand," he told the reporter, beginning a ritual practiced after most shootings: looking to make sense of what just happened—and then defending the honor of the deceased. "My son wasn't involved in any kind of gang activity or anything of that nature," he told the reporter, in an effort to offset what he knows everyone's thinking: *Your son did something to deserve this.* He continued, "To tell you the truth, he was a pretty likable kid. He got good grades in school. He loved basketball, made music. He loved to rap. He worked. He was planning to go to college. He didn't cause any kind of problems."

Before George headed back to the halfway house, another reporter, from *DNAInfo,* a news website, asked him about his son, and George recounted what he said was his fondest memory of Daquan: when he was seven, he sat at the kitchen table reading a newspaper. "I asked him what he was doing, and he said, 'I'm looking for a job,'" George told the reporter. "I said, 'But you're only

seven.' And he said, 'Someone has to take care of you and Mom.'"
What George didn't tell the reporter is this: this memory of his son,
his fondest, occurred right before he went to prison. "A part of me
has been taken away. Stolen," George told the reporter. "For what?
Because you thought he was someone else." The *you* referred to the
shooter, but in some ways, though George didn't say this—he didn't
have to—*you* could be referencing all of us. *My son,* he was trying to
say, *wasn't who you think he was.*

I n the following months, once George got out of the halfway
house, he worked as a cabinetmaker and spent the evenings by himself, drinking, Crown Royal and Hennessy. He put on
more weight. He lived with his grandmother. He rarely went out.
And then he logged on to a dating site, PlentyOfFish, and went on
a date with a young woman, Chrishion Spriggs. They had dinner at
MacArthur's, the soul-food restaurant on the West Side, and then
rode the Madison Street bus downtown and back, lost in conversation. It felt good. He didn't talk much about Daquan, but he did tell
her that he had had a son who'd been killed. On the next date, when
George came by her house, he showed her pictures of Daquan on his
iPhone and shared with her the *Chicago Tribune*'s video interview
of him, which had been posted online. George seemed so proud of
him, she would tell me later, and regretful that they never had a
chance to fully repair what had been broken. He found videos of
Daquan dancing and would play them for Chrishion. She admired
George's reticence but could also be frustrated by it. She had never
dated anyone who had had someone close to them murdered, and
wanted to know more so she could console him. "When he talks,
just let him talk," she told me, "because you might not have that
opportunity again." He struggled with what to tell people when
they asked if he had children. She told him to be honest, and so he
would say, "I have twins, but my son is deceased."

When they moved in together, in an apartment in a near West suburb, George placed his Chicago Bulls cap on the top shelf of their closet. He explained to Chrishion that Daquan had given this to him on the day he was killed. He wasn't letting go of it. He had had it dry-cleaned and kept it in the clear plastic. Sometimes George sits on their beige living room couch, flipping through Daquan's Facebook page, which is still live and which his friends still post to.

> I miss you so much bro. On everything, it annoys me it's been soo long, like I'm making this shit up bro. This ain't no dream man, why you had to leave me? We were never apart, I ain't gone get another you. Everything I love bro, I'm hurting. I love you man. Lamark Gray

> Remember dat day we got suspended for arguing about pouring milk on me . . . We wasn't even gone fight . . . I just know wasn't no milk touching me lol Tarik Taylor

> Heyyy I jus wanted to say miss yu nd happy thanksgiving I wish yu was here to see all ur friends cause we have all grown up and family Makayla Jackson

> In my dream, you was laying right next to me ☹, only for me to wake up and realize its my pillow Priesha

> I don't want to be on Facebook bro ☺ 💯 but I ain't got nobody else to talk to. Come back . . . Where can we meet? Lamark Gray

The day is like an itch. George scratches and scratches at it, and at times it seems to work. It goes away. He forgets about it. And then it's back again. One time I sat with George in his apartment's living room, on the couch, dirty clothes piled in a corner, his DJ's turntable on a high table, and as we spoke he seemed distracted, as if he had just remembered an appointment. "Everything okay?" I asked. He seemed startled. He nodded. "I hate talking about this," he said. That was a half-truth. I hadn't seen George in several months, and he had emailed to check in, to ask if we could get together again. This is grief. You feel ripped in half. Half of you wanting to retreat, to disappear, to find a place where no one asks questions. And then there's the part of you that wants to remember, has to remember because if you don't, not only will the day cease to exist but so will the reality of that moment. And if that happens, you start to think the person is still there, in the next room, down the street, at school, in the park, somewhere near enough that you start thinking about what might have been. George wonders if he and Daquan would've gone fishing together. If Daquan would've gone crazy over his Chevy Malibu with its twelve speakers. If Daquan and he would've played music together.

George told me that after Daquan was killed and after he got out of the halfway house, he sought out Daquan's friends. "They told me Daquan was so glad I was home," he said. George then got up and told me he had somewhere to be.

Chapter 15

I Ain't Going Nowhere, part two

AUGUST 20 . . . AUGUST 21 . . . **AUGUST 22** . . .

Dressed in loose-fitting gray sweatpants and sweat-shirt, Anita Stewart, the Harper High School social worker, pulls up in front of Thomas's house midafternoon. The mechanical lift in front and the NO TRESPASSING sign affixed to the beige siding mark the location. Earlier in the summer she had learned that because of budget cuts at the Chicago public schools, she wouldn't be returning to Harper. The school would have to make do with one social worker. She hadn't broken the news to Thomas yet. She told me that she worried how he'd respond, but in truth I think she was also worried how she'd hold up, worried that she might break down.

Thomas's mother, who floats in and out of his life, stands on the front porch, her arms across her chest to keep warm in the unseasonably chilly air. Anita explains why she's there. "It's going to break his heart," Thomas's mother muses. "You've come a long way with him." Anita smiles. It feels good that Thomas's mother appreciates her efforts. The front door opens and Thomas emerges, dressed in an oversized sweatshirt that reads "Lincoln U Township," his long hair pulled back into a ponytail. He seems groggy, as if he's recently awoken, though he has actually just returned from a day of summer school classes.

"What's up, Thomas? You didn't get none of my texts? Did you finish your Spanish class? Where's your paper?" Anita can't help herself. She's on him from the get-go, desperately wanting to see him graduate.

"I don't know what I did with it," Thomas says, not so much apologizing as matter-of-factly explaining the situation.

"You don't know what you did with it? You got to keep it. That's proof you took it. What you been doing?"

"Nothing," Thomas replies, as he picks at his fingernails.

"So what do you think this year's going to look like, Thomas?" Anita asks, trying to ease into the news. She has a habit of invoking his name when she wants his attention. "You remember, Thomas, when they were talking about all those budget cuts and not having the money for certain positions?"

"Yeah."

"They didn't have the money to fund my position. So when you step in there, there won't be a bunch of old faces. I won't be there." Thomas pulls the sleeves of his sweatshirt over his hands. "But Crystal will."

"Y'all got to find new jobs?" For all of Thomas's frostiness, he can be empathetic. Anita thinks to herself, *Here I am worried about him—and he's worried about me.*

"I found a new job, at an elementary school. What exactly does that mean for you? That doesn't mean you're not going to be going to class. That doesn't mean you won't graduate. I'll be over there to see you. It means you go to school and do what you got to do to get out. It means you got to listen to whoever the social worker is. Thomas?"

"Yeah." Thomas pulls his sweatshirt up over the bottom half of his face. He's finding distance, drifting, like flotsam at sea. Anita senses it and tries to pull him back in.

"You think you could find that paper for me?"

Thomas shakes his head. "I got a C."

"You got to find that paper."

Thomas has a knack of changing direction to deflect what he perceives as disapproval, and so he quickly shifts the conversation to a subject that will undoubtedly elicit sympathy from Anita, about the boy who allegedly shot and killed Shakaki. It's been on his mind because of the pressure being applied on him to testify.

"We was looking Monkey Man up online. They shipped him to County," he said, referring to the jail.

"I don't think he likes to be called Monkey Man," Anita says.

"That's his name," Thomas asserts.

A scraggly middle-aged man with an unkempt beard and jeans hanging off his hips staggers down the middle of the street, talking to himself, and he notices Thomas on the porch. "What's up?" he hollers, giving Thomas a thumbs-up before returning to the conversation he was having with himself.

"I like that," Anita says to Thomas. "He says 'What's up?' and then gets back to talking to his own people. I think that's pretty good." She gets a laugh out of Thomas. She tells him to keep texting, that just because she isn't at Harper anymore doesn't mean she won't be around. Thomas is disappearing into his sweatshirt. He looks either deeply sad or lost, or both.

"How come they didn't have me testify when Nugget got killed?" he asks by way of wondering why he needs to testify in the trial of Shakaki's assailant. "What if I tell 'em I don't remember anything?"

"You afraid?" Anita asks.

"No. I don't want to sit on the stand and tell them everything. It's snitching. You can get killed for that. I ain't scared. It's just like that."

Anita can feel him slipping away, not necessarily in this moment, but she sees it coming. She tells him how he owes it to Shakaki to appear at the trial. It seems only right. She was his best friend. Justice of any kind feels so ephemeral in Englewood, and this feels like a moment that you can actually grab on to it, a moment when things can be made right, that Thomas can be made right. But Anita knows. And Thomas knows. As Anita later told me, "You need to be honest—Thomas is afraid. I understand that."

Afterward, in her car, she starts to cry. She tells me that she can tell it's hard on Thomas, knowing she won't be around this coming year. "If I had known this was going to happen, I would've never gone to Harper," she tells me. "It's like I'm giving up on them. It's so unfair to him." She pauses to wipe her cheeks and drives down the narrow one-way street: past the two-story home where Shakaki was shot, the downstairs windows covered by sheets of warping plywood; past the sidewalk along a waist-high fence where Dwayne "Duck" Duckworth had been shot so many times—thirteen—it took hours for neighbors to scrub the blood from the pavement; past the home where Nugget was killed at her birthday party by a bullet piercing the large front window, shot by a young man who at the age of thirteen had himself been caught in crossfire and shot in his leg; and past a shuttered home on which someone has scrawled "Fuck 7-0." Some, Anita tells me, call this "the block of death."

Ur child is in jail. Anita received this text from Thomas's sister, Stella.

As the trial of Monkey Man—his real name is Antuan Joiner—approached, Thomas became more and more skittish. At one point, the prosecutor on the case asked Shakaki's mother if she felt she might need protection or if she wanted to move. Thomas was in the room at the time, and after he returned from the courthouse, he told Anita, *Miss Stewart, they was asking the wrong person.* He worried that he might be the one targeted, not Shakaki's family. Thomas received a subpoena to appear in court, but he refused to comply, and as a result the judge ruled him in contempt, sending him to the county jail, a place he'd never been. He was miserable. He kept to himself. He would've called Anita, but he hadn't memorized her phone number. After a week locked up, he promised he'd appear at the trial, and so he was released on house arrest. When he arrived home, he learned that a few days earlier someone had driven by and shot up his house, a bullet piercing his grandmother's bedroom window. The bullet hole was still in the wall. He called Anita, who told him, *You need to be in protective custody.*

The case dragged on; the trial was postponed several times. In June 2014, Thomas graduated from high school in a ceremony at Trinity Church, and Anita and Crystal cheered and yelled, "Hey, Big Baby!" as he received his diploma. The school also awarded an honorary diploma to Shakaki and one other slain student, a not uncommon occurrence at Chicago public school graduations. The next day Anita texted Thomas: *I am so proud of you! You are really growing into a responsible young man. I love you very much and I am still in charge.* ? ☺ Anita also celebrated the graduation of her oldest daughter, who was awarded a full scholarship to Carleton College. (Her two youngest, twins, would end up at the University of Wisconsin Madison and at the University of Michigan.)

Anita called me one day, noticeably upset, trying to keep from crying. She told me that the week before, as Thomas was walking home from Harper after picking up his transcript, he had noticed a figure furtively moving alongside his house. Thomas was crossing a vacant lot across the street when the figure emerged and shot at him. Thomas changed direction and kept low, making himself small, sprinting to the alley. Nine shots. Fortunately, they all missed. "It's heartbreaking," Anita said. "How can this be happening in America?"

When the trial finally commenced, Thomas told Anita his plan was simple: he'd attend, but to all questions he would reply that he didn't remember. He didn't want to testify. When he arrived at the courthouse, he was told to go upstairs and wait in a small room along with Shakaki's mother, Kim Shumake, until they called for him. Earlier he had told the prosecutor, his voice gruff and pointed, *They're still shooting at us.* The prosecutor, Don Lyman, told me Thomas was so agitated that morning that he couldn't have a conversation with him. Thomas told a victim's advocate, *I don't want to be here. This is bullshit.* As he waited in that room with Shakaki's mother, he began to soften. Kim Shumake was alternately crying and trying to hold herself together. Earlier she had relayed a message through Thomas's mother. *Tell him,* Kim said, *how are you a gangster outside and then you're afraid to come testify?* Thomas became unsettled and discomforted by her deep, penetrating sobs as she awaited the trial, and as he sat there, hiding behind his dreads, he told himself that Shakaki had been there for him, so he'd be there for Shakaki.

It was a bench trial, and Judge Vincent Gaughan had a reputation for his no-nonsense gruffness. As we waited for the trial to begin, an older woman stood up in the back of the courtroom, waving at her son, whom she spotted through an open door near the judge's bench. Gaughan called her up, admonished her for interrupting proceedings, and held her in contempt, ordering a deputy sheriff to take her into custody. He then heard the charges against a woman who'd been arrested by undercover officers for selling loose cigarettes. The judge shook his head at the pettiness of the crime and told the prosecutor to pass a message on to the police: "They need to get a life."

Antuan Joiner, or Monkey Man, sat next to his attorney behind a long table. Dark-skinned, he wore his short hair tightly braided and had a small goatee. His expression stoic, he spent much of the trial taking notes on a legal pad. What was most noticeable was his age; he looked like a boy. He was sixteen at the time of the shooting. The case was not a slam-dunk for the prosecution, even if they could get Thomas to testify. Shortly after the shooting, a block away, in the basement of an abandoned house, police recovered a 9mm handgun resting atop a gray hoodie, along with a baseball cap. The police sampled all three objects for DNA, and none of the DNA matched Joiner's. Moreover, Joiner had no record. Leon, Thomas's brother, who was twenty-one at the time, testified that he recognized the shooter as Joiner, but his remarks were so inaudible that at one point the judge admonished the prosecutor that if Leon didn't speak up, he wouldn't admit his testimony as evidence. Moreover, Joiner's attorney, Tony Thedford, in his cross-examination suggested that Leon was gang-affiliated (which Leon didn't completely deny), in an effort to impeach his testimony.

Thomas was called as the second witness. Anita had planned to attend the trial, but she had gotten the days wrong and so wasn't able to get the day off from her new job working at an elementary school. When Thomas entered the witness box, wearing a black nylon jacket and jeans, he slouched into the high-backed chair, his dreads falling in front of his face. It was as if he were trying to make himself invisible. "Young man, sit up straight," the judge admonished him. I thought to myself, *He so doesn't want to be here. Even if he tries, he's not going to be believed.* But as Thomas recounted that evening, he prefaced all his responses with a "yes, sir" or "no, sir." He appeared to sit straighter and taller, his tone uncharacteristically direct and firm. It was as if someone had hit a switch, as if he knew that if he was to be believed, he needed to project an air of self-confidence and calm. He recounted the evening. Shakaki, he said, sat on the porch railing, her legs swinging over the side, while he sat on the front steps and his brother on the front lawn. He volunteered, "We was smoking." And then, he explained, this boy with a hood tied over his head ran out of the gangway. "He started firing a gun," Thomas said, his voice even and matter-of-fact. "Toward Shakaki first . . . It was a lot of times. Then he started shooting at me. I started scooting back to the door . . . and then I jumped off the porch and ran straight across to the lot." He explained that once the shooter had run away, Thomas returned, and as he sat with

Shakaki on the porch, she moaned, *It burns. It burns.* Thomas said he recognized the shooter as someone he knew from the neighborhood. "Monkey Man," he said.

On cross-examination, Thedford, Joiner's attorney, on a hunch asked Thomas whether he'd been smoking cigarettes or marijuana. Unfazed, Thomas told him that he and his brother had been smoking marijuana. He also confirmed that it had taken two days for him to identify Joiner to the police, and conceded that he did so only because the police sought him out. "You knew this girl your whole life and you probably heard the last words she uttered and you didn't go to the police?" Thedford asked in disbelief. Thomas replied simply, "That's right." It was, for Thomas, a remarkably even-keeled performance. He never lost his cool, never seemed uncooperative.

In the hallway later, visibly relieved, he told me, "I'm glad it's over with. It was like they needed me there. Miss Stewart, she's gonna be happy to know."

In his closing arguments, the prosecutor, Don Lyman, made clear how proud he was of Thomas's appearance. "You saw Thomas," he said, "and you saw how he rebutted this [defense] counsel." Lyman went on to emphasize how Thomas remembered small details. "Thomas," he continued, "did a great job testifying in this case. He was confident. He was certain . . . the certainty that this is the person he saw." Antuan Joiner was convicted and sentenced to seventy-one years—though his attorney, Tony Thedford, is convinced that Thomas and his brother identified the wrong person. Joiner, who claims he wasn't the shooter, is appealing his conviction.

After the trial, Shakaki's mom thanked Thomas. *I'd been angry at you because you were letting Shakaki down,* she told him. *But I appreciate you stepping up.* She asked if Thomas needed anything, but he told her, I *don't need anything for doing that. She was my friend.* Shakaki's father wanted to pick him and Leon up to take them out for dinner, but Thomas told him that it was too dangerous for him to come around his block. Shakaki's mom sighed when she heard this. "It's like Russian roulette every time they walk out the door," she told me.

S hortly afterward, Thomas, with Anita's help, moved to St. Louis, where he moved in with a cousin and her boyfriend. There he found a job cleaning offices, and every now and then he called or texted to let me know he was doing well. He and Anita talked or texted every day. "I'd say, isn't it nice to be in a peaceful environment?" Anita told me. "You can just walk down the street without looking every which way. He would say he was bored, but he got to a place where he was happy. He was safe." But after a year the boyfriend told Thomas's cousin he no longer wanted Thomas living there, so Thomas returned to Chicago.

Thomas is back living with his grandmother at the house with the blowing blue tarp on 70th Place, the block where death whispers at you, nags at you, dances about, before swooping down and interrupting the living. Anita doesn't visit as often as she used to, and when she does she won't tell her husband, because he worries that death will seek her out, too. Thomas doesn't hang on the porch like he used to, and when we go out for lunch he insists that it not be a restaurant in the neighborhood, and at the restaurant he insists on sitting away from the window. He often talks of when he was younger, of building a robot in grade school and how he thought he wanted to be an engineer. Or the dollhouse he built in his sophomore year, or almost built. He never got to putting the roof on, because his carpentry teacher suddenly left the school. He talks about having flashbacks, moments when he can't get certain images out of his head. Nugget lying on the living room floor, her left eye wandering as if she was looking for someone to help her. Duck on the stretcher, a cigarette dangling from his lips. Shakaki lying on the porch, telling Thomas, *It burns. It burns.* He tells me he's lost much of his taste. Sometimes he goes a day or two without eating. He says he's lost twenty pounds.

One afternoon, while he was sitting on the porch of a friend on another block in the neighborhood, someone walked up and started shooting at him and his two friends. The young woman with him was shot in the face. She survived. Thomas had a bullet enter his back and another graze his side, along his right hip. He called Anita from the porch, even before the ambulance arrived, but she didn't pick up. When she learned what had happened, she rushed to the hospital and embraced Thomas as he lay in his hospital bed, still wearing a bloodied white T-shirt. Thomas told Anita that the police were convinced that he had shot himself because of the trajectory of the bullet, from back to front, along the hip. *That's stupid,* Thomas told Anita. *Miss Stewart, I kept trying to tell them, I didn't shoot myself.* Anita bent down and gave him another hug. *I'm just glad you're okay.*

When I was writing this story, I went back through the notes which I had accumulated over the course of four years. I feel sheepish admitting this, but I wasn't fully paying attention to all that Thomas was telling me. I started to make a list. Shakaki's cousin, Kywante Shumake, shot two times on Thomas's block. Thomas's friend Tim, who held two jobs, invited Thomas to come by to celebrate his birthday; Thomas went to the corner liquor store to buy Tim a bottle of Hennessy, and when he returned found Tim lying beside his house in a pool of blood, a fatal bullet wound in the back of his head. While Thomas was in jail on the contempt charge, Antonio Clark, a friend and fellow Harper High graduate, died, an apparent victim of the accidental discharge of a pistol. His friend who's a rap artist and goes by the moniker Skully TV was shot six times, including in both eyes; he lost his sight. Thomas's friend's older brother, Vido: killed. Thomas's friend Nukey: shot and killed by a fourteen-year-old boy. Thomas had indeed mentioned each of these incidents to me, but the casualness of his remarks belied what he was telling me. The shootings, the killings, accrue like so many teardrops. Nobody's keeping count. Not even Thomas. He just tells me he's tired, that he's stopped going to funerals.

"You can't cry about it," he tells Anita and me one day over lunch at Ms. Biscuit, a soul-food restaurant a few miles east of Thomas's home. "I've seen people go crazy because of all the violence they seen. People lose their mind. They don't care 'bout nothing. But I'm stronger than that. I ain't gonna let it break me down. I don't let that stuff get to me. I think about it, but I don't let it get to me." He pauses. "I be thinking about a lot of crazy stuff, about revenge." He's talking more than usual, and neither Anita or I want to interrupt. And then, as an afterthought, almost to convince himself, he assures us, "It's not gonna happen overnight, but it's gonna get better."

Chapter 16

This Is What He Remembers

AUGUST 23 . . . **AUGUST 24** . . . AUGUST 25 . . .

Quinntellbua Benson asked me to arrange the meeting with Calvin Cross's mother. It troubled him that he had been there when Calvin had been killed. He didn't know Calvin. He wasn't even from the neighborhood; he'd been visiting his sister. But he can't get the evening out of his head. He remembers it so clearly: When he heard the gunshots, he threw himself on the sidewalk, flattened out, low to the ground, not moving. From his time in the military, because of the rhythm of the reports, he could tell it was a semiautomatic weapon. Ten. Fifteen. Twenty rounds. He lost count. With such a large magazine, he thought, it must be an assault rifle. He heard a bullet hit metal. *My truck,* he figured. All he knew was to stay down, pancaked, as if he and the sidewalk were one. But over his left shoulder, out of the corner of his eye, he could see a boy in shorts and a black T-shirt sprinting across the street toward a church, a squat red-brick building. *Safety,* Benson thought. But then the realization. *Not now.* Not at ten at night. He could make out the locked gate pulled across the church's front door. And so the boy ran north of the church into the thick brush of a vacant lot, out of sight, his pursuers running, too, one with the assault rifle, the other with a semiautomatic pistol, the rounds just coming and coming.

Benson, a forty-eight-year-old former long-haul truck driver who had returned to school to become a computer specialist, holds things tight, but he did tell me that he thinks of that night a lot. Too much, he said. He wanted to tell Calvin's mother all that he knew, tell her what he saw, what he heard. He wanted to explain why he didn't talk to the police. He wanted to make it right. He wanted to get it out of his head. Maybe meeting with the family would be a move in that direction. Could I make it happen? he asked. When I mentioned it to Calvin's mother, Dana Cross, she immediately said yes, and so we found a Saturday afternoon that worked for everyone.

B enson, as he likes to be called, arrived on time. He has a shaved head and wears a small gold loop earring in his left ear. He's trim and fit and still has the erect bearing from the time he served in the Army's 82nd Airborne. He was dressed in jeans and a gray henley which had a food stain he clearly hadn't noticed. He wore a Chicago Cubs hat, backward. Although Benson can seem aloof, if not distant (though I wonder if it's simply a general suspicion of strangers), he greeted Dana warmly. "It's so nice to meet you," he told her. "Please, just call me Q or Benson." Dana introduced him to the youngest of her two daughters, Senetra, who's twenty-four and a manager of a local restaurant. Where Dana is restrained, Senetra is direct, saying what comes to mind. Where Dana dresses in grays and browns, Senetra wears large, floppy, colorful hats. She dresses to be noticed. They made small talk, mostly about the weather. Benson folded his arms across his chest. He wanted to get to why he was there. "I'm sure there are questions you want to ask me," he told mother and daughter.

Dana directed him to the kitchen table, on which sat a jar of cookies and an elephant-shaped ceramic bowl for sugar, and asked if he wanted anything to drink. Water would be fine, he said. This ranch home didn't belong to Dana. She had been hired to care for her pastor's eighty-nine-year-old father, who has dementia, and so Dana lived here, trying to keep him and the home in order. Before Calvin had been killed, she worked at a day-care center where she'd been for fifteen years. But afterward she found she couldn't concentrate—the kids got on her already highly taut nerves—and so two months after his death she quit.

Dana, who's forty-seven, is sturdily built and missing two front teeth, which I suspect leads many to underestimate her will and her thoughtfulness. She's been through a lot. When she was six-teen, she became addicted to crack cocaine. Six years later, when she had her second child and started attending church, she quit, on her own. She hasn't touched cocaine or any drug since. She went on to have three more children: two girls and then Calvin, the young-est. Their father disappeared from their lives, and so Dana raised them herself. To some she seemed restless, but she moved regu-larly because she worried about her two sons; it was like search-ing for the perfect wave, searching for the perfect place where she could feel assured that her sons were safe.

Benson told Dana and her daughter that he had been visiting his sister, to loan her $200. She lived at the northeast corner of Wal-lace Avenue, where it intersects with 124th Street. The neighbor-hood, West Pullman, has been beaten down over the years, with the loss of the steel mills and a Sherwin-Williams paint factory, but it's holding on, knowing that with each foreclosed home, with each overgrown vacant lot, with each street robbery, it teeters like a cat on a ledge fearful of falling. As if to fight back, people take great care of their homes and post signs of hopeful thinking, including one hand-painted in three different colors along a wood fence which reads: US AS PEOPLE NEED TO BELIEVE THAT IF WE

STAND TOGETHER THAT SHOOTING CAN AND WILL STOP. On the night when the shooting began, twenty-one different neighbors called 911 to report multiple shots fired. They cared. They wanted the police to protect them. They were doing what neighbors do.

On the eastern side of this narrow, tree-lined street, along with Benson's sister's brick house, is a row of tightly packed single-family homes, most of them wood-framed, some with small vegetable gardens. Across the street, on the western side, sits the Spiral Temple of Truth church. It looks tired, a tarp covering one corner, where the roof is damaged. The city has a propensity to name streets after famous and not-so-famous Chicagoans, and this street has been given the honorific title Rev. Gladys P. Harrell Street, named after the founder of the church and mother of the current pastor. A chain-link fence runs along the back of the church, separating it from a paved bike path which extends three miles north and three miles south. On the other side of the bike path is an eyesore, precisely what neighbors worry about: four abandoned three-story apartment buildings, the windows covered with sheets of plywood, the courtyards littered with broken beer and cognac bottles. Adjacent to the church, just to the north, is an empty lot, which at the time of Calvin's death was overgrown with weeds, so high and so thick that it had the feel of a tropical forest.

Taking a sip of water, Benson began at the *end* of that evening. It just occurred to him, he told Dana, that he remembered seeing her minutes after the shooting. She lived around the corner, heard the shots, and so drove her purple van to the scene. There, Benson recalled, he saw her get out, dressed in a full-length housedress, clearly panicked. He remembered her asking the police something, and while he couldn't quite hear her question ("What was he wearing?" she had inquired, wanting to know if the victim was her son), he clearly heard the officer's response, a bellowing *Move! Get this car out of here! Get this damn van out of the street! Move on!* Benson remembered the officer had his pistol unholstered and was gripping it in his hand. He told Dana that he remembered she looked scared, and that she got back in the van and quickly turned around and took off. Dana nodded. *Whooo.* She let out a breath, like she had been holding it in all this time. "That's just how it happened," she told him. She thought to herself, *He really was there.* At this point, before Benson told her everything he had seen, she knew she could trust him.

Benson sensed that, and visibly relaxed. He removed his Cubs cap, placed it on the table, and leaned back in his chair, his arms still folded across his chest. Dana told him, "I appreciate you coming forward. I want these policemens off the street."

"I want them dead," Benson proclaimed, the words seemingly at odds with his unemotional tone. He can seem restrained at times, like he's holding on to a lot. Dana saw that. "I don't know how they live with themselves," she told him. "They don't have no heart." Benson offered an almost imperceptible nod of agreement.

Benson has his own history with the police. He lost both his parents by the time he was twelve, and he was subsequently shuffled from one older sister to another. His mother had been a preacher, and he regularly attended church with her, but in his teens he became a part of the Black P Stones, a gang on the South Side. He doesn't like to talk about it—"That's a part of a chapter that's closed"—except to say he saw a lot, too much, really, and that some of it involved untoward run-ins with the police.

"Ask me questions," he directed Dana. "Anything." Senetra interrupted and asked if it would be okay if she filmed him with her smartphone. She said she wanted to put this on Facebook for others to see. Benson consented, and so she filmed the exchange, her elbows planted on the table so they formed a makeshift tripod. She framed him so that you can see the jar of cookies in front of him, and on the wall behind him two flyswatters hanging from elaborate hooks resembling sunflowers.

Senetra asked the first question, really the only question, the one both she and her mother had wanted answered: "I just want to know, what did you see on the night my brother was killed?"

Benson seemed unfazed by being filmed, took a breath, and continued. "What I saw," he explained, "I was standing in front of my sister's house and we was talking through the gate." At the front of his sister's home she had erected a seven-foot-high iron gate, which she kept locked. Along the south side of the home she had erected a wood fence made of slats, which had enough space between them that you could make out movement on the sidewalk.

"I heard your brother and his friend walking down the street, having a nice conversation, just laughing and joking," Benson told Senetra. "I don't know what they was talking about, but they was laughing."

Dana already knew that on this night, May 31, 2011, her son Calvin, who had just turned nineteen, and his friend Ryan Cornell had left her house to meet some girls at a nearby bus stop. They were planning to walk the girls back to the house. Calvin and Ryan had met in the Job Corps in southern Illinois, and when Calvin returned to Chicago he convinced his mother to let Ryan stay with them, since he came from a fractured family. Calvin was like a big brother to Ryan. When Calvin got a job during tax season, he helped Ryan get one, too. The two were hired to dress up as the Statue of Liberty and hand out flyers for a local tax-filing service. At home, Dana ran a tight ship. She insisted that her children attend church with her, and so Calvin was a member of the choir. The church's pastor, a Chicago firefighter, was his godfather. Most of Calvin's friends were from church. The only time Calvin got into trouble with the police—at fifteen, he got picked up for violating curfew—Dana had him sit in the police station for three hours before picking him up. She wanted to teach him a lesson. Calvin was a playful kid, and so Dana wasn't surprised to hear from Benson that he and Ryan were joking and laughing as they walked to the bus stop that night, just a few blocks away from her home.

"Next thing I know, I saw a spotlight flash through the fence." Benson paused before continuing. "I heard a car. And before the car stopped moving, shots rang out, and when they rang out, I took one or two steps back and I dove on the concrete, on the sidewalk." His sister, he said, ran into her house. "I looked over my left shoulder. I saw Calvin run and I saw two police officers run after him, going across the street, never coming down the sidewalk. And I mean I heard so many shots I wouldn't move until they stopped shooting."

Indeed, on those twenty-one 911 calls, as neighbors spoke to the dispatcher, the shooting continued in the background. There were so many shots that some callers tried to count them for the dispatcher. One woman simply declared, "They're shooting like crazy."

According to the police, the city's Law Department and the Independent Review Authority, a civilian agency established in 2007 to examine police shootings and alleged police misconduct, here's how events unfolded that night: Three police officers riding in a marked squad car came upon Calvin and Ryan walking on the sidewalk, just along the wood fence by Benson's sister's house. All three officers were a part of the department's Mobile Strike Force Unit, which was deployed to high-crime areas, and so they were dressed in all-black uniforms. The officer in the backseat, Macario Chavez, had a military-grade assault rifle strapped to his chest. The officers said they saw Calvin fidget with something in his waistband, leading them to believe he may have had either drugs or a gun, and so they pulled to the curb, illuminated the two with a spotlight, and ordered Calvin and Ryan to freeze. One of the officers yelled at them, "Show me your hands." Ryan, who had been stopped by the police before, remained in place and raised his hands in the air. Calvin ran. Two of the officers told investigators and later recounted in depositions that as Calvin fled, he pulled a revolver from his cargo shorts and from over his shoulder shot at them. In a deposition, one officer testified that Calvin shot "more than three times." Another recalled that "as I got closer to him, I saw Calvin Cross reach into his front waistband and he began to fire his gun . . . toward my direction and in my partners' direction." One testified to seeing the muzzle flashes. The officers continued shooting as they chased Calvin around the corner and across the street, behind the church, and then into the high brush in the adjacent lot. Altogether the three police officers fired forty-five rounds of ammunition. Officer Chavez fired the full twenty-eight rounds from his rifle, and then shifted to his Beretta pistol when they found Calvin lying in the bushes.

Benson continued his story. He told Senetra and Dana that once the gunfire subsided, he got up, cautiously, and had his sister unlock her front gate so he could take refuge in her house. A few minutes later he poked his head out the front door to see what had happened to the boy in the brush across the street. He couldn't make out anything, so he walked to the sidewalk and continued past where he'd been lying down. There, he told them, "I stepped over a pistol."

Senetra leaned in with her phone. She couldn't help herself. She knew what was coming. "When you seen that gun on the ground, you knew that that wasn't my brother's." It was less a question than a statement. "My brother did not have a gun."

Benson felt reasonably certain that he knew that, too. The gun on the sidewalk lay in the spot where he had taken cover, where he had lain on the ground. He was perplexed, because Calvin Cross never ran anywhere close to him. He couldn't understand how the gun got there. "Yes, I knew," he told Senetra, "because your brother never ran past me. He ran directly across the street, behind the church." Benson went on to explain that as he stood there, "This white police officer, he didn't say nothing to me, didn't say 'go back into the house' or 'get on the sidewalk'—he just went straight to the gun, shined a spotlight on it . . . And then started asking me questions. Did I see anything? And then he said, 'You know, there's people going around here shooting and killing people.'" In Benson's mind, the officer was already trying to justify what had taken place.

The recovered gun, it turned out, was a Smith & Wesson revolver, so old and clogged with "dirt and grime," according to a state police examination, that it was inoperable. Nearly a hundred years old, it had been manufactured in 1919. Moreover, all six bullets were still in the chamber. Investigators found no gun residue on Calvin's hands and no fingerprints on the gun. Given all this, the natural question is, how could Calvin Cross have shot at the police as they contended?

Benson continued, "The officer said something to that effect. I was like, 'Oh, really.' And he was sweating. Big balls of sweat coming off of him. He said, 'What did you see?' I said, 'I didn't see a thing.' And then he asked for my ID. I gave him my ID. I said I didn't see nothing. I said that because I didn't want to give these low-down cops—I knew they were low-down cops—any information. I just held it."

Benson caught himself. He didn't want Dana and Senetra to think he had let them down, and so he reminded them of how they connected, of how, in the end, he came forward. "It was God that led me to that McDonald's that day to y'all family," he said. Two weeks after the shooting, Benson had stopped at a nearby McDonald's for a cup of coffee, and while he was there he heard a gaggle of kids, all of whom looked to be in their late teens, talking and crying. He could make out bits of their conversation, and it became clear that they were talking about the shooting he had witnessed and that some of them were related to the victim, whose name he didn't know at the time. Benson approached them and introduced himself, told them he was there at the shooting, and said that if the family needed him or wanted to get in touch with him, to give him a call. He wrote down his phone number on a napkin and handed it to one of the boys, who, it turned out, was Calvin's cousin LaVell. The family passed along Benson's phone number to

Tony Thedford, the lawyer they had hired (and who coincidentally also represented Antuan Joiner). They planned to file a civil suit against the police.

Senetra leaned forward. "Thank you so much," she told Benson. Benson nodded, still leaning back in his chair. "No problem."

At this point Senetra stopped filming, and the three sat around for another half hour, relieved, more relaxed. Dana had remained quiet during much of this. She revealed little, though it was clear she was taking it all in. It was almost as if she was angry with Benson, just for being there, just for being privy to the death of her son. Something occurred to Benson. He turned to Dana and said, "Another thing, I still don't know how your son look." Senetra went into the living room and returned with a framed photo of Calvin. He's smiling, in a button-down plaid shirt and a Yankees baseball cap. Benson held the photo. "You have a very handsome family," he told Dana. "Thanks," she replied. "It's been hard. After we get over one stumble, we hit another."

This is how it often happens in Chicago. One act of violence follows another which follows another and so on. Sometimes there's a causal relationship between them, and sometimes they just happen, almost like an infection being passed along from friend to friend or family member to family member. For Dana, it didn't matter why it happened. It just happened. And each time it took a little more out of her.

First there was Virgil, who was Calvin's cousin but was really more like a big brother to him. They grew up together; Virgil lived with Dana and her family for a number of years. He was three years older than Calvin, and like brothers they fought. Once when they were young they got into an argument. Calvin burned Virgil's thigh with a hot iron, leaving a scar. "I'm kind of glad it's down there now," Virgil told me at one point. "Something to remember him by." Virgil seemed more unmoored by Calvin's death than just about anyone. He'd periodically visit Calvin's gravesite and sit there and just talk to him. I once accompanied him, and Virgil stood at the gravesite, which was unmarked. "What's up, bro? Just stopped by to tell you I love you. You know me and LaVell took the fire department test and we all passed. If you were here, you would've been right with us." Virgil, who worked for a private security company, had aspired to become a police officer, but that changed after Calvin's death, for obvious reasons. He took the firefighter's test instead—his dad had been a firefighter for twenty-three years—but Dana mused that that seemed an unlikely job for him, since he was afraid of heights. The summer after Calvin was killed, Virgil worked security at a housing complex in Richton Park, a southern suburb. At 11:30 p.m. on August 12, 2012 ("I'll never forget that date and time," he told me), Virgil was on patrol with an off-duty deputy sheriff who was moonlighting when they saw a young man shoot a gun from inside a car. They approached him, their weapons drawn, and ordered the shooter to drop his weapon. The shooter replied, 'No, y'all drop y'alls.' He shot at Virgil and his partner. They shot back. Virgil was so disoriented that he didn't know how many rounds he'd fired until he checked his magazine afterward. He'd shot three times; his partner shot twice. The young man was killed instantly. When Virgil found out that the victim, the person he'd shot, was the same age as Calvin, he couldn't forgive himself, he couldn't go on. He quit his security work. He had flashbacks. He couldn't get rid of the smell of burning flesh, of the fresh wound made by his bullet. "He didn't see that young man laying on the ground," Dana told me. "All he could think about was Calvin."

Then there was Ryan Cornell, who was with Calvin the night he was killed. Ryan, who was a tall, narrow kid, had a troubled childhood. By his own account, he'd been kicked out of two high schools, both times for fighting, and so his mom, who was worried about his idleness, insisted he join the Job Corps, which had a location in Golconda, Illinois, at the very southern tip of the state, a six-hour drive from Chicago. He and Calvin ended up in the same dorm. One day Ryan needed to borrow $60, since he was making his biweekly run to Walmart. He needed odds and ends, mostly toiletries, and no one would loan him the money except for Calvin, who barely knew him. Ryan paid him back, and they soon became close friends. Both attended the brick masonry program together. Calvin completed the program, but again, Ryan got kicked out because of fighting. Both Ryan's father and his brother were in prison, and when the two returned to Chicago, Calvin invited Ryan to move in with his family. He slept in the basement with Calvin. He got so close to Dana that he came to call her "mother." Ryan became so much a part of the family that he was given a key to the house.

Ryan remembers the night well. He'd been hanging out at his cousin's nearby, and when he returned to the house, Calvin was asleep on his mother's bed, the first game of the NBA Finals on television, the Mavericks versus the Heat. Ryan woke Calvin, who had lost interest in the game because the Mavericks were losing; the two retreated to the kitchen and heated up chicken noodle soup. Calvin convinced Ryan to join him as he went to meet some girls a few blocks away, and as they walked, Calvin showed off his new G Shock watch and seemed pleased with himself that he had figured out how to turn on the watch's green light. Then the squad car pulled up. Ryan remembers the headlights were off and that the police shined a spotlight on them. The officers jumped out of the car, one of them with an assault rifle strapped to his chest. "Freeze," they yelled, and Ryan did just that. He stopped moving. But Calvin ran. Ryan doesn't know why. No, he insists, Calvin did not have a gun on him. That wasn't Calvin. The last thing Ryan remembers before he ran to get Dana was the officer with the assault rifle held to his shoulder, using the sights to zero in on his target.

After Calvin's death, Ryan says, "I just didn't care anymore. I didn't care about living." When he tells me that, it's as if there's nothing else to say. I ask whether he ever thought about hurting himself. He shakes his head vigorously but then tells me he thought about hurting others. He got into fights. He smoked a lot of weed, popped Ecstasy, anything to take him away from the images in his head. Some rivals in the neighborhood taunted him, claimed that earlier that evening it was they who had shot at the police and that the police shot at Calvin thinking it was them. He started stealing cars, robbing people on the street. Dana asked him to leave the house. He got tattoos on both fists. On the left it reads: *RIP May 26, 1992*. On the right: *Jack May 31, 2011*. (Jack was Calvin's nickname.) Ryan served a year in prison after leading the police on a high-speed chase in a stolen car. When he got out, he moved in with an uncle in Burlington, Iowa, thinking that if only he could put some distance between him and Chicago, maybe it would muffle the memories. Maybe he could stop thinking about revenge. Maybe some of the anger would dissipate. But in Burlington, a down-and-out town along the Mississippi, he continued to get into trouble, and got arrested again for trying to rob a drug dealer. "My mind wasn't right," he told me. "I just felt like my temperature was going up."

I visited Ryan in prison, and it was there, in the brightly lit visiting room, that he recounted all of this for me. He's bulked up from lifting weights. We sat across from each other in plastic chairs, and Ryan leaned back in his, speaking in a soft, quiet voice. Sometimes he'd turn to the side when he was talking. He'd invited me to visit him, but I felt like once he had his curiosity sated, he wanted to go back to his cell. He seemed almost embarrassed by his pain. Often I had to ask him to repeat things. He told me that every May 26 he celebrates Calvin's birthday and makes a special drink, a mixture of coffee, Kool-Aid, and pop, so loaded with caffeine and sugar it gives you a rush. To accompany the cocktail he'll make tacos on his hot plate, stacking summer sausage, cheese, packaged chili, and barbecue sauce on a tortilla. I stopped asking about that night right after he muttered, "I hate talking about this stuff." He paused. "I just wish I stayed at my cousin's or that the Mavericks were winning. We woulda stayed [inside]." For a moment he imagined what might have been. "When he died," he told me, "I didn't have anyone to motivate me."

Two years later, after Benson's visit, Calvin's cousin LaVell Southern, whose father was Dana's pastor and who was the one Benson met at the McDonald's, was at a nightclub near downtown Chicago with Senetra and some friends. Outside, an argument erupted. One of the young men pulled a gun. As Senetra tells it, as LaVell tried to get people to calm down, someone emerged from the crowd and started shooting. LaVell was shot in the back of the head, and was pronounced dead at Stroger Hospital.

And then there was a close friend of Calvin's, a pallbearer at his funeral. Dana didn't want to give his name. She said he was torn up about Calvin's death and then devastated by the murder of LaVell, whom he was also close to. One weekend afternoon, according to Dana, this young man told his grandmother he was headed to the garage to unwind, and about fifteen minutes later the grandmother smelled smoke. She rushed to the garage and tried to open the door, but it was jammed shut. She called the fire department, and once they had squelched the flames, they found the young man hanging from the rafters by his belt. When Dana told me this story, I thought that of all the stories I've heard over the years, stories of wending one's way through the aftermath, on some level this made the most sense. It felt understandable. You lose two best friends within the span of a couple of years, and you give up, you sink into your grief, you think you're next.

O n the day of Benson's visit, Dana's thoughts wandered. She seemed to speak in non sequiturs, but if you listened closely enough, there were connections. "I'm not moving yet," she declared. "I got too much to do." In other words, she wasn't going to stumble like the others.

Standing by the door, Benson assured her, "Any help you need, I'm right here."

Dana leaned into Benson and to me, and again she was moving somewhere else in her mind. "At first—I've never said this." She spoke so low we needed to move closer. "I never seen Calvin with a gun. But I wondered. You never know what your child's doing around others. I thought to myself, he must've shot at them the way they shot at him. I needed to give myself an excuse for the pain. But the next day, when I talked to the coroner on the phone for half an hour, he was so sympathetic. He was almost crying. He told me which bullets hit first. He said he first got shot in the back." But, she continued, that wasn't the shot that killed him.

The two officers who chased Calvin into the vacant lot, into the thick brush, told investigators that Calvin, who had been wounded at this point, lay in the high weeds on his stomach and refused their orders to show his hands. One of the officers said it appeared as if he was trying to hide from them. At close range, they fired again—with their handguns. The bullet that most likely killed Calvin entered at the bridge of his nose. The bullet exploded as it entered his skull, and fragmented rather than passing through. He died on the scene. The coroner determined he had been shot a total of five times.

"When we saw him at the coroner's, it was like he was saying no," Senetra told Benson. "The way his mouth looked, the way it was shaped." Senetra and her mom argued. Dana insisted that the fatal bullet had entered under one of his eyes. Senetra said no, it was above. They realized, almost simultaneously, what did it matter? "They meant to kill him," Dana declared, putting an end to their disagreement.

As they were saying goodbye, Dana told Benson, "Continue to pray for me. I don't wish this on nobody." Each of them—Dana, Senetra, and Benson—seemed unsure, hesitant, almost as if there was more, or they hoped there was more, to say. In what felt like an afterthought, Benson blurted out something he had forgotten to mention. "They were dressed in black op uniforms," he said. It's not revelatory, nothing Senetra and Dana didn't already know. But it was clear that Benson wanted to make sure he told them everything he could remember. "If we ever go to trial," Dana told Benson, "you can come and sit there with us." Benson hugged Dana, then Senetra, and then he was gone.

After Benson left, Senetra put the video on Facebook with this explanation: "I don't know him. All I know is it took courage for him to speak in the defense of my brother Calvin Cross—'Jack' . . . This is the first time my mother and I met with Mr. Benson. For those of you who don't know, my brother was killed by Chicago Police officers . . . but nothing can bring my brother back. Where are the officers? What are they doing? Are they looking for their next victim? My nephew doesn't have a father. I'm sharing this touching video with you hoping justice will be reached sooner than later. Rest up Jack. We love you and haven't and will not forget."

Many months later I met Benson for coffee at a Starbucks on the South Side. He told me that he'd been jittery and nervous when he'd gone to meet with Dana and Senetra. "I just wanted to tell her what I saw," he told me. "I wish I could do more." He told me he's never been contacted by detectives or by investigators for the Independent Police Review Authority. "I think about that night all the time," he told me. He paused. "I try not to."

Two years later, Dana told me she was ready to visit her son's gravesite. She hadn't been there since she'd buried him. Virgil, who'd been there often and knew how to find Calvin's plot, joined us. It was unmarked, in part because Dana had been unable to afford a headstone. But she also worried that when they did lay a headstone, it would feel permanent, and she wasn't ready for that. "I needed to think he was gone for only a while," she told me. "That he'd be back." It was a warm, windy day, and Virgil knew from previous visits that Calvin's gravesite lay atop a small hill next to the grave of a gentleman named Melvin Jackson, and so it was reasonably easy to find. Virgil, with a bottle of orange juice in one hand, spoke to Calvin, as he often did, while Dana stood by in silence, the long, windblown grass dancing at her feet. It had been a hard few years. The night Calvin was killed, just hours afterward, she noticed about a dozen packets of crack cocaine in a decorative vase that sat in her living room. She knew right away that they belonged to her half-brother, who had come by to comfort her and who dealt drugs and who must have panicked with all the police around. She was tempted. She threw the bags in the garbage but couldn't stop thinking about smoking just a little, just enough to calm her. Then she thought, *I'm not going back there,* and took the bags from the garbage and emptied them into the toilet. She took medicine to help her sleep. She started smoking cigarettes again. She developed boils from the stress; they became so infected she needed to take antibiotics through an IV. "It made me mad when people said, 'I know what you're going through,'" she asserted. "No, you don't."

Dana has kept fighting. The Independent Police Review ruled that "the use of deadly force by Officers Mohammed Ali, Macario Chavez and Matilde Ocampo was in compliance with Chicago Police Department policy." The officers were not disciplined. They were awarded certificates of valor. When Calvin was killed, his girlfriend was pregnant with their child, and so Dana sued the city and the police on behalf of her grandson. After taking depositions from the officers and learning the status of the gun found on the sidewalk—that it was inoperable, with all six bullets in the chamber—the city's lawyers settled and agreed to place $2 million in a trust fund for Calvin's son. In the ten years preceding Calvin's case, the city had paid a total of $521 million to families of victims of alleged police misconduct, often the only acknowledgment that an officer might have acted unprofessionally. The city's lawyers were troubled by what they learned about Calvin's death, so they turned the case over to the state's attorney's office. No charges were ever filed. "They paid us off," Dana Cross told me at one point. She was reluctant to settle, but in the end agreed to because the money would go to her grandson. "It feels like blood money," she told me. "I just want those police officers off the street. If they did it to my baby, they'll do it again." At Dana's insistence, the case has since been reopened.

A few months after her visit to the cemetery, Dana had a headstone made. She kept it simple. It reads:

CALVIN (JACK) CROSS

IN LOVING MEMORIES

WILL NEVER BE FORGOTTEN MAY 26, 1992–MAY 31, 2011

Six years after the police killed Calvin Cross, I was driving with Thomas, the boy who had attended Harper High School, on our way to get lunch, and as we motored down 124th Street, we noticed a makeshift memorial at the exact spot where Calvin and Ryan had been stopped by the police. The memorial was small: a vase holding plastic flowers, along with three empty liquor bottles—tequila, Rémy Martin, and Hennessy Cognac—and four candles, all of which were extinguished because of the rain. I, of course, assumed this memorial was for Calvin, though it didn't fully make sense, since the anniversary of his killing wasn't for another few weeks, and as far as I knew he hadn't been much of a drinker. Driving away, I noticed two gentlemen who looked to be in their forties sitting on lawn chairs in their open garage, out of the afternoon rain. I rolled down my window and told them I was writing about the shooting by the police of a young man here. I told them I had seen the memorial. They nodded, and one of them said, "Yeah, I guess he was trying to rob someone and that someone turned out to be an off-duty cop. Shot him. Died right there, I hear." I was perplexed. I told him that the young man in question had actually died across the street, in the lot by the church. Six years ago, I said. Now the man looked puzzled. Six years? No, this just happened a few months ago, he insisted. There was some more back-and-forth, some more confusion, but it became clear— confirmed by police reports I read later—that six months earlier, twenty-year-old Joshua Jones had allegedly tried to rob a police officer from a nearby suburb who was serving papers on someone in the neighborhood. When we realized that two young men had been killed by the police at the same exact spot six years apart, we all just shook our heads. "That's some crazy shit," one of the men commented before Thomas and I drove on.

ing on what their stats look like. The most important question he asks: Are violent crimes up or down? The department uses the numbers to figure out where to deploy officers. McCarthy was so proud of these gatherings—called CompStat, derived from the term *computer statistics*—that he opened them up to visitors, from politicians to academics to journalists. His refrain among his officers was, "This isn't your father's police department." I attended a number of CompStat gatherings, and there were often well over two hundred in attendance, including visitors from other cities and other countries. It felt at times like performative art, a commander at a podium talking about data from the last week or the last month, facing a seated line of top officers, including McCarthy, who posed questions and passed judgment. During this summer CNN was filming what would be an eight-part series on Chicago's violence, which featured McCarthy as one of the city's heroes, and so the TV crew was there, often with two cameras focused on McCarthy, who at times seemed to be addressing not his officers but rather those observing and recording. "We're having a pretty good year," he boasted at one CompStat gathering. Homicides and shootings, indeed, were down. "None of this is by accident," he continued. "This drill works. It's not easy, but holy crap, it works." McCarthy and other top police brass seemed obsessed with the gangs and at times spoke with the bravado of military officers at war. In responding to a series of cell-phone street robberies, McCarthy lectured one of his commanders, "The way we prevent robberies is find patterns—and when we have multiple offenders we don't just lock up one. We get them all. Basically, target them, destroy them. The object here is to swat and destroy that gang."

McCarthy's approach impressed Kirk, who as a naval officer had worked in counter-narcotics in Afghanistan and employed what's called "human terrain mapping," essentially mapping people's connections, using informants and cell-phone data. At one point McCarthy invited Kirk on a ride-along, and while they were out one night, they got a call that someone had been shot. Because of his stroke, Kirk was susceptible to motion sickness and so threw up in the backseat as they sped to the scene. There a young man lay in his front yard, apparently shot three times in the buttocks. Kirk remembers McCarthy telling him, *The shooting of someone is expenditure of ammunition and effort and risk. And the reason to do that is part of a battle. Like ninety percent of the shootings, it's gang-related.* So Kirk asked himself, *Why not simply get rid of the gangs?*

In January, Kirk, like so many others, had been deeply unsettled by the murder of a fifteen-year-old girl, Hadiya Pendleton. Hadiya had been a drum majorette at her high school, and just a week earlier had performed with her school's marching band at President Obama's second inauguration. On the afternoon of Tuesday, January 29, earlier this year, Hadiya, after taking final semester exams, headed to nearby Harsh Park with some friends. It was raining, so the thirteen of them took shelter beneath a metal canopy, huddled together, talking, unwinding, when a boy just a few years older than Hadiya hopped a nearby fence and, mistaking them for a rival gang, opened fire with a black handgun, shooting six times. Two of the bullets wounded two of the students. A third bullet entered Hadiya's back. She died at the hospital. (A few hours after the shooting, the police department released a statement which they later had to retract: "Preliminary information indicates that most of the members of the group were gang members.") Her killing became national and international news. A bevy of dignitaries attended her funeral, including Michelle Obama; the city's mayor, Rahm Emanuel; the secretary of education, Arne Duncan; and the state's governor, Pat Quinn. Michelle Obama famously said afterward, "Hadiya Pendleton was me, and I was her."

For reasons no one can explain, Chicago has been the epicenter for murders by and of young people. They've served as markers for the city. On October 13, 1994, two boys, aged ten and eleven, dangled Eric Morse, who was five, out of a fourteenth-floor window at a public housing complex. Eric had refused to steal candy for them, and so they dropped him to his death. Eric's eight-year-old brother raced down the fourteen flights hoping, thinking, praying that he might be able to catch his younger brother before he hit the ground. That same year, eleven-year-old Yummy Sandifer made the cover of *Time* magazine when his bloody body was found under a viaduct. Sandifer, who was nicknamed Yummy because of his love for junk food, had shot and paralyzed a rival gang member and mistakenly killed a young girl while aiming for someone else. His own gang members were afraid he might snitch, so they executed him. In 1998 two boys, aged seven and eight, were arrested and charged with the sexual assault and murder of eleven-year-old Ryan Harris. Again it made national news. It turns out that the real assailant was a man in his twenties, not these two boys—but virtually everyone in the city had become so accustomed to children killing children that they assumed their guilt. In the afternoon of September 24, 2009, fellow students beat to death sixteen-year-old Derrion Albert with pieces of a railroad tie; the incident was caught on a cell-phone video which went viral. In the wake of Albert's death, President Obama sent Attorney General Eric Holder and Secretary of Education Arne Duncan to Chicago. Each of these deaths rattled an already shaken city. Each time politicians vowed it wouldn't happen again. Each time, to borrow from Yogi Berra, it felt like déjà vu all over again. So many children were killed that for many years the local press kept a running tally of public school students killed, a kind of measuring stick for the health of the city. So many that some feel that there's something nefarious at work. Earlier this summer Monique Davis, a state representative who represents a part of the South Side, offered her conspiracy theory to a radio host: "I'm going to tell you what some suspicions have been and what people have whispered to me. They're not sure that black people are shooting all of these children. There's some suspicion, and I don't want to spread this, but I'm just going to tell you what I've been hearing: they suspect maybe the police are killing some of these kids . . . It's time to make it known. It's time to stop being quiet."

Disturbed by Hadiya's murder and encouraged by his time with Police Superintendent McCarthy, Kirk, early in the summer, floated a proposal, one that was probably more contentious than he intended. He told a television reporter, "My top priority is to arrest the Gangster Disciple gang, which is eighteen thousand people. I would like to do a mass pickup of them and put them all in the Thomson Correctional Facility. I will be proposing this to the assembled federal law enforcement: ATF, DEA, and FBI." Soon after, he explained, "I'm pretty focused on crushing the Gangster Disciples. It's payback for Hadiya Pendleton's death. In my case, personally, I want to take out the GDs because they killed Hadiya."

Bobby Rush, whose congressional district covers a wide swath of the city's South Side, is best known for two moments in his past: in the 1960s he was the minister of defense for the Black Panther Party in Illinois, and in 2000 he defeated an upstart challenger for his seat, Barack Obama. It was the only election Obama would lose. (Rush also received a good deal of publicity when he was removed from the floor of Congress after donning a hoodie to honor Trayvon Martin.) But what isn't talked about as much are two deeply personal moments that have come to shape him. In October of 1999, during the campaign against Obama, his twenty-nine-year-old son, Huey Rich, who bore his mother's surname and was named after Huey Newton, was killed in a robbery. Two men approached Huey as he carried groceries into his home, and one of them pulled out a badge identifying himself as a police officer. Huey, according to Rush, must have sensed that they weren't in fact police and took off running; one of the men shot him in the leg, rupturing his femoral artery. Rush told me that when he got word of his son's shooting, he sped to the hospital, where he found his son unconscious after losing a lot of blood. After ten hours of surgery and massive blood transfusions, Rush said, the doctors seemed hopeful and believed Huey's condition had stabilized, so Rush flew to D.C., as he was in the midst of negotiating the Telecommunications Act. The evening he arrived in D.C. the doctors called to tell him his son had taken a turn for the worse. It was too late to catch a flight, so Rush had to spend the night in D.C., and a staff member and two of her friends stayed up with him, keeping him in conversation and praying with him. When he arrived in Chicago the next morning, his son was bloated, twice his normal size, Rush recalls, breathing with the help of machines. He died that day. Rush's daughter fell to the cold, polished hospital floor and yelled, *Daddy, Daddy, do something!* "I never felt so powerless," Rush told me. And then he remembers his daughter's and Huey's mother's piercing cries of torment, coming from somewhere deep and remote, a place that felt primal. "I can't get that scream out of my head to this day," Rush told me.

Then, in 2002, Rush's nephew, Dennis Rush, who was seventeen, killed a drug dealer while trying to rob him. Dennis was convicted of murder and sentenced to twenty-two years. "It was devastating," Rush told me. "He was kind of wild-eyed and thought that the world owed him something. He wasn't hostile, not a lot of rage. He just got caught up in the streets and thought that would get him status and stature."

Rush isn't the only high-profile Chicagoan to be personally touched by the city's violence. Jennifer Hudson's mother and brother were murdered, as was the son of alderman Robert Shaw. NBA star Dwayne Wade's nephew was shot and injured (in the coming years his cousin would be killed). Local activist Hal Baskin's younger brother and his nephew were shot and killed. So was Derrick Rose's childhood friend. Last summer the up-and-coming rapper Lil JoJo was gunned down riding a bicycle; another rap artist lost his brother. I could go on.

"The violence, it's like a virus," Rush said. "It's part of this rage and anger, and the need to express power. It's about absolutely nothing except for seeking a sense of validation."

When Rush heard Kirk's proposal to arrest 18,000 gang members, he became infuriated. He knew that the police kept a database of all those they suspected of gang involvement. It numbered over 100,000, and for many in the African-American community it felt like an arbitrary manner of labeling black and Latino youth. The police didn't inform you if you were listed on the database, nor would they tell you how you got on it. The list, as many would learn, was often wrong, and if a person was murdered, the police often issued press releases linking the deceased posthumously to a gang, as if that somehow made the person's death inevitable or warranted. Of Kirk's proposal, Rush told a reporter for the *Chicago Sun-Times*, "It's a sensational, headline-grabbing, empty, simplistic, unworkable approach. I am really very upset with Mark." Rush then let loose, adding that Kirk's approach was an "upper-middle-class, elitist, white boy solution to a problem he knows nothing about."

This public feud played out in the press (including one charged headline that read "Bobby Rush Plays the Race Card"), and though no one said as much, it hit a nerve because it got to the crux of the debate: Kirk believed that the violence was a police problem; Rush believed it was a problem growing from the economic distress and physical isolation of his community, which is why Rush, in the wake of their dispute, invited Kirk on a tour of his district, to see what his constituents, especially young men, were up against.

They began at noon at Ryan Harris Park, a place purposefully chosen by Rush to underscore the upside-down nature of the violence. Rush and Kirk knew each other mainly from time spent traveling together between Chicago and D.C. They were in many ways remarkably different, from remarkably different backgrounds. One liberal, the other conservative. One from Chicago's West Side, the other from Kenilworth, one of the country's wealthiest communities. But they have both struggled with health problems, Kirk's recent stroke and Rush's cancer of the salivary glands. For both, illness affected their speech. Kirk seemed to hesitate when he spoke, as if he were searching for the right word. Rush sounded like he was talking with cotton in his cheeks, his words garbled and pebbly like he was speaking from deep within his throat. After Rush had calmed down, he had invited Kirk to spend a day with him in his district which encompassed much of Englewood. Kirk took him up on the offer. "There was no upside to starting a public spat with Bobby on this," Kirk told me. "That's part of the rules of the game, that the assumption is that the congressman is the greatest expert on his own district, and so for me I wanted to go knowing what I don't know."

So they met early this morning at this small park alongside raised railroad tracks. It was named after eleven-year-old Ryan Harris. In 1998, Harris, who lived in a suburb, was spending the summer with her godmother in Englewood, babysitting and attending a local swimming program. On a Monday afternoon she left on her bike for the corner store and disappeared. The next day neighbors organized a search, distributing 250 Xeroxes of Harris's school portrait. Shortly before three in the afternoon, a teenage boy found Harris's body lying among a thick grove of trees and high weeds that ran along the rear of a vacant lot and behind a two-story red-brick home just on the other side of the railroad tracks from the park. Her face and head were badly swollen and beaten, and her flowered panties, which had been ripped off her body, had been stuffed in her mouth. Her red-striped short-sleeved shirt had been pulled up, partially exposing her breasts, and her lime-green shorts lay in a curled mess around her right ankle. She still wore her white Nike sneakers, the only articles of clothing which were undisturbed.

Twelve days later the police announced they had arrested Harris's killers. They were two boys, whom I'll call Ricky and Isaac, who were eight and seven years old. The police said that the boys had wanted Harris's blue Road Warrior bicycle, so the seven-year-old threw a rock and knocked her off the bike. Then, the police suggested, the boys beat her before suffocating her. The police said they confessed to the killing.

When the boys were brought into court and charged with first-degree murder, people fixed on some detail that unnerved them, mostly having to do with their diminutive size. (One weighed fifty-six pounds, the other sixty-two pounds.) A local reporter remembered the two boys being escorted into the courtroom, the small hands swallowed up in the long fingers of adults. A television sketch artist remembered she had to lean over the raised bench where she sat to make out more than just the boys' scalps. A public defender who represented one of the young boys described the doodles he made on her yellow legal pad; on one sheet he drew a house with heart-shaped balloons overhead, on another he simply wrote his name and his father's all over the page. Another attorney, the mother of young children, took one look at the boys and began to cry. But there's one shared memory everyone mentions: when the boys entered the courtroom, there was silence followed by an audible gasp, as if to collectively say, "Oh my God, what has society wrought?"

Nobody—the press, the police, the prosecutors—was listening to the mothers in Englewood, all of whom looked at Isaac and Ricky and saw their own children. There's no way, the mothers said, that boys that young could've done what they'd been accused of. They—and they alone—were convinced that the police did not in fact have Harris's killer. No one heard them. No one listened. But four weeks after the boys' arrest, the police found semen on Harris's panties and quickly determined that children that young could not have produced this. All charges were dropped—and the DNA was matched to a twenty-nine-year-old man who at the time was in the county jail awaiting trial for allegedly raping three girls, two of them under thirteen. He had not been incarcerated at the time of Harris's murder. A short time later Rush held a press conference outside the local police precinct and asked for the Department of Justice to investigate possible civil rights violations of the two boys. "Obviously, there's a growing pattern of malfeasance, misconduct, and shoddy investigations," he said at the time. The Ryan Harris case represented for Rush the topsy-turvy world of relations between his constituents and the police. The police, he believed, sometimes saw themselves as an occupying force, detached from the very people they were there to help.

Today Rush, dressed in an open-collared shirt and a brown blazer, chastised Kirk's staff. "Why do you got him in a red tie and black suit?" he said, commenting on Kirk's formal attire. "This is Englewood." Rush then thanked Kirk for agreeing to come and asked for applause from the couple of dozen people gathered there. Kirk, his press officer, Rush and a staff person, and I loaded onto the party bus, the disco light flashing. "So this is a church bus?" Kirk joked, knowing that Rush is also a pastor. Rush laughed along with him, and asked the driver to turn off the laser lights.

We drove north up Racine Avenue, and it was apparent that there was little civic life here. It used to be that in the warm months adults would gather after work at a place called "the Hump," a raised vacant lot across the street from two taverns. Those taverns are gone, and jobs are in short supply. What civic life remains seemed centered outside the small bodegas and currency exchanges and the storefront churches. They're on every block, sometimes two to a block: Word and Holy Ghost Apostolic Faith Church, Life Giving Ministries Church, Travelers Rest Spiritual Church. Most of them are windowless, with locked gates pulled shut across their front doors. It's as if even God takes precautions here.

"Bobby, what was the foundation of Englewood?" Kirk asked. Rush informed him that it had been the steel companies in the southwestern corner of the city and in northern Indiana, which in the 1960s employed 80,000 men and women and produced more steel than anywhere else in the world. Deindustrialization is a tired story, one told over and over again, and yet it has had a profound impact on vast strips of our cities. Work is the thread that holds the social fabric together, and without jobs that fabric begins to unravel. "You're jobless, living in the land of plenty," Rush later told me. "You're constantly reminded that others have and you don't."

We passed boarded-up properties. Single-family homes. Small apartment buildings. Storefront businesses. Kirk asked about the large red X's drawn across front doors, which looked as if someone had come in to metaphorically cross out the community. Rush explained that they were there to warn police and firemen that the structure was unsafe. His aide told Kirk that there were 3,500 vacant buildings in Englewood, that the community had never recovered from the 2008 housing crisis. "This is a despair tour," Rush said. "What you're going to see here is desperation, without real hope. How do you operate with individuals who don't operate from a vantage point of hope?"

At one point during the tour we passed a fresh crime scene, where uniformed police officers were stringing yellow tape from telephone pole to fence to tree and back again. Detectives searched the ground for evidence, presumably for shell casings. Given the number of police and the presence of detectives and a police helicopter overhead, it appeared that someone may have been shot. It felt too ironic, so much so that no one really had anything to say.

Rush had designed the tour to drive by two elementary schools which had closed at the end of the year, among forty-nine the mayor deemed unworthy of remaining open because of declining enrollment, most in neighborhoods that are predominantly black and Hispanic and among the poorest in the city. It's been a source of deep controversy, as many residents complain that the loss of a neighborhood school is yet one more brick pulled from the foundation of their neighborhood. Some argue, too, that it means their children will be transferred to schools controlled by rival gangs—though it hardly seems right that public policy should be conscribed by gang boundaries. (At the opening of the school year, just a couple of days earlier, the city was so nervous about families having to cross gang boundaries that they supplemented extra police with city workers driving up and down blocks in their street sweepers.)

The last stop was at the corner of 63rd Street and Racine, where in 1994 the city closed the El stop, which Rush sees as a kind of metaphor for the shunting aside of Englewood. He's convinced that it's contributed to the isolation of the community and the closing of numerous businesses which once made this stretch of avenue a place of bustling commerce.

Kirk, I've got to say, was a good sport. "I'm willing to play the role of the educable white guy," he told me. "To come here with a sense of openness and humility." Moved by what he saw, he told me at one point that he had once had a girlfriend who was Ghanaian, and, sadly, Englewood reminded him of conditions in Ghana. "I worry that this is America," he said. "Nobody up on the North Shore [where he lives] knows about this."

After the bus tour, Rush had arranged for a small town-hall gathering at the Englewood United Methodist Church, where members of the community—most of them activists, many of them parents of murdered children—could talk directly to Kirk, who opened it by declaring, "I don't think we can economically survive if we're known as one of the most violent places in America." This drilled down to the core of their disagreement. Do you directly target the violence because it so discourages any kind of economic development? Or do you bring in jobs and rehab homes, knowing that with a sense of opportunity the violence will diminish? Those at the church told Kirk they wanted jobs and activities for the children and better housing. Deanna Woods, the aunt to Siretha White, the ten-year-old girl who had been shot at her surprise birthday party, the one Thomas had attended, wore a T-shirt that read "The Good Die Young." Embroidered on her sleeve was the nickname of her niece: Nugget. "I am Englewood," she declared. "When Nugget got killed we had so many cameras there. But when the cameras went away, nobody was there. All the resources we need don't have to do with policing. Jobs is where we need to start. People need to be able to put food on the table. Put some money in these community centers."

Kirk, who along with Rush sat behind a fold-up table, Kirk in his wheelchair, Rush in a folding seat, listening to residents, asked, "This plan of mine to destroy the Gangster Disciples, is there anyone here who agrees with what the Gangster Disciples do?" No one raised their hand. "Often times people say you cannot police your way out. I just say thank God Chicago didn't believe that. We could've let Al Capone run the whole place, but our grandparents brought the feds in and we crushed the Capone organization."

"This is the reason why we're here," Rush responded. "When he made that statement, I went ballistic, because I knew that wasn't the problem. I wanted to disabuse Mark of the notion that the GDs are the root of the problem in Englewood." Besides, Rush pointed out, the Gangster Disciples really didn't exist anymore and instead had been replaced by the groups of young people who live on a certain block, many of whom knew that their only protection was to be identified with a particular clique or crew.

The crowd murmured. People started shouting, not so much out of anger but to agree with Rush. One man rose and pointed his finger at Kirk. "They happen to be our uncles, our nephews, our brothers," he said. And this may be the real heart of the issue. There is no real enemy out there, but instead a conflagration, a firestorm of forces which have led young people to make choices constricted and directed by the burden of circumstance. One woman at the town-hall gathering, Tonya Burch, who's middle-aged with a hesitant smile, lost her son, Deontae Smith, who was shot at a block party he attended with his girlfriend. "I raised my kids in Englewood. My son died in Englewood," she told both Kirk and Rush. "The first thing they want to do is stereotype our kids as gang members." Indeed, in online comments to the *Chicago Tribune* story on her son's murder, readers suggested that her son must have belonged to a street gang. "My kid wasn't a gang member," she explained. "He was nineteen, on the way to the Air Force. People just assume how the community is." To that, others declared "Amen."

In the end, Mark Kirk never pursued his initiative.

Chapter 18

The Witnesses, part two

I n his first-floor bedroom, Ramaine Hill awoke to a late-summer thunderstorm, reached for his iPhone and his earbuds, lay back down, and disappeared into the beats of R. Kelly. He had his job that afternoon at Jewel, a local grocery store, where he worked in the meat department, but he didn't need to rise for a while. His younger brother, Jeremiah, walked in, as he often does in the mornings, and plopped down on the white rocking chair at the foot of the bed. Jeremiah just liked being around Ramaine. He looked up to his brother and in his presence felt relaxed, like he could be himself. Jeremiah thought Ramaine seemed out of sorts this morning, more withdrawn than usual. Ramaine shared with him that yesterday he had gotten into a verbal altercation with another boy in the neighborhood, who at the end of their tiff warned him, *Them boys gonna kill you.* Ramaine seemed unnerved, and as he told Jeremiah about yesterday's argument, he dropped his head into his hands. Unbeknownst to Jeremiah, his brother had told his boss at Jewel that he felt like someone was following him.

A quiet nineteen-year-old devoted to his longtime girlfriend, Kaprice, Ramaine had been the victim of a shooting by a fifteen-year-old on a bicycle. By most measures he had done the right thing: he had identified the shooter to the police. The shooter, Deantonio Agee, was convicted and sentenced to fifteen years. Because Ramaine had come forward, over the past two years the shooter's friends had been threatening him, offering him money to recant his identification and once even trying to kidnap him. At one point he told Kaprice, *"These niggas after me. They're trying to kill me. I'm tired of this. I didn't do nothing."* Kaprice begged Ramaine to stop walking with his headphones on. *It's too dangerous,* she'd tell him.

To get to work, Ramaine walked south along a side street and then turned east toward a neighborhood which in recent years had turned from ghetto to glitz. Homes sold for as much as $2 million. A Starbucks opened, as did a Panera Bread. Moreover, the neighborhood had become predominantly white. The area's anchor was Seward Park, which included a small but well-groomed lawn encircled by tidy rows of honey locust trees. In the summer the park district showed movies and held jazz concerts here. The four full-sized basketball courts attracted talented players. In fact, it was here that Kyrie Irving, the NBA star point guard, filmed one of his Uncle Drew's Pepsi ads; in it, he enters a pick-up game disguised as an elderly, potbellied, bearded man, along with Nate Robinson and Maya Moore, each of them also looking well past their prime. The park sits just half a mile north of the city's Magnificent Mile shopping strip and is adjacent to the high-priced apartment buildings along the lake known as the Gold Coast.

As Ramaine walked east, nearing the basketball courts, Kaprice, who was with a friend, spotted him in the distance. She stopped, because something didn't seem right. She would've approached, but she and Ramaine had an up-and-down relationship, and in recent days they'd been arguing. Ramaine was smoking, which he did infrequently, and appeared to be pacing, walking in a tight circle, shaking his head. Kaprice told me, "I was being nosy. I stopped and looked at him for a minute to see what he was doing—if he was on his phone. But he wasn't. Then we kept walking."

To get to Jewel, Ramaine had to walk through Seward Park, and as he walked north past the fieldhouse, nearing the park's manicured lawn, a young man briskly approached from behind. Across the street, Ramaine's cousin, a member of the Jesse White Tumbling Team, sat in one of the team's vans eating a croissant from Dunkin' Donuts, but he looked up and saw Ramaine. He waved and Ramaine waved back. The cousin then got out of the van and in the parking lot bent down to tie his shoes; through the brush he made out a man in a red hoodie and red jogging pants, with a distinctive limp, advance toward Ramaine, raising his arm, a pistol in his hand. The cousin shot up and bellowed, *Watch out! Watch out!* but at that moment an El train roared by, drowning out his warning. Moreover, Ramaine had his earbuds in, listening to his music.

A short time later Jeremiah strolled past Seward Park on the way to visit his cousin's tutor, who lived downtown. The street had been cordoned off. Police cars—lights flashing, sirens wailing—soared past, so many that Jeremiah assumed that President Obama was in town and that this was part of his motorcade. Jeremiah kept walking to his cousin's tutor's high-rise apartment.

Kaprice, who had heard the gunshots, ran toward the park, and as she got there she saw the paramedics lift a young man, his head hanging off the stretcher, into the ambulance. She lifted the yellow crime tape, but a police officer stopped her. *I just wanted to see if it's my little brother*, she told the officer, figuring that if she was an immediate relative he'd be more likely to let her through. But the officer held her back. She then spotted Ramaine's cousin, but he turned his gaze. "I don't think he wanted me to know that he'd seen me," she said. Kaprice collapsed on the sidewalk, and the officer asked again who she was to the victim. *I'm his baby mama,* she replied. The officer asked for Ramaine's birthdate and his middle name. She supplied both. *Is he dead?* she asked. *It's not looking too good,* the officer replied.

When detectives arrived on the scene, they discovered three, possibly four witnesses to the shooting. There was Ramaine's cousin, who knew the shooter by his distinct limp. As the shooter approached Ramaine, a middle-aged woman, the mother of another Jesse White tumbler, sat in her Kia, waiting for her son to get across the street. She was so close to Ramaine that if she had opened her passenger door she could've touched him as he fell. She, too, saw the assailant. Ten yards down the street, a postal worker sorted his mail at the rear of his parked car. The shooter ran right past him. And across the street, a young man walked on the sidewalk on his way to work. This all happened at 1:30 in the afternoon on a Saturday, and so people were sitting in the park or out for midday strolls or driving to the grocery store or the Starbucks across the street or sitting on their terraces overlooking the scene, so the police are reasonably certain there were other witnesses as well. But no one else stayed around to talk with them. No one else came forward.

For nearly thirty-two hours Ramaine held on. He'd been shot four times: once in each shoulder, in his neck, and behind his left ear, a wound the doctors didn't discover right away. After surgeons worked to stop the bleeding, doctors told the family that one bullet had destroyed his voice box and so if he survived, he might not speak again. They also worried that a nerve had been severed, so he might lose movement in his right arm. In the ICU, according to family members, doctors discovered the gunshot wound behind his ear and realized that he'd been hemorrhaging in his brain. When Jeremiah visited Ramaine, he found his breathing assisted by a tracheostomy tube, blood running from his mouth and pooling about his head on the pillow. Jeremiah did all he could to keep from crying and took Ramaine's hand in his, trying to get a response, hoping to elicit some movement in his fingers. *I'm here. I'm here for you,* Jeremiah assured his older brother. Jeremiah said Ramaine's hand was limp, but he told me, "When I looked at him, I got this sense that he was there, that he could hear me." Jeremiah left to get some rest, and while he was at home his brother died of cardiac arrest. Jeremiah and his sister chose to donate Ramaine's organs.

Ramaine's death has been hard on his family, but especially on Jeremiah. He tells me that the smell of the pooling blood lingers. It's like concentrated vinegar, he says. It's a nauseating odor that he can't seem to shake. It follows him everywhere. He'll try to brush it away, but then it'll return, and with such power it's as if he's back in the hospital room with Ramaine. He wears his brother's clothes— especially Ramaine's Ruthless Art bright-red jacket with epaulets— and slept in his bed in the months following his death. Soon after Ramaine's murder, Jeremiah dropped out of Trinity Christian College, where he was a freshman hoping to study microbiology. He has dreams, nightmares really, that he comes across Ramaine in the park after he's been shot, but before he can speak to his brother he's jolted awake, unable to get back to sleep. For a while he moved to live with relatives in Madison, Wisconsin, thinking the distance would help. But it didn't. More than anything, Jeremiah feels secluded, like he's on an island watching everyone paddle by. He tells me that he's never spoken about Ramaine's death—to anyone—until now. "I just feel like I'm always gonna feel this way, so it won't do any good talking about it," he tells me. "I know for a fact I'm not the same anymore. I put a smile on, but that's not how I feel inside . . . It's natural, but I don't want to become bitter. I have to learn to cope with it. I don't know how I cope with it, honestly. It'd be nice to speak to someone who's been through the same thing. Nobody understands . . . I wouldn't say it's a hundred percent anger. It's like I feel nobody cares." Nobody? I ask. He gets more specific. "I honestly, genuinely feel the police don't care," he says, a notion that others in his family hold, as well.

Everyone knows who killed Ramaine. I know his name. And his nickname. I've seen numerous photographs of him. I can describe his tattoos. I can find him on Facebook. But he will probably never be charged with Ramaine's murder.

Through some friends at the police department, I heard second-hand that the lead detective in this case was indignant, tired of the no-snitch code of the streets. Authorities and the press have clamped on to the notion that those living in distressed urban communities refuse to cooperate with the police because they see it as dishonorable or unprincipled. It's not that that culture doesn't exist, but it's so much more than just the idea that people won't work with law enforcement because they see it as betraying their peers. In a city like Chicago, where maybe 10 percent of the shooters are arrested, many simply take justice into their own hands. Or, as is so often the case, they're simply afraid.

After months of trying, I was finally able to meet with the detective. The police department asked that I not name him. We met at a restaurant in Little Italy, where he sat in a corner in white shirt and tie, middle-aged and white, sipping an iced tea. He seemed surprised that the department had asked that I not quote him by name. His hands were resting on an inch-and-a-half-thick file on Ramaine's case. "I told them I had no problem talking to you but that I'd tell it straight," he said.

He began by telling me that he was never able to corroborate that Ramaine had been repeatedly threatened. It's not that he doubted it happened, but rather that he had no evidence, no records of calls from Ramaine or his family. Nonetheless, in his report when he filled out the line for "Possible Motive" he wrote "possible retaliation." He told me that Ramaine's family refused to give him the name of his cousin who had witnessed his murder. He said at one point a family member told him, *That's your fuckin' job to learn his name.* Now this is where many detectives might get their backs up, where they might deride the no-snitch culture that so many speak of, but this detective saw something different. He told me in no uncertain terms that this lack of cooperation had little or nothing to do with some street code. "People who tell you that are lying," he told me. "I don't blame them for not coming forward. If you saw something, you'd ask yourself, 'How am I going to protect my family?' I can't get mad at those people."

Fear runs through these communities like a steady rip current, pulling people out to sea, where they're on their own, flailing to stay afloat. Fear is everywhere. You see it in the language. In the street signs. In acts, both small and large. At Harper High School, Crystal Smith, one of the two social workers, once asked a student how his summer was, to which he replied simply, "Safe." A number of years ago, when Myra Sampson, the principal at Lawndale Christian Academy, walked me through her school, poking her head into classrooms, asking students how they were doing, many of the boys would answer simply, "Staying out of trouble." As Myra told me later, this is what their parents tell them before they leave each morning: Stay alert. Keep your head up. Look around you. Be safe. In other words, maintain a stance that assumes the worst. In Chicago, neighbors often come together to form block clubs, small block-by-block organizations which host barbecues and beautify their street. I've been photographing block club signs on the city's West and South Sides, because they all announce their intentions not in language that speaks to their dreams but rather in language that speaks to their fears. In bold letters, the block clubs have printed all that's prohibited, including:

NO DRUG DEALING

NO GAMBLING PENNY PITCHING OR DICE

NO LOITERING

NO LOUD MUSIC

NO SOLICITING

NO BALL PLAYING

NO ALCOHOL

NO GANG ACTIVITY

These are communities, to borrow a term from the world of psychology, that are hyper-vigilant. They are wary and weary, collectively looking over their shoulder, trying to fend off all that feels like a threat to their well-being. Many parents take out life insurance policies on their children, not because they're looking to profit off a child's death but rather so they are assured of having the funds to pay for their funeral. I've seen that fear even among those whose very job it is to make people feel safe. Earlier in the summer, a teenage boy, Jose, was shot in the face. Doctors put him in an induced coma for three weeks, and according to his mother, little by little he regained consciousness. One bullet had entered his mouth and exited his jaw. His right cheekbone had been blown away. He needed extensive reconstructive surgery. Jose knew his assailant, but his assailant's friends sent him text messages offering to pay him not to testify. In court the assailant's friends muttered loud enough for him to hear, *You fuckin' trick.* When he eventually had to testify, he responded to the prosecutor's questions with *I don't recall* or *I don't remember,* and was threatened with contempt. Jose's mother, it turns out, works as a victim's advocate in juvenile court. Her job is to offer reassurance and encouragement to victims as they wait to testify, but she couldn't or wouldn't insist that her son testify. In fact, she told him not to. "What guarantee would there be to protect him?" she asked rhetorically. "I love my work. The attorneys here will tell you that I can bring in anyone in the world." She paused. "Except my son . . . I'm a victim advocate at my job, but not at my home." That's where we're at: that someone whose job it is to help give people the courage and support to testify knows better. Not when it comes to her own family.

This is what the detective in Ramaine's case was up against. Plain and simple, people are afraid to come forward. They see what happens to those who do. Indeed, when the detective visited the woman in the Kia who witnessed Ramaine's murder from just a few feet away, her husband came out on the stoop and told the detective, *We can't get involved. We know people from that neighborhood.* The detective, who's good at what he does, told him he would feel the same if he was in their shoes, but convinced him to let him inside. He got the man's wife to look at a photo lineup and so spread six photos on a coffee table. He watched as she scanned the images, her sight each time involuntarily resting on the key suspect. He could tell. She knew. In the end, though, she asserted that she couldn't decide between him and one other individual. The detective didn't believe her, but he understood. The postal worker said he couldn't pick the suspect out of a photo lineup either. Nor could the young man who'd been walking across the street. At one point the detective got a call from an FBI agent who said that one of his informants had heard who did it. But the FBI agent refused to let his informant talk to the police—though the detective doubts it would've been of much help anyway, since it was hearsay. Then there was the cousin.

A gang officer found the cousin on social media, and after a search learned he was appearing in court on a misdemeanor drug charge. The detective went to the courthouse and in the hallway introduced himself. The detective recalls that the cousin got emotional, started crying, and then recounted everything he had seen, including identifying the man with the limp. So finally the police had reason to arrest the suspect, who was twenty-one and who had his gang name tattooed on both fists. Under law they could detain him for forty-eight hours without pressing charges, and so while they held him, the detective went back to the cousin to have him come to the station to pick the suspect out of a lineup. He also tried to reconnect with the woman in the Kia. She wouldn't answer his calls. And he couldn't locate the cousin, who, once he learned that the detective was looking for him, went into hiding. In those forty-eight hours the detective visited the cousin's home over a dozen times and reached out to two uncles, who agreed to help find him. (The detective concedes that even if he had located the cousin, it might not have been enough to bring charges, since the cousin had waited so long to come forward.) As he told this story, the detective was clearly irritated, but not without sympathy for the cousin's predicament. "It's fear," he told me. "I think it's justified—if you're not a criminal yourself." As Ramaine's brother starkly pointed out in explaining why no one would come forward, "Look what happened to my brother."

I asked the detective if the case was still active. He looked sheepish. He explained to me that it had been listed as "cleared exceptionally," a phrase of art that suggests they'd done an exceptional job. There are two ways to clear a case. The most prevalent is that there's been an arrest and prosecution. But a case can also be considered cleared if the offender is deceased or there are no witnesses left to interview or no more evidence to be found. This second explanation is what the police department calls "cleared exceptionally." Even though neighbors, family, friends, witnesses, and the police are certain who killed Ramaine Hill, there has not been, and may never be, an arrest or a prosecution. Nonetheless, the case is considered solved. If you look at the police department's end-of-the-year report which lists murder cases that have been cleared, a rather important statistic in a city of over four hundred homicides, Ramaine Hill's murder will be classified as a closed case. When this detective explained all this to me, he shook his head in resignation, an acknowledgment that it really made no sense. "It's frustrating," he told me, on every level, not least because Ramaine Hill, as much as, if not more than, anyone, deserved some justice. He did the right thing: he identified the boy who had shot him two years earlier. And this is what everyone in Chicago's neighborhoods know: if you do the right thing, bad things often happen.

I tracked down the cousin at a two-story graystone building on the city's far West Side. It was a rainy summer day, and so he and I talked on the small porch under an overhang, the rain coming down so hard it was at times hard to hear each other. He wore his hair in long braids, and his eyes were bloodshot, suggesting that he might be high. In the humidity he had unbuttoned his shirt, revealing a well-sculpted yet lean body. He told me he had been a Jesse White tumbler for fifteen years; they've performed their acrobatics at halftime of Chicago Bulls and Chicago Bears games, on the *Tonight Show,* and in two presidential inaugural parades. He told me that after he heard the gunshots, he sprinted across the street and kneeled by Ramaine, who lay on his side. Ramaine, he said, had a large gunshot wound in his neck, a gaping hole, really, and was laboring to breathe. *You're gonna make it. You're gonna make it,* the cousin told him over and over again, hoping that if he said it enough it'd come true.

He told me that over the previous year he, too, had heard that Ramaine had been offered money not to testify in a possible upcoming hearing. He had urged Ramaine to accept the cash. *Take the money,* he had told Ramaine. *You'll sleep better.* But Ramaine had responded, *Cuz, why would I take their money if I didn't do anything wrong?*

The cousin confirmed what the detective had told me, that he indeed had identified the shooter, that he had broken down and cried when recounting the shooting, and that after that first encounter he had hidden from the detective. He insisted, "I ain't afraid," but continued, "If I testified, they'd come after me. I'd just need to be prepared. I know I couldn't be out here lacking. I know I'd have to have a gun on me." He paused, and seemed to guess my next question. "I'm not picking him out of a lineup. I'm not testifying in court."

I asked him, "But don't you want justice? Don't you want him in prison?" The cousin leaned against the railing, nodding to himself, considering my question. He took his time. He brushed his braids from his face, and he extended his hand beyond the porch, letting the raindrops fall on his outstretched palm. The rainwater ran down his forearm. He turned to me, and mused, "Karma is a motherfucker."

Chapter 19

The Tightrope, part four

L ate one evening Marcelo went to the bathroom to wash up and brush his teeth before bed. As he leaned over the sink, he noticed hair circling the drain. He knew right away the hair belonged to a boy down the hall, and so Marcelo went to the boy's room and cursed at him, completely out of proportion with the offense. He later apologized. Another time a staff person told Marcelo he had to move away from another boy working on a computer. He yelled at the staff that it was a stupid rule and then turned, retreated to his room, and headed to the shower, where for nearly an hour he let the hot water soothe him. "I struggle with my identity," he told me. "I'm just scared."

D uring the summer, on Sundays, I would come by to visit Marcelo at Mercy, since he couldn't go anywhere because of the electronic monitoring. We had a routine. Marcelo, like I said, doesn't like surprises, anything that pulls him away from what he knows. At a nearby Italian deli, I'd pick up a sandwich—turkey, lettuce, and tomato and easy on the mayo—along with chips, a pickle, and a Coke and go by in the early afternoon. We'd sit at a table in his suite, eat lunch, and then sit in plush chairs by the television to play chess. Marcelo usually won. And we talked.

Marcelo is reasonably private, and so it wasn't until we had spent a number of Sundays before he spoke about the morning he and his friends went on a string of street robberies. "Where's the real Marcelo?" he asked rhetorically. "I don't really know yet, to be honest. I mean, I do know, but my mind goes in different directions during different situations." He's been diagnosed with post-traumatic stress disorder, a result of being shot. He takes melatonin to get to sleep at night. He asks questions three or four times, not trusting each answer, sometimes not remembering. He has what he calls "reruns" of the night he got shot, sometimes retreating into a trancelike state, clearly somewhere other than in the present. He angers easily. The sound of running water soothes him. When it rains, he'll sit by an open window, especially during thunderstorms, the steady patter comforting him. Sometimes he'll sit by a running sink just to hear the flow of water. He'll take long showers. He doesn't know what it is about running water, but it's the one thing that calms him down. It makes his body tingle, he told me. It makes him feel good.

Mercy, which is housed in a three-story building near the city's downtown, has a contemporary feel. Bright lights and large windows give the place a sense of openness. Each child is assigned to a "home" or suite, and this summer Marcelo lived in Mahoney, which housed nine other boys. Marcelo didn't like me coming into his room because he felt it was too messy ("Remember, I'm a teenager," he'd say), but a few times he let me into the narrow space. On the wall he's hung a Chicago Bulls 1996 championship banner, a gift from his first-grade teacher. On his desk, next to a Chicago White Sox helmet, he has a photo of his older brother, Elio, when he was at Mercy. He's close to both brothers but feels responsible for Omar, who's two years younger and also is now at Mercy. Omar, like Marcelo, is a good student, but is more withdrawn. Marcelo worries about him, that if he goes back into the neighborhood people will mistake Omar for him. His old gang, Marcelo tells me, has put an SOS order out: shoot on sight. So he has told Omar to stay at Mercy, where he's secure.

On this particular Sunday, rather than sit in the TV room, Marcelo suggests we talk in a small alcove in the rear of his suite, which is considerably more private. We sit by a floor-to-ceiling window which gives the illusion of being outside, something he welcomed, given that he was still on house arrest. Marcelo's small frame is swallowed up in an oversized red Jordan hoodie and gray sweatpants. He plays with a rubber band he wears on his wrist and picks at a pimple on his nose. He bites his fingernails, leaning back in a cushioned chair, his legs extended. On the couch, reclining on his side, is Tom Gilardi, a Mercy vice president, who has become especially close to Marcelo. Dressed in a plaid button-up shirt and jeans, Tom, who's forty-six, is a beefy man, tall and broad-shouldered, who played nose tackle for the football team at the College of the Holy Cross. He has a young son and a young daughter and lives next door to the facility. With a booming voice, he's a straight shooter and buoyant, which Marcelo appreciates. A few weeks earlier, Tom had told me he still wasn't sure they had done the right thing. Mercy had never bailed someone out of jail. Ordinarily, if you get in trouble with the law, you're out. But there was something about Marcelo that felt different. As a sixteen-year-old, Marcelo had persisted in convincing Mercy to let him in. On his own. And once in, he became a mentor to other kids, and studied such long hours he made the A Honor Roll at De La Salle, earning a 4.1 average his junior year.

"Over the years I've been worn down by working with kids who I see potential in and then I see that same child do something that's wicked bad," Tom told me. "I've just learned over time that those two worlds are not that far apart . . . Even with Marcelo struggling, I literally want to wring his neck. Like, wake up! And then part of me is like, he's seventeen. He's a knucklehead and he's hurting. I waffle. I go back and forth."

Tom and Marcelo clearly enjoy each other's company, and Marcelo seems especially relaxed with Tom, who is taking good-natured jabs at Marcelo's effort to grow a goatee.

"That Fu Manchu thing you got going there . . ." Tom joshes.

"The what?"

"Fu Manchu."

"If anything, this is helping me," Marcelo says, stroking the scraggly hair growing from his chin.

"That's what I'm saying. That's your Samson hair right there. Don't cut it off."

"Yeah, I'll just get bored and I'll play with it. I need to tame it."

"You eating good?" Tom asks, concerned that Marcelo looks bonier than usual. "You eating at school?"

"Yeah, I mean, I'm eating every day, so I'm good."

"Get the hot lunch!"

Marcelo laughs.

"Do you have any friends at school now?" I ask.

"Uh, a couple. I mean, they're obviously white kids."

"Why do you got to say it like that, man?" Tom asks. "You sit together at lunch and study together and stuff?"

"Yeah. I can tell they're really good kids. Like they're positive."

"What's their names?"

"Uh, one is Connor, the other one is Rob, and the other one is Michael. There's a lot, so that's pretty cool."

"Do they ask you about yourself?"

"Yeah, but I've put my distance. I just say that I'm just from the city. I transferred over here, you know, obviously for better grades and stuff, but I don't tell them anything. I don't." Marcelo shifts in his seat, sits up, his right leg pumping.

"Yeah? Why?"

"'Cause they're not going to understand at all. At all at all. It's like everything over there is so comfortable."

After Marcelo's arrest, De La Salle refused to take him back. Scott Donahue, the priest who runs Mercy, convinced his alma mater, St. Viator, a Catholic school in the northwest suburbs, to take a chance on Marcelo, and so Marcelo gets up every morning at 4:30 to catch a commuter train to Arlington Heights, a forty-five-minute ride. St. Viator is a school of privilege, and Marcelo marvels at the wealth of his fellow students. "They drive some wild-ass cars," he tells me. BMWs. Porsches. Range Rovers. "I look at my life and I look at their life and my life sucks." The other students ask him where he's from in Chicago, and Marcelo is purposefully vague. "South Side," he says. They'll respond, *It's crazy over there. Is there shooting?* Marcelo brushes it off and tells them, *Nah, not that I know of.* He doesn't think they'd understand. Besides, he says, "Getting shot is not cool at all." He's excused from gym class so that he doesn't need to wear shorts, which would expose his ankle bracelet, a source of great embarrassment. In the coming months, he'll run into trouble on two occasions. One time, two sheriff's deputies came to Mercy to take Marcelo in. According to their records, Marcelo had thirty-seven violations, meaning he had gone places he wasn't authorized to go. When they showed up at Mercy, Marcelo was working in the cafeteria, and got so upset he started shaking, then went to the bathroom to throw up. Fortunately, at Mercy the staff records each resident's whereabouts every thirty minutes, and it became clear that there had been a malfunction on the sheriff's end. The other time, in the fall, Marcelo, who had moments where his mood turned dark, called his girlfriend, Tania, from the train station and urged her to meet him downtown, which she did. They sat in a park, and Tania told Marcelo she was mad at him for not going to school. "I just wanted things to stop for a minute," he told me. He was tired of the constraint and decided he needed a day to stretch his legs. "Sometimes I don't trust myself," he told me. Again a deputy sheriff came by later that day to arrest Marcelo for violation of his house arrest, but he was so taken by Marcelo's honesty and directness that he let it slide. Other than that incident, Marcelo abided by the rules of house arrest and electronic monitoring for 488 days, or for a year and four months, after which the prosecution inexplicably shifted its stance and agreed to reduce Marcelo's charges to a misdemeanor, to which Marcelo pled guilty.

Marcelo's industrious. He wrote nearly two dozen prisoner advocate organizations around the country until he got one to help fund a trip for him and his family to visit his father at a federal prison in West Virginia. He nags and steers and protects his younger brother, Omar, who's now an honor roll student at De La Salle, Marcelo's old school. They have dinner together every Thursday. Marcelo's mom has moved out of the neighborhood, so that when Marcelo is off house arrest he can visit her. "I was ashamed," she told me. "But now I'm so proud of Marcelito. He doesn't think like a kid anymore." From Mercy, Marcelo had written his mother a long letter of apology. Marcelo's trying to get his best friend, Javier, who participated in the robbery spree, out of the gang. Marcelo told him, *I'm not going to fuck up my life just because you're fucking up yours.* He finally got the bullet taken out of his leg, and though he asked to keep the bullet as a reminder—"a souvenir," he called it—the police took it as evidence should there ever be a case against the shooter. He's still dating Tania, who has aspirations to become a social worker and who has stood by him even though for two years they could get together only at Mercy. And Marcelo got into DePaul, a Catholic university in the city, where he plans to major in accounting.

Marcelo still gets agitated easily, and as his older brother, Elio, says, he's "spookalacious." That is, he spooks easily. He'll cross the street if he sees a car with tinted windows. He won't walk in his old neighborhood. He tells me that when a driver honks at him, "I want to beat his ass."

"The light and dark forces in Marcelo are fighting," Tom says. "You see the battle in Marcelo's eyes. It's probably why we fight for him so much. It's why he's beloved around here. We know he's a good soul."

Many months later I visit Marcelo on a Sunday afternoon, and Tom is there, too. This time we meet in a boardroom on the first floor of Mercy. Marcelo's limping, as he's just had the bullet removed and is fighting a subsequent infection. He's in a DePaul sweatshirt and sweatpants, and he has put on some weight and grown his hair out, both of which make him seem older—and healthier. He's in this strange place, between worlds, trying to figure out where he fits in, how, or if what he's done in the past has shaped who he is now. He proceeds guardedly, fiercely independent, resolute to make this work on his own terms. He worries about being judged, and especially when it comes to family, he holds things close.

"You hear from your pops?" Tom asks.

"He's not doing really good. His health. He's on painkillers. His back. I just want to spend time with him when he gets out of prison. Seventeen years. He needs to stay alive. That's why I tell my girlfriend's brother—he's fourteen—to shut the fuck up, to stop yelling at his dad." He pauses—and grins. "I'd be a good youth worker."

"Yeah, you love to drop the *f*-bomb."

"It gives texture to the conversation," Marcelo says with a glint in his eyes. He then gets reflective. "I feel like everyone here looks at me differently."

"Is it something I'm saying?" Tom asks. "Something I'm doing?"

"I know you care about me, but I feel like you look at me differently. I feel like I betrayed you."

"A lot of that shit might be your own shit. Was I disappointed that this happened? Yeah. Great people make stupid-ass decisions . . . You are who you are. Is this going to define you? Or is it going to motivate you? I'm just saying."

Marcelo deliberates for a moment, his right leg pumping. "Sometimes," he says, "I feel like I'm in this alternate universe."

Chapter 20

False Endings

As the summer wound down, the days growing shorter, a chill blowing through the streets, some in the city, mainly those in positions of authority, declared that all was looking up for Chicago. Police Superintendent McCarthy touted the numbers—the lowest murder rate since 1965—and publicly bemoaned the city's image as a place riddled with violence. "We're struggling with perception," he declared. In early September, Mayor Emanuel appeared on the David Letterman show. Letterman made the observation that people warn, " 'Oh, don't go to Chicago. The violence is unbelievable.' " Letterman asked, "Now, tell us why people say that." Emanuel replied, "Actually, it's on its way down."

It seemed the summer would quietly melt into fall. Then, on a Thursday night, September 19, a group of men, women, and children casually gathered in a park in a neighborhood known as "Back of the Yards" because of its proximity to the long-ago-shuttered Union Stock Yards. While some played a pick-up basketball game and others threw dice on the side, two men approached. One carried a semiautomatic assault rifle and the other a .22-caliber revolver. Without a word, they knelt down on the basketball court and opened fire. Thirteen people were shot, including a three-year-old boy; the bullet entered the back of one ear and exited his cheek. Somehow, everyone survived. The shooting made national and international news. The mayor interrupted a trip out East and flew back to Chicago. Clearly the summer had not quite ended.

Three years later, in 2016, the number of people killed in the city would soar to 795, a 61 percent rise from the previous year. Another 4,369 would be wounded by gunfire. It would be the deadliest year in Chicago in two decades. Nobody could offer an explanation. The University of Chicago's Crime Lab, a think tank on urban violence, examined weather (it was no hotter than past years), city spending on social services (which remained stable), and changes in policing, among other factors. In an unusually candid report, the Crime Lab concluded, "What caused Chicago's sudden surge in gun violence in 2016 remains a puzzle."

The shooting doesn't end. Nor does the grinding poverty. Or the deeply rooted segregation. Or the easy availability of guns. Or the shuttered schools and boarded-up homes. Or the tensions between police and residents. And yet each shooting is unlike the last, every exposed and bruised life exposed and bruised in its own way. Everything and nothing remains the same.

For those who buried their loved ones in the summer of 2013, what's left in death's wake? I was once told the story of a mother who stood her daughter's coffin upright so that she wouldn't be remembered for the way she was left to die, lying in the street. People find a way to defy death's touch.

The interviews I conducted for this book were the toughest I've ever done. It's not that people were emotional—they were at times—but rather it was that often for the first time people were giving voice to memories and feelings they'd held tight. Many spoke with a surprising candor. One man talked about getting shot and paralyzed by a close friend. A sixteen-year-old girl recounted saving the life of a woman—a complete stranger—shot in the neck. A young man spoke about his obsession with finding the person he suspected of murdering his father—twenty years earlier. They'd spin yarns. They'd cry and laugh and scold. It was no doubt cathartic. And then they'd vanish. They'd stop returning phone calls. They'd unfriend me on Facebook. They'd not answer my knocks on their doors. I understand. Violence has a way of catching up with you. Best not to stand still. Best to keep moving. Violence has a way of making you feel sullied. Best not to raise questions. Violence has a way of taking over your narrative. Best not to let it shape who you are. Violence has a way of exposing cracks in your universe. Best not to speak of those you love. Cathlene Johnson, who owns Johnson Funeral Home with her sister, once told me, "Your death will tell on you." And what she might have added, on everyone around you as well.

I have deep admiration for those in these pages. They spoke with such honesty and thoughtfulness and often kindness about the moment when the tectonic plates on which they walked shifted and quaked, leaving fissures so wide their journeys momentarily halted and then took unexpected turns. I, too, was shaken, often by the fury and mistrust vented by the storytellers at those around them, including me. I remember once David Kelly, a Catholic priest who has spent twenty-eight years working with youth in the city and who has comforted both the living and the dying, told me, "Void is even worse than hate. If you have hate, at least you have something." And so I came to understand people's capacity to hold on, to aspire, to move forward—and, yes, hate—even when there is good reason to give up.

People have a capacity to keep going even when their world has been shattered. We all long for connection, for affirmation that our lives matter. I can't shake a brief encounter I had that summer of

2013. Schwab Rehabilitation Hospital is a kind of way station for shooting victims, a place for those who have lost use of some of their limbs (sometimes all their limbs). It's an edifice of tragedy and hope. One afternoon at Schwab I was introduced to a thirty-four-year-old man, Edward, who was there with his mother. At the auto repair shop where he was employed, Edward had been shot in a robbery by a man wielding an AK-47. He'd lost his right leg to an infection and so he was in a wheelchair, rolling toward the exit after a physical rehab session. His mother did all the talking. "It's embarrassing," she told me. "When people learn he was shot, they think he's a bad person, that he had to be selling drugs or that he was gangbanging." Edward seemed uninterested, like he wanted to be somewhere else. I didn't even think he was paying attention to what his mother was telling me. As mother and son turned to leave, Edward, a burly man in a gray T-shirt, twisted around in his wheelchair, faced me, and in a surprisingly commanding voice issued a directive: "Don't forget about me." He then pivoted and rolled away.

A Note on Reporting

When I set out to report this book, my intention was to spend the summer of 2013 reporting and then come fall begin writing. I imagined it would be a fast turnaround. I was so wrong. I should've known better. To capture just a snapshot in people's lives would have been both unfair and incomplete, and so as many of these stories unfurled in the months and years to come, I stayed with them. Time has a way of revealing things.

These stories, I suppose, are subject to a little trickeration (a word I first heard uttered by an older former gang member). Many of the tales, as I'm sure you're now well aware, move back in time as well as forward, in some cases taking us well beyond the summer of 2013. I think of each of these chapters as a kind of portal into the particular tale at hand. It requires, I know, a small leap in both trust and temporal imagination.

Over the course of four years I interviewed roughly two hundred people, most of them numerous times. Some asked for anonymity, and so in a few stories I changed names to protect people's privacy. For this book I interviewed people in their homes, at their jobs, over a meal, or, in the case of Marcelo, over regular Sunday chess games. I attended bond hearings and trials, hung out on street corners and on front porches, attended funerals and vigils, visited people in prison, showed up at crime scenes, spent time at a funeral home and in a hospital trauma unit, and on one occasion drove from Chicago to Texas with Eddie, to spend time with his family. That summer of 2013, I also embedded with a homicide unit on the city's South Side, and while it was both exhilarating and enlightening, I ended up not using any of that material, mainly because it felt too familiar. Nonetheless, my time with the detectives in that unit informed my reporting.

In recreating moments from the past, I tried when possible to interview more than one person who was present. I also relied on several thousands of pages of documentation to flesh out people's stories and to ensure their accuracy. These included police reports, criminal records, civil court records, trial transcripts, medical examiner reports, school records, hospital records, records from the Independent Police Review Authority, journals, letters, surveillance video, and in a few instances video or audio recorded by local reporters. All quotes in quotation marks I heard firsthand. Those in italics I reconstructed, when I could with the help of more than one person who was present at the time.

In my reporting I was especially informed by those in the field, including the work of Ted Corbin, a Philadelphia emergency room physician who runs a program for shooting victims called Healing Hurt People; Father David Kelly, who runs Precious Blood Ministry of Reconciliation in Chicago; Eddie Bocanegra, who founded the program Urban Warriors and now runs an anti-violence effort at Heartland Alliance; Kathryn Bocanegra, a PhD candidate at the University of Chicago School of Social Service Administration, who runs two groups of grieving mothers and who has worked with youth reeling from the violence; Susan Johnson, the executive director of Chicago Survivors; Jens Ludwig, Harold Pollack, and Roseanna Ander at the Chicago Crime Lab; and those I've spent time with over the years—including Ameena Matthews, Alphonso Prater, and Tim White—who are in the streets putting their own safety at risk in an effort to stem the violence.

Acknowledgments

My deepest debt is to those in these pages, for their candor and thoughtfulness and their trust in me to tell their stories. Their courage and openness inspired.

Myrna Roman taught me so much. As did Cobe Williams whose gentle ribbing and regular conversations kept my spirits up. So many in Chicago gave generously of their time and their insights. My time with each of you profoundly informed my reporting. Michelle Gittler, Tony Thedford, Bob Garza, Kristi Battolini, Crystal Smith, Anita Stewart, Jamie Kalven, the staff at Mercy Home for Boys and Girls, Cathy Johnson, Maria Pike, Don Sharp, Carolyn Frazier, Shobha Mahadev, Evelyn Diaz, Mike Morrissey, Donya Smith, Carol Reese, Jeffrey Granick, Leonetta Sanders, Annie Purtell, Miles Harvey, and Janey Rountree. Juliana Stratton alerted me to Marcelo's story. And a big thanks to Carey Stephenson, who introduced me to Ramaine's family, and to Bob Fittin, who introduced me to George Spivey.

To Dave Isay who one evening in the spring of 2013 called me excitedly from the New York subway suggesting the idea for this book. He insisted, "This is the book you were meant to write." I hope he was right.

Meribah Knight was with this book from the beginning, tracking down documents, sussing out stories, knocking on doors, reading draft after draft. A remarkable journalist in her own right, her insights helped shape this book. When she took a job at Nashville Public Radio, Kalyn Belsha stepped in to assist with both research and fact checking which she did with such thoroughness and diligence. Any mistakes in this book are my own. To Zoraida Castilblanco for transcribing hours upon hours of interviews.

I can't thank enough my friends Kevin Horan, Melissa Fay Greene, Julie Snyder, and Vera Titunik, all of whom read partial or full drafts of the book. They sharpened my prose and my storytelling, and gently nudged me along. And to my friend Doug Foster who early on patiently helped me figure out the book's structure.

A few of the stories sprang from seeds planted while reporting for *This American Life*, WBEZ, and for the documentary *The Interrupters*. And so thanks, respectively, to Ira Glass, Ben Calhoun, Linda Lutton, Robyn Semien, and (again) Julie Snyder; to Amy Drozdowska and Cate Cahan; and to Steve James and Zak Piper. Thanks to John Freeman who invited me to write about the city's violence for *Granta*.

Many friends kept me company along the way and kept my head above water. Chris Ware, Joe Margulies, and Jeff Bailey for the regular conversations. And to Liz Taylor, Carlos Javier Ortiz, Julie Justicz, Mary Rowland, Reg Gibbons, Ben Calhoun, John Corbett, John Murphy, Nancy Horan, John Houston, James Adler, and my brother, Dan Kotlowitz. I'm indebted to the support of my colleagues at Northwestern University, which has been my home for the past twenty years. Dave Sanders for his invaluable legal guidance. And a thanks to Hannah Scott and Miriam Feuerle of the Lyceum Agency for helping make the writing life possible.

A shout-out to reporters Linda Lutton and Natalie Moore, who each generously provided me with raw audio tape of two events in this book. And to the photographer Andrew Nelles who provided video.

For thirty years, David Black, agent extraordinaire, has had my back. Always. I don't know where I'd be without his friendship and his steady encouragement. Nan Talese: What can I say? This is the third book we've done together, and her guidance, her friendship, her editorial wisdom have made me a better writer. Nan and David, you've always had faith. Even when I didn't. And to the brilliant Doubleday team—Carolyn Williams, Dan Meyer, Emily Mahon, Daniel Novack, Bette Alexander—a big thank you.

Finally, my family. They're my ballast. Over the course of one summer, Lucas sat with me in the mornings as I read him an early draft of the book. His wise insights and his enthusiasm for what he heard kept me going. I treasured those mornings together. To Mattie who never stopped asking questions and who kept me smiling. And to my beloved wife, Maria, who never stopped believing and who kept me upright (and who tried, in vain, to bring order to my office). Her presence in my life has been a gift. Her work with immigrant children is heroic. This book is for her.

ALSO BY

ALEX KOTLOWITZ

THE OTHER SIDE OF THE RIVER
A Story of Two Towns, a Death, and America's Dilemma

In this gripping and ultimately profound book, Alex Kotlowitz takes us to two towns in southern Michigan, St. Joseph and Benton Harbor, separated by the St. Joseph River. Geographically close but worlds apart, they are a living metaphor for America's racial divisions: St. Joseph is a prosperous lakeshore community and 95 percent white, while Benton Harbor is impoverished and 92 percent black. When the body of a black teenage boy from Benton Harbor is found in the river, unhealed wounds and suspicions between the two towns' populations surface as well. The investigation into the young man's death becomes, inevitably, a screen on which each town projects their resentments and fears. *The Other Side of the River* sensitively portrays the lives and hopes of the towns' citizens as they wrestle with this mystery—and reveals the attitudes and mispercep- tions that undermine race relations throughout America.
Sociology/Race Relations

ALSO AVAILABLE
There Are No Children Here

ANCHOR BOOKS
Available wherever books are sold.
www.anchorbooks.com